Walk in the Light Series

Restoration

An Examination of Pagan Influences in Christianity and the Need for Scriptural Restoration

Todd D. Bennett

Shema Yisrael Publications

Restoration
An Examination of Pagan Influences in Christianity and the Need for Scriptural Restoration

First printing 2007

Unless otherwise noted, Scripture passages are translated by the author.

For information write: Shema Yisrael Publications, 123 Court Street, Herkimer, New York 13350.

ISBN: 0-9768659-4-7
Library of Congress Number: 2007904380

Printed in the United States of America.

Please visit our website for other titles:
www.shemayisrael.net

For information regarding publicity or author interviews call (866) 866-2211

Restoration

An Examination of Pagan Influences in Christianity and the Need for Scriptural Restoration

""In that day I will restore David's fallen tent [succa] I will repair its broken places, restore its ruins and build it as it used to be ¹² so that they may possess the remnant of mankind and all the nations that bear My Name."

Amos 9:11-12

TABLE OF CONTENTS

Acknowledgments

I must first and foremost acknowledge my Creator, Redeemer and Savior who opened my eyes and showed me the Light. He never gave up on me even when, at times, it seemed that I gave up on Him. He is ever patient and truly awesome. His blessings, mercies and love endure forever and my gratitude and thanksgiving cannot be fully expressed in words.

Were it not for the patience, prayers, love and support of my beautiful wife Janet, and my extraordinary children Morgan and Shemuel, I would never have been able to accomplish this work. They gave me the freedom to pursue the vision and dreams that my Heavenly Father placed within me and for that I am so very grateful. I love them all more than they will ever know.

Loving thanks to my father for his faithfulness along with his helpful comments and editing. He tirelessly watched and held things together at the office while I was away traveling, researching, speaking and writing.

Special thanks to Sonia Bowling and Carolyn Adams for all of their help in editing this work. Their efforts are greatly appreciated.

Introduction

"²⁰Everyone who does evil hates the light, and will not come into the light for fear that his deeds will be exposed. ²¹But whoever lives by the truth comes into the light, so that it may be seen plainly that what he has done has been done through God."
John 3:20-21 NIV

This book is part of a larger body of educational work called the "Walk in the Light" series. It is intended to lay the foundation for the rest of the series because it is critical for a person to see the pagan influences in their life and their religious beliefs before they can see the need for restoration. If a heathen does not know they are a heathen then they will never see the need to change. If they think that their heathen beliefs are, in fact, the truth then they will never be restored to the truth.

The book and the entire series were written as a result of my search for the truth. Having grown up in a major Protestant Christian denomination since I was a small child, I had been steeped in doctrine which often times seemed to contradict the very words contained within the Scriptures. I always considered myself to be a Christian although I never took the time to research the origins of Christianity or to understand exactly what the

term Christian meant. I simply grew up believing that Christianity was right and every other religion in the world was wrong or deficient.

Now my beliefs were founded on more than simply blind faith. I had experienced a "living God," my life had been transformed by a loving Redeemer and I had been filled with a powerful Spirit. I knew that I was on the right track although regrettably, I always felt something was lacking. I was certain that there was something more to this religion called Christianity; not in terms of a different God, but what composed this belief system which I subscribed to, and this label which I wore like a badge.

Throughout my Christian walk I experienced many highs and some lows, but along the way I never felt like I fully understood what my faith was all about. Sure, I knew that "Jesus died on the cross for my sins" and that I needed to believe in my heart and confess with my mouth in order to "be saved." I "asked Jesus into my heart" when I was a child and sincerely believed in what I had done but something always felt like it was missing. As I grew older, I found myself progressing through different denominations, each time learning and growing, always adding some pieces to the puzzle, but never seeing the entire picture.

College ministry brought me into contact with the baptism of the Holy Spirit and more charismatic assemblies yet, while these people seemed to practice a more complete faith than those in my previous denominations, many of my original questions remained unanswered and even more questions arose. It seemed that at each new step in my faith I added a new adjective to the already ambiguous

label "Christian." I went from being a mere Christian to a Full Gospel, New Testament, Charismatic, Spirit Filled, Born Again Christian; although I could never get away from the lingering uneasiness that something was still missing.

For instance, when I read Matthew 7:21-23 I always felt uncomfortable. In that Scripture, the Messiah says: *"Not everyone who says to Me, Lord, Lord, will enter the kingdom of heaven, but he who does the will of My Father Who is in heaven. Many will say to Me on that day, Lord, Lord, have we not prophesied in Your name and driven out demons in Your name and done many mighty works in Your name? And then I will say to them openly (publicly), I never knew you; depart from Me, you who act wickedly [disregarding My commands]."* The Amplified Bible.

This passage of Scripture always bothered me because it sounded an awful lot like the modern day Christian Church, in particular, the charismatic churches which I had been attending where the gifts of the Spirit were operating. According to the Scripture passage it was not the people who **believed** in the spiritual manifestations that were being rejected, it was those who were **actually doing** them. I would think that this would give every Christian pause for concern.

First of all "in that day" there are **many** people who will be calling the Messiah "Lord." They will also be performing incredible spiritual acts allegedly in His Name. Ultimately though, the Messiah will openly and publicly tell them to depart from Him. He will tell them that He never knew them and specifically He defines them by their actions, which is the reason for their rejection - they acted wickedly or lawlessly. In short, they disobeyed His

commandments.

Also, it seems very possible that while they thought they were doing these things in His Name, they were not, because they may have never known His Name. In essence, they did not know Him and He did not know them.

I think that many Christians are haunted by this Scripture because they do not understand who it applies to or what it means and if they were truly honest they must admit that there is no other group on the face of the planet that it can refer to except for the "Christian Church." This series provides the answer to that quandary and should provide resolution for any who have suffered anxiety over this verse.

Ultimately, my search for answers brought me right back to the starting point of my faith. I was left with the question: "What is the origin and substance of this religion called Christianity?" I was forced to explore the very foundations of my faith and to examine many of the beliefs which I subscribed to and test them against the truth of the Scriptures.

What I found out was nothing short of earth shattering. I experienced a parapettio, which is a moment in Greek tragedies where the hero realizes that everything he knew was wrong. I discovered that many of the foundations of my faith were not rocks of truth, but rather the sands of lies, deception, corruption and paganism. I saw the Scripture in Jeremiah come true right before my eyes. In many translations, you will read: "*O LORD, my strength and my fortress, My refuge in the day of affliction, The Gentiles shall come to You from the ends of the earth and say, Surely our fathers have inherited lies, worthlessness and*

unprofitable things. Will a man make gods for himself, which are not gods?" Jeremiah 16:19-20 NKJV

I discovered that I had inherited lies and false doctrines from the fathers of my faith. I realized that the faith which I had been steeped in had made gods which were not gods and I saw very clearly how many could say "Lord, Lord" and not really know the Messiah. I found that these lies were not just minor discrepancies but critical errors which could possibly have the effect of keeping me out of the New Jerusalem if I continued to practice them. (Revelation 21:27; 22:15).

While part of the problem stemmed from false doctrines which have crept into the Christian religion, it also had to do with anti-Semitism imbedded throughout the centuries and even translation errors in the very Scriptures that I was basing my beliefs upon. A good example is the next verse from the Prophet Jeremiah (Yirmeyahu) where most translations provide: *"Therefore behold, I will this once cause them to know, I will cause them to know My hand and My might; and they shall know that My Name is the LORD."* Yirmeyahu 16:21 NKJV.

Could our Heavenly Father really be telling us that His Name is "The LORD"? This is a title, not a name and by the way, won't many people be crying out "Lord, Lord" and be told by the Messiah that He never knew them? It is obvious that you should know someone's name in order to have a relationship with them. How could you possibly say that you know someone if you do not even know their name? So then we must ask: "What is the Name of our Heavenly Father?" The answer to this seeming mystery lies just beneath the surface of the translated text. In fact, if most people took the time to read the translators notes

in the front of their "Bible" they would easily discover the problem.

You see the Name of our Creator is found in the Scriptures almost 7,000 times. Long ago a false doctrine was perpetrated regarding speaking the Name. It was determined that the Name either could not, or should not, be pronounced and therefore it was replaced. Thus, over the centuries the Name of the Creator which was given to us so that we could know Him and be, not only His children, but also His friends, (Isaiah 41:8, James 2:23, John 15:15) was suppressed and replaced. You will now find people using descriptions, titles and variations to replace the Name such as: God, Lord, Adonai, Jehovah and Ha Shem ("The Name") in place of the actual Name which was given in Scriptures. What a tragedy and what a mistake!

One of the Ten Commandments, also known as the Ten Words, specifically instructs us not to take the Name of the Creator "in vain" and *"He will not hold him guiltless who takes His Name in vain."* (Exodus 20:7). Most Christians have been taught that this simply warns against using the Name lightly or in the context of swearing or in some other disrespectful manner. This certainly is one aspect of the commandment, but if we look further into the Hebrew word for vain - שוא (pronounced shav) we find that it has a deeper meaning in the sense of desolating, uselessness or naught.

Therefore, we have been warned not only to avoid using the Name lightly or disrespectfully, but also not to bring it to naught, which is exactly what has been done over the centuries. The Name of our Creator which we have the privilege of calling on and praising has been

suppressed to the point where most Believers do not even know the Name, let alone use it.

This sounds like a conspiracy of cosmic proportions and it is. Anyone who believes the Scriptures must understand that there is a battle between good and evil. There is a Prince of Darkness, Ha Shatan, who understands very well the battle which has been raging since the creation of time. He will do anything to distract or destroy those searching for the truth and he is very good at what he does. He is the Master of Deception and the Father of Lies and he does not want the truth to be revealed. His goal is to steal, kill and destroy. (John 10:10). The enemy has operated openly and behind the scenes over the centuries to infect, deceive, distract and destroy Believers with false doctrine. He truly is a wolf in sheep's clothing and his desire is to rob the Believer of blessings and life.

As you read this book I hope that you will see how he has worked to deceive mankind from the very beginning. Since the temptation in the garden the adversary has continually tried to get mankind to disobey the commandments. We are given wonderful promises in the Scriptures concerning blessings for those who obey the commandments. Sadly, many Believers have been robbed of those blessings due to false doctrines which teach them to not keep the commandments thus turning them into lawless individuals. Their belief is not followed by righteous works making their faith empty and, to some extent, powerless.

My hope is that every reader has an eye opening experience and is forever changed. I sincerely believe that the truths which are contained in this book and the

"Walk in the Light" series are essential to avoid the great deception which is being perpetrated upon those who profess to believe in, and follow the Holy One of Israel.

This book, and the entire series, is intended to be read by anyone who is searching for the truth. Depending upon your particular religion, customs and traditions, you may find some of the information offensive, difficult to believe or contrary to the doctrines and teachings which you have read or heard throughout your life. This is to be expected and is perfectly understandable but please realize that none of the information is meant to criticize anyone or any faith, but merely to reveal truth.

In fact, the information contained in this book had better stir up some things or else there would be no reason to write it in the first place. The ultimate question is whether the contents align with the Scriptures and the will of the Creator. My goal is to strip away the layers of tradition which many of us have inherited and get to the core of the faith which is described in the Scriptures commonly called "The Bible."

This book should challenge your thinking and your beliefs and hopefully aid you in your search for truth. My prayer for you is that of the Apostle Paul in his letter to the Ephesian assembly: *"¹⁷that the Father of glory, may give to you the spirit of wisdom and revelation in the knowledge of Him, ¹⁸the eyes of your understanding being enlightened; that you may know what is the hope of His calling, what are the riches of the glory of His inheritance in the saints, ¹⁹and what is the exceeding greatness of His power toward us who believe, according to the working of His mighty power."* Ephesians 1:17-19 NKJV.

I

In the Beginning

Every person has a frame of reference through which they view their lives and the world around them. Their unique paradigm is influenced by numerous factors including their cultural and national heritage, inherited religious doctrines and political ideologies - to name a few. Our paradigm becomes the filter or lens through which we view and interpret our surroundings.

If you are interested in truth you must recognize the existence of this mental framework which has been constructed from your youth. While there may come a time when we start to become the masters of our own destiny, every person must admit that during the most formative years of their life they probably had little control over their environment or the influences which helped to mold them. We all have been provided with information from parents, teachers, television, radio and numerous other sources which played a role in developing our perception of life - our world view.

We owe it to ourselves, as well as those within our sphere of influence, to revisit our core beliefs from time to time in an effort to identify any preconceived notions or ideologies we hold which are not grounded in truth. In doing so we all must be willing to consider information

which challenges our core beliefs and, if necessary, discard or adjust them should they prove to be flawed. We also must be willing to adjust our worldview if it is based upon erroneous information.

For instance, most Americans probably enjoy Christmas as one of their favorite times of the year. They typically believe that Jesus was born on December 25th and they celebrate this time as a religious holiday. If I were to tell people that the Messiah was not born on December 25th - which is a traditional date celebrated by pagans - they would have a choice to make. They could either disregard me, believe me or investigate the matter for themselves. If they are a truth seeker then they should do their own investigation and they will inevitably find that I am correct. The date, December 25th was the Winter Solstice, and was a time when pagans would celebrate the rebirth of the sun. Christianity adopted this pagan tradition, as well as many others over the centuries, and made them Christian. Once this truth is discovered a person has another choice to make - they can disregard the information and carry on with their inherited traditions or they can change those traditions.

Change is not always easy nor is it comfortable but it should be a common occurrence in the lives of those who desire to live an upright, set apart and righteous existence. Change is an integral part of restoration and restoration is the essence of this book - which is the first of twelve books that constitute the Walk in the Light Series.

In reality, the entire series is about the process of restoration which is taking place throughout creation. This first book is intended to awaken the reader to their need for restoration because a person will not experience

restoration unless they recognize their need to be restored. The goal of this book and this series is to send out an alarm for those who have ears to hear and provide much needed information so that they can make the changes necessary to walk in the light of truth.

If you desire truth then I suggest that you look to the source of all truth - The Creator of the Universe. I grew up in a mainline Protestant Denomination which claimed to serve, worship and obey the Creator that they called "The LORD." Quite often they called the Creator "God" although I later discovered that He is more properly called Elohim[1] in Hebrew. "God" is an English word derived from the Teutonic language and was originally used to describe a Germanic deity - not the Creator of the Universe described in the Scriptures.

The Scriptures were initially written in Hebrew and that is the language selected by the Creator to reveal Himself. In those Hebrew Scriptures He uses the word Elohim which properly describes Him as the most powerful being in the universe. There are hundreds of different "gods" worshipped in numerous religions and referring to the Creator with the same descriptor as these false deities is a disservice to Him. Therefore throughout this book, and every book in the Walk in the Light Series for that matter, you will not read the word God when referring to the Almighty, but rather Elohim.

When I first discovered this truth I was pleased to learn that the Creator was called Elohim but I was not completely satisfied because I wanted to know His Name. Understanding the significance of names is a critical part of the restoration process since every name has a meaning in the Hebrew language.[2] As was stated in the introduction the Prophet Jeremiah - whose true Hebrew name is Yirmeyahu[3] - prophesied that in the end days many Gentiles would recognize that they have inherited lies from their fathers.

Let us read the prophecy in a modern English translation of the Bible: "O LORD, *my strength and my fortress, My refuge in the day of affliction, The Gentiles shall come to You from the ends of the earth and say, Surely our fathers have inherited lies, worthlessness and unprofitable things. Will a man make gods for himself, which are not gods? Therefore behold, I will this once cause them to know, I will cause them to know My hand and My might; and they shall know that My Name is the LORD.*" Yirmeyahu 16:21 NKJV.

This translation encompasses numerous lies, some of which will be discussed throughout this book. We are currently experiencing the realization of that prophecy as many people are discovering the true Name of Elohim which has been hidden and suppressed for centuries.[4] Nearly 7,000 times the Name of Elohim is found in the Hebrew Scriptures yet you will rarely, if ever, find it in English translations, or any other translation for that matter. The reader should take note that two times in the prophecy it refers to LORD and even states that the Name of the Almighty is "The LORD." This, of course, is not true and therefore: It is a lie. "The LORD" is simply a title which has been inserted in every instance where the Name of the Almighty is found within the Scriptures.

The Name of the Almighty, The Elohim of Yisrael, is spelled 𐤉𐤄𐤅𐤄 in Ancient Hebrew Script and 𐤉𐤄𐤅𐤄 in the earliest known paleo-Hebrew pictograph script. The paleo-Hebrew pictographic script may reflect how the Name looked on the Tablets of the Ten Commandments,

which were written in stone by the Hand of Elohim, or in the first Torah Scroll[5] written by Moses - whose proper Hebrew name is Mosheh.[6]

Today, most people use Modern Hebrew script which is much different from the ancient script that resembled hieroglyphics and actually related the meaning of letters and words through pictures.[7] In Modern Hebrew the four letter Name, known as the Tetragrammaton,[8] looks like this: יהוה. In English, which reads from left to right, the Name is often shown as: YHWH or YHVH. There is much debate concerning the pronunciation of the Name. Some popular transliterations are Yahweh, Yahuwah and Yahovah.[9]

For far too long people have been suppressing and replacing the Name with titles such as God, The LORD, Adonai, Jehovah and Ha Shem. None of these are accurate transliterations of the Name which saves mankind and which is supposed to be praised and magnified by all of the nations. Thankfully, there is a great awakening occurring concerning the Name of the Creator which is being manifested and revealed throughout the world. This marks a significant point in the restoration process, and because correcting names is so important in studying the Scriptures and restoring the truth, we will be correcting names throughout this book.

Before we proceed any further though, it might be beneficial to actually define what is meant by restoration. The word "restoration" means the act or process of restoring or returning something to its original existence, state or condition.[10] In Hebrew the word which is often translated as "restore" is shuv (שוב) which involves action - a change in direction or thought. Interestingly, this same word is translated as "repent." Therefore, restoration and repentance are intimately connected because they both involve change, and one could argue they are the same.

If you believe that you are perfect, have perfect knowledge and have not inherited any lies or false traditions, then this book is not for you. Also, if you believe that you, and the entire human species, derived from an evolutionary process and were not created by an all powerful Creator, then you certainly have no desire to be restored since that would mean a digression back to an inferior status.

If, on the other hand, you believe in an Almighty Creator Who fashioned the Universe in a perfect state which is currently in a fallen condition, then you should be interested in restoration because that is, in essence, the plan outlined in the Scriptures.

In order to properly examine and participate in restoration it is essential to start at the beginning; because if we fail to understand where we came from it will be difficult, if not impossible, to ever achieve the knowledge of truth. Most people are familiar with the story of creation found in the Book of Genesis, more accurately called "Beresheet," which means "In the Beginning."[11] The text tells us that "In the Beginning" Elohim created the heavens and the earth. He made man and woman and placed them in the Garden known as Eden. The word Eden, which derives from the Hebrew word adan (עדן), means: "pleasant, delightful or to live voluptuously."

The Scriptures describe a firmament which was set above the earth. "[6] *Then Elohim said, Let there be a firmament in the midst of the waters, and let it divide the waters from the waters. [7] Thus Elohim made the firmament, and divided the*

*waters which were under the firmament from the waters which were above the firmament; and it was so. *⁸ And Elohim called the firmament Heaven."* Genesis (Beresheet) 1: 6-8.

Many who study the Scriptures have a hard time visualizing this firmament because it talks about dividing the waters, which you would think is land, but then we see that the firmament is called heaven - shamayim (שמים) in Hebrew. Therefore some simply think of it as the sky or air, but this would not be sufficient to explain how it would separate the waters above from the waters below.

The word firmament in the Hebrew text is raqiya (רקיע), which derives from the root raqa (raw-kah) which means: "to pound the earth (as a sign of passion); by analogy to expand (by hammering); by implication, to overlay (with thin sheets of metal)."[12]

The implication from this word raqiya (רקיע) is a metal plate which has been beaten thin. In the past this might have been difficult to imagine, but with modern scientific advancements we understand much more about water and the characteristics of the elements that it contains - hydrogen and oxygen. Some scientists now believe that the firmament was located approximately 11 miles above the Earth where a heat sink exists and temperatures range between -130 to -180 degrees Fahrenheit. If this firmament was made of water it would be in solid form - pure, transparent - no more than twenty feet in thickness. The compressed hydrogen would be in a near metallic state, thus creating a metallic dome or shell around the earth which filtered light, radiation and radio waves.[13]

This firmament would have resulted in a greenhouse effect and, as a result, most Creation scientists believe that the planet was a much different place than

we currently observe. They describe a world where temperature, light, oxygen levels and even atmospheric pressures were optimal.

The conditions which existed allowed for enormous vegetation growth along with the existence of the largest vegetative consumers - dinosaurs. Mankind was larger, stronger and smarter - not the animal-like cavemen which evolutionists promote to naïve youth during their formative years in school.  Most importantly, original man was connected both to his Creator and to the Creation over which he was given dominion.

Quite simply, the early Earth was a perfect ecosystem formed by a perfect Creator Who described His handiwork as *"exceedingly good."* It was far different from the earth that we currently live on, a planet which has since been plagued by sin and death due to the fall of man. The Scriptures describe a paradise that was disrupted due to disobedience which led to death and destruction. Man, who was originally intended to live forever with his Creator, now experienced both a physical and spiritual death along with all of creation.

Adam (אדם) was a unique creation and he was intimately connected with the entire created world. His name is directly associated with the word "ground," adamah (אדמה), from which he was created, although he then received the "Breath of Life" - nishmat chayim (נשמת חיים) from Elohim. He was the special link between

the Creator and the Creation and was a bridge, so to speak, between the two. The Scriptures record that he was made *"in the image of Elohim"* and so long as he remained obedient he could partake of the Tree of Life. He was created to live, as a complete being, forever.

For those familiar with the Creation account, it is well known that both the woman and the man disobeyed a command and were expelled from the Garden and denied access to the Tree of Life. Adam failed to watch over the Garden by allowing the serpent to enter and tempt his mate whose name is Hawah (חוה) - not Eve as she is commonly called in modern translations of the Bible.[14] Hawah then engaged in a discussion with the serpent who tempted her to transgress the commandment not to eat of the Tree of knowledge of good and evil.[15] She then ate and gave to Adam who also ate.[16]

The transgressions of the man and the woman resulted in sin and death entering mankind which again - was directly linked to the rest of creation. The impact was immediate, although the process of both physical and spiritual death took their own unique courses. Adam and Hawah did not immediately experience physical death for their deeds.

We read that: *"for Adam and his wife YHWH Elohim made tunics of skin, and clothed them."* Beresheet 3:21. This meant that something had to die; blood was shed because of their transgression. They were then literally covered by the death of another being, which gives us a vivid picture of substitution and the atonement provided by YHWH. Both Adam and Hawah deserved to die immediately, but instead, innocent blood was shed to provide atonement for them.

2

The Fall of Creation

While evolutionary concepts generally portray mankind on an upward journey from chaos to perfection, those that believe the Scriptures see a once perfect creation on a downward spiral toward destruction, judgment and ultimately - renewal and restoration. These are two diametrically opposed paradigms which result in very different views of the universe - one sees purposed creation and the other sees random chance. Each paradigm requires faith - faith in man or faith in Elohim.

In fact, belief in evolution takes much more faith than belief in Elohim. Those who believe in evolution exercise "blind faith" because there are no witnesses to evolution nor is there any evidence that this world was created by chance or that mankind evolved from simple matter. The laws of probability make evolution so improbable[17] that you can safely say it is impossible. An evolutionist cannot even explain how matter or energy came into existence to form all that exists and supposedly evolved.

Make no mistake about it, evolution is a religion or rather an anti-religion cloaked behind science. Instead of faith in the Creator, evolutionists exercise faith in the

various hypotheses and theories of men, science and the instrumentation and technology which they use in their attempts to explain away the Creator and Creation. The Scriptures truly are correct when they proclaim: "*A fool says in his heart that there is no Elohim.*" Psalms (Tehillim)[18] 14:1.

There was a time when scientists understood that they were studying creation. Now, sadly, science has "evolved" to the point that most scientists have no need for a Creator and instead of viewing creation as miraculously complex and "intelligently designed" they see it as merely the result of countless random and chance mutations and deviations over an enormous period of time which somehow inexplicably always improves upon itself - which is then proclaimed as a marvel of "nature."

Interestingly, evolutionists fail to provide proof of the existence of billions of scrapped prototypes that their theories rely upon and only through very creative artistic  ad-libbing can they even attempt to portray mankind's progression from Homo habilis to Homo erectus to Homo sapiens archaic to Homo sapiens neandertalensis to Homo sapiens sapiens. These artistic renderings are more the result of a wild imagination and are unsupported by any real tangible evidence. In fact, recent archaeological findings at Lake Ileret, Kenya appear to show that there is no direct "link" between Homo habilis and Homo erectus.

While this book is by no means an attempt to disprove evolution I merely hope to emphasize how pathetically absurd and disprovable it is as a theory.

There are plenty of resources available on the subject that discredit both the theory of evolution as well as its' major proponents such as J. B. Lamarck and Charles Darwin.[19] Sadly, most will not receive this vital information in the public educational system or any secular university for that matter. As a result, the fancies of a few select misguided individuals have become accepted truth because that is what is being taught in most modern schools and universities.

For those who believe the Scriptural account of creation, one of the most significant events that occurred after Creation was the disobedience of mankind, known as - the fall of man. The fall was a complex and multifaceted event which is worthy of much study. It is discussed throughout the Walk in the Light Series but for the purposes of this discussion it is important to recognize that since that event, mankind and the entire creation has been deteriorating from perfection to death and destruction.

Interestingly though, while Creation has been experiencing a decline - at the same time there has been a parallel process of restoration that the Creator has been working through the ages. It is through this restorative process that He will find a people who willingly obey Him. Immediately after the fall an interesting prophecy was declared: "*And I will put enmity between you and the woman, and between your seed and her Seed; He shall bruise your head, and you shall bruise His heel.*" Beresheet 3:15 NKJV.

Through this promised Seed the Almighty continues to seek a people who will obey Him - a people whom He will redeem from their fallen state to dwell with Him in a restored Creation. Sadly, at the same time we see men attempting to prove that Elohim does not

exist in order to justify their own disobedience. This is the epitome of fallen man who puts himself in the place of Elohim and lives according to his own desires and in contradiction to the Ways of the Creator.

Mankind has increased in knowledge with incredible speed and is now deluded into thinking that his abundance of knowledge and scientific achievements make him a higher evolved species than his predecessors. I see the same type of attitude surface when a westerner visits a third world nation. Westerners used to see themselves as more civilized or advanced because of their advanced technology or weaponry. It is important to distinguish the difference between cultural and scientific advancement and physical evolution.

Sadly, many have failed to make this distinction which historically has aided in the justification of slavery and genocide.[20] The technological and industrial revolutions that have taken place over the recent centuries are, in large part, an illusion that has blinded "civilized" man from his fallen state. For as much as he excels, he is chased relentlessly by famine, hate, corruption and disease. For as many problems that he solves, there are hundreds more that await his attention.

Philosophers have declared that "God is dead"[21] and one of the ways that man has attempted to accomplish

this grand plan of declaring that "God is dead" is through the sciences. The modern sciences have, in large part, become hijacked by atheists and science has now become the preferred method of "disproving" the existence of Elohim. In particular, they believe that if they can

discredit the creation account they can discredit the Creator.

While there are numerous individuals who are responsible for this, one of the most notable individuals is Charles Lyell who in the 1830's wrote his 3 volume geological opus entitled: *The Principles of Geology: Being an Attempt to Explain the Former Changes of the Earth's Surface, by Reference to Causes now in Operation.* "Lyell advocated what William Whewell later dubbed a uniformitarian view of geology. This assumed first of all the constancy of natural laws (except as regarded the origin of new species which was left rather vague). The kinds of causes which affected the earth in the past must be  assumed to have been exactly those we see in operation today (such as erosion, sediment deposition, volcanic action, earthquakes etc.) . . . Lyell was obsessed with the implications of the evolutionary theory of J.B. Lamarck. In Lyell's view, if Lamarck was right then religion was a fable, Man was just a better beast, and the moral fabric of society would crumble to dust.

A concerted refutation of Lamarck's theories of progress and evolution became a central part of the Principles. However, by devoting such extensive treatment to Lamarck, Lyell paradoxically made Lamarck's views better known in the English-speaking world than they ever had been. (Lamarck's evolutionary work was not translated into English until 1914.) For example, the oft heard remark that Lamarck believed that a giraffe's neck was long because each generation stretched its neck to reach higher branches and passed on its stretched neck to its offspring is a mocking example from Lyell, not from Lamarck himself."[22]

Charles Darwin read the works of Lyell and used them to support his hypothesis of evolution which he expounded upon in his work published in 1859 entitled *On the Origin of Species by Means of Natural Selection, or the Preservation of Favoured Races in the Struggle for Life*. While Lamarck and Darwin agreed on certain points, their theories  fundamentally differed on how evolutionary changes occurred. Regardless of their differences, both theories required a lot of time and Darwin latched onto the theories of Lyell which gave him just that - an old earth which would provide time for his process of natural selection to occur. It is through the efforts of men like these that we can see a change from the young earth theories to the old earth models.

Modern scientists now use radiometric, Carbon 14, K-Ar, as well as other methods of dating in support of the old earth theories but there are critical flaws with all of these methods.[23] What they all fail to take into account is the cataclysmic geological and global climatic changes that took place on the planet during and after the flood described during the days of Noah.

Creation scientists have constructed models which provide incredible insight into a pre-flood earth which was covered by a protective firmament that filtered light and

radiation. The planet was, in essence, a perfectly tuned thermonuclear reactor with optimal lighting, temperature, atmospheric pressures and oxygen levels which provided for lush vegetation and very large mammals - thus the existence of dinosaurs which were necessary to keep the vegetation in check.

If the model presented by Creation Scientists is accurate and the Earth was actually operating as a thermonuclear reactor and experienced a "meltdown" this would have resulted in the shattering of the firmament and there would also be nuclear material strewn throughout the planet. When Scientists rely on dating based upon the decay patterns of radioactive isotopes they assume that these materials existed in an old earth evolutionary model and they fail to recognize that Elohim could have created these materials at any state that He desired which makes their methodology flawed. By discounting the Scriptural record of history many modern scientists have blindly accepted theories and hypotheses which can never be proven and which lead people away from truth.

The Scriptures detail a planet which is around 6,000 years old and declare that in the beginning there was a lush garden planted by Elohim eastward in Eden. The word for garden is gan (גן) in Hebrew and it envisions a place which is hedged about - a protected place. We are told that YHWH placed the man - Adam - in the Garden and gave him a specific purpose. He was placed in the Garden of Eden "to tend and keep it." Beresheet 2:15 NKJV.

The Hebrew word for "tend" is abad (עבד) and the Hebrew word for "keep" is shamar (שמר). Both of these words are verbs and they involve action. These concepts are very important as we shall see throughout our discussion

and another way of describing Adam's mission is *"to work and to watch"* or *"to do and to guard."*

After we are told what Adam was <u>to do</u> in the Garden, we are then told of one specific commandment which he was given. The Scriptures record: *"¹⁶And YHWH Elohim commanded the man, saying, 'Of every tree of the garden you may freely eat; ¹⁷ but of the tree of the knowledge of good and evil you shall not eat, for in the day that you eat of it you shall surely die.'"* Beresheet 2:16-17.

Now this was by no means the only command given to mankind, but it happened to be the first one that was transgressed - that is why we are provided the specific details of this particular command. Adam was surely given instructions concerning his duties and what was expected of him as he and his Creator walked and fellowshipped together in the Garden.

It was his job to protect and nurture this special place where he had direct communion and fellowship with his Creator. The use of the Hebrew word shamar (שמר) gives us the picture that Adam was the watchman over the Garden. The garden represented the paradise which Elohim desired for His Creation. It was a state of existence where mankind could fellowship directly with YHWH as long as he obeyed His instructions - His commandments, also known as His Torah.

The word Torah is uniquely Hebrew, although many have attempted to translate it into English as "Law" which is not accurate. The word Torah (תורה) in Hebrew refers to the *"utterance, teaching, instruction or revelation"* from Elohim. It comes from horah (הורה) which means: *"to direct, to teach"* and derives from the stem yara (ירה) which means: *"to shoot or throw."*

Therefore, there are two aspects to the word Torah: 1) aiming or pointing in the right direction, and 2) movement in that direction. This gives a much different sense than the word "Law." Consistent with this definition we see that the Hebrew word for sin - hata (חטא) means: *"to miss the mark."* In other words, sin is a failure to walk in the way set forth in the instructions which is disobedience to the Torah.[24]

Now it can plainly be seen that Eden represented mankind living within the hedge of protection provided by the Torah. Man was given a choice: 1) obey and commune with Elohim - which is life, or 2) disobey and be separated from Elohim - which is death. We know that both the man and the woman disobeyed Elohim and were expelled from the Garden and the presence of their Creator. This incident, commonly referred to as the fall of man, set off a chain reaction - not only with mankind, but with all of creation.

After the transgression in the Garden both Adam and Hawah were expelled and denied access to the Tree of Life. This resulted in death entering mankind, which again, was directly linked to the rest of creation. The spiritual impact was immediate. Prior to the fall, Adam could commune directly with Elohim in an intimate fashion which no created being was able to do subsequent to the fall. After being expelled from the Garden, he was separated from that communion.

Death also began to take hold of his physical body as well as the rest of creation. Those things which were made to last forever began to die and while mankind was originally created in the image of Elohim, the offspring of Adam, beginning with Seth, were born in the image

of Adam, NOT in the image of YHWH. (Beresheet 5:3). Adam contained the "breath of Life" which cannot be killed, but he existed in a body which was once eternal, but now was dying. As a result, his offspring were born in this same state.

With sin and death present on the Earth, mankind continued to sin and become more evil as time passed. (Beresheet 6:5). This sin took its toll on mankind and all of creation until judgment was rendered through the flood. The Scriptures record that "the windows of heaven" opened as well as the foundations of the earth which resulted in the global flood. The windows of heaven was the transparent firmament that we discussed in the previous chapter which contained an enormous amount of water - enough to flood the entire planet. The foundations of the deep were likely opened through a meltdown or series of meltdowns.

One can imagine the enormous impact that such an event would have upon the planet. As scientists in the order of Lyell attempt to explain the geological column based upon the constancy of natural laws and assuming the kinds of causes which affected the earth in the past have been exactly those we see in operation today (such as erosion, sediment deposition, volcanic action, earthquakes etc.) their theories will clearly fall short when the constancy which they rely upon is removed.

The flood did not fit within their construct of constant orderly changes and thus they become stymied because of the effects of the flood. Of course it was foolish of them to expect order and constancy when their own theories were premised on randomness, chaos and cataclysmic events that formed the universe. Interestingly, another matter that evolutionists cannot explain through their hypotheses' is the existence of giants. Throughout the Scriptures we read detailed accounts of giants - yet the evolutionists have no explanation for this race of beings. There have been numerous archaeological digs throughout the world which have found the remains of giants yet the scientists have no idea how to categorize these anomalies  because giants do not fit within their e v o l u t i o n a r y paradigm. In ancient days it was common for people to place these giant remains in temples because it was believed that they belonged to the gods. The Scriptures have answers to questions which baffle scientists.[25]

Contrary to the evolutionists, the creation models have very logical explanations for the variations that secular geologists use to support their evolution-based hypotheses which contradict with the Scriptural account of creation. Sadly, there are those "Believers" who feel the need to accommodate the old earth scientific theories and try to force them into the Scriptural account which does nothing but open the door to discredit and weaken the Scriptures, which is exactly what evolutionists are attempting to accomplish.

For instance, there are some well known Christians who try to squeeze millions, even billions of years into the first week of creation. In other words, they postulate that maybe a day is not really a day but rather millions or

billions of years. They do this to accommodate science and to supposedly make the Scriptures fit within the findings of science rather than the other way around. If you start reinterpreting the Scriptures in order to appease the wild imaginations of evolutionists then you have, in essence, elevated science above the Scriptures.

In my opinion, there is absolutely no need to discount or diminish the Scriptures in light of scientific findings because the Scriptural account is supported by science - just not evolutionary science. The Scriptural account of Creation is not only supported by science - it is the only explanation that makes any sense. Therefore, it is within this construct that we will examine history in the light of the Scriptures.

3

Babylon

The Scriptures record that YHWH judged the world by a great flood that covered the entire planet. (Beresheet 7). The flood was a cleansing, and all of creation was ritualistically purified through this process so that they could start afresh; only this judgment altered the paradise which once existed. The planet had changed and it did not take long after the flood for mankind to, once again, fall away from YHWH. A significant occurrence in that process can be seen in what is commonly referred to as the Tower of Babel. There is much that we can learn from the incident at Babel which gives insight to many of the problems that we see today in the world. We read a very brief but telling portion of history in the Scriptures when it describes Babylon.

"¹ Now the whole earth had one language and one speech. ² And it came to pass, as they journeyed from the east, that they found a plain in the land of Shinar, and they dwelt there. ³ Then they said to one another, 'Come, let us make bricks and bake them thoroughly.' They had brick for stone, and they had asphalt for mortar. ⁴ And they said, 'Come, let us build ourselves a city, and a tower whose top is in the heavens; let us make a name for ourselves, lest we be scattered abroad over the face of the whole earth." Beresheet 11:1-4 NKJV.

The inhabitants of the Earth had established their own economic, social, political and religious system. They were going to build a city *for themselves* and make a name *for themselves.* Contrast this city with Jerusalem which was to be a city where YHWH would place His Name and dwell with His people. Babylon was in direct contrast with the desire of the Creator for his Creation. Mankind had become haughty and arrogant - they gloried in their own intelligence and abilities rather than giving the honor and esteem to YHWH. We see that much of modern civilization shares the same haughty attitude as mankind once had in Babylon as they built a Tower *"to the heavens."* (Beresheet 11:1-9).

Today we share more with Babylon than mere attitude or architectural ambitions. In fact, what many fail to recognize is that it was the false religious system established by men that was at the heart of the

Babel incident. While many popular paintings show a round tower reaching to the heavens, the tower was more likely an ancient ziggurat which served as the centerpiece to the sun god worship established through Nimrod and his mother Semiramis.

It was at Babylon that we see Nimrod being worshipped as a god. Legend has it that Shem, the righteous son of Noah, killed Nimrod for this abomination and scattered his body throughout the earth.[26] Despite his death, a religious system developed wherein Nimrod became deified and an entire trinitarian religious system

developed which directed worship away from YHWH toward a false system of worship which is commonly called sun god worship.

History reveals a very ancient struggle between the worship of the Creator of the Universe and that of the sun or other related deities, which dates back to Babylon when Nimrod built the Tower of Babel. As we shall see, most of the religious systems in existence today derive some of their practices from Babylon and Babylon represents the attempt of mankind to establish a system of worship which is not condoned by Elohim. It was a religious and political system that challenged the authority and government of Elohim.

The Scriptures tell us that Noah's son Ham had a son named Cush who married a woman named Semiramis. Cush and Semiramis then had a son and named him Nimrod. They further report that Nimrod *"began to be a mighty one in the earth. He was a mighty hunter before YHWH: wherefore it is said, even as Nimrod the mighty hunter before YHWH. And the beginning of his kingdom was Babel, and Erech, and Accad, and Calneh, in the land of Shinar."* Beresheet 10:8-10.

Most people do not quite understand the meaning of this passage and believe that maybe Nimrod was simply good with the bow and arrow. There are many different legends concerning Nimrod - some claim that "mighty hunter" should actually be interpreted as "giant hunter" because he slew giants and conquered lands. Others claim that his great success in hunting was due to the fact that he wore the coats of skin which Elohim made for Adam and Hawah. These coats were handed down from father to son, and thus came into the possession of Noah, who took them with him into the ark, whence they were stolen by Ham. The latter gave them to his son Cush, who in turn gave them to Nimrod, and when the animals saw the latter clad in them, they crouched before him so that he had no difficulty in catching them. The people, however, thought that these feats were due to his extraordinary strength, so they made him their king.[27]

Determining fact from fiction is not always possible but one thing is clear - at some point Nimrod became opposed to YHWH. "Until Nimrod, mankind was governed by the patriarchal system where the heads of families heard from [Elohim] and guided their individual tribes. Nimrod, more accurately a "mighty hunter against [YHWH]", usurped patriarchal rule, and crowned himself the first human king in all of history. Now man ruled instead of [Elohim]."[28]

Common tradition indicates that Nimrod became a god-man to the people and Semiramis, his mother and later his wife, became the Queen of ancient Babylon. Nimrod was later killed and his body was apparently cut into pieces and sent to various parts of his kingdom to demonstrate that he was a man and he was dead. This was supposed to put an end to his being  worshipped as a god but here is where it gets interesting. Semiramis allegedly had all of Nimrod's body parts

gathered, except for one part that could not be found - his phallus.

Semiramis claimed that Nimrod could not come back to life without it and told the people of Babylon that Nimrod had ascended to the sun and was now to be called "Baal" the sun god. Baal actually means "Lord" in the Semitic languages. She was creating a mystery religion, and claiming she was immaculately conceived, established herself as a goddess. She became known as Ishtar or Easter and claimed that she came down from the moon in a giant moon egg that fell into the Euphrates River at the time of the first full moon after the spring equinox. Ishtar soon became pregnant and claimed that it was the rays of the sun-god Baal that caused her to conceive.

The son that she brought forth was named Tammuz who was believed to be the son of Baal – thus the first pagan trinity. Tammuz, like his supposed father, became a hunter. When Tammuz was 40 he was killed during a freak accident by a wild pig. Ishtar proclaimed that Tammuz  was now ascended to his father, Baal, and that the two of them would be with the worshippers in the sacred candle or lamp flame as Father, Son and Spirit. Ishtar, who was now worshipped as the "Mother of God and Queen of Heaven", continued to build her mystery religion.

She also proclaimed a forty day period of sorrow  each year prior to the anniversary of the death of Tammuz. It was called "Weeping for Tammuz" and it lasted for forty days - one day for each year that Tammuz was alive. The concept was to

deprive oneself of an earthly pleasure and during this time no meat was to be eaten. Worshippers were to meditate upon the sacred mysteries of Baal and Tammuz and to make the sign of Tammuz in front of their hearts as they worshipped. This is where the act of making the sign of the cross originated as well as Lent, which is simply a modified version of weeping for Tammuz. Worshippers also ate sacred cakes with the marking of a "+" or cross on the top. This is the origin of the wafers marked with the Tammuz "+" which some Catholics still use during their Eucharist services.

Every year, on the first Sunday after the first full moon after the spring equinox, a celebration was made. The celebration was known as Ishtar's (Easter) Sunday and was celebrated with rabbits and eggs. Ishtar also proclaimed that because Tammuz was killed by a pig, that a pig (ham) must be eaten on that Sunday.[29] Historically, the priests of Easter would impregnate virgins on the altar of Easter during their Easter sunrise service to celebrate the rebirth of the sun. The following year, the three-month old infants would then be sacrificed and eggs, the ancient symbol of fertility, would be dipped in the blood of the slaughtered infants. This is the origin of the modern Easter celebration - it is a pagan fertility rite which the Christian religion adopted to replace the Scriptural Feast of Passover. Christianity rejected a Scriptural Feast, claiming it was only for "Jews" and instead adopted a pagan celebration into their religion.

Sadly, many people who read the Bible get confused on this issue because it appears that the Early

Disciples of the Messiah celebrated Easter or that Passover was somehow replaced by the Easter celebration. This confusion traces back to an erroneous translation of Acts 12:4 found in the King James Version of the Bible which reads as follows: "*And when he had apprehended him, he put him in prison, and delivered him to four quaternions of soldiers to keep him; intending after Easter to bring him forth to the people.*"

For many who grew up in the Christian religion the problem might not be so evident because Easter is an accepted celebration and their English Bibles appear to support the celebration of Easter. It is important to remember that this celebration predates Christianity by centuries, even thousands of years. When we look at the Greek translation of the text the problem becomes evident. You will not find the word Easter in the accepted manuscripts but rather the Greek word Pascha (πασχα). The word is Pesach (פסח) in Hebrew and Passover in English. Passover is not the same celebration as Easter, so whoever translated this text from Greek to English changed the meaning of the passage by inserting a different word with a very different origin and meaning.

As part of the restoration process it is important that we carefully examine our Scriptures and clean up any poor translations which may foster or support bad doctrines - such as Christian participation in the Easter celebration.

Easter has nothing to do with Passover except that they happen to occur at a similar time each year. Easter was the Great Mother Goddess of the Saxon people in Northern Europe and the Teutonic dawn goddess of fertility. Her name was derived from the ancient word for

spring: "eastre." Similar goddesses were known by other names in ancient cultures around the Mediterranean, and were celebrated in the springtime such as Aphrodite in ancient Cyprus, Ashtoreth and Astarte in Ancient Canaan, Astarte in ancient Greece, Demeter in Mycenae, Hathor in Ancient Egypt, Ishtar from Assyria/Babylon, Kali from India and Ostara the Norse Fertility goddess. All of these fertility goddess myths trace back to Babel and they are all pagan.

4

Paganism

The Scriptures record that YHWH scattered the inhabitants of Babylon "over the face of the Earth." (Beresheet 11:8). Those citizens of Babylon were dispersed throughout the world and new languages were given to them. Does this mean that they forgot their form of false worship which was created in Babylon? Absolutely not. They still worshipped their gods, only now they had different names for them as the languages were confused.

This is why when we examine religions throughout the world we see many similar forms of worship, and even similar building techniques - such as the pyramids and ziggurats which are an integral part of sun worship. The people continued their pagan practices in their new locations, only now they had their own unique languages and building materials as they implemented their familiar religious systems. Sun worship has continued to this day in almost every culture and language. Again, the names of the gods are often different, but beneath the superficial labels,

they are very similar in substance.

You may have heard the phrase "history repeats itself" and so it does. Those who fail to know and learn from history are destined to repeat its' mistakes and this is evident in the religious systems that we see developed over time. Of course, with the passage of time, each system then followed its' own unique and individual progression to the point where it would become somewhat unique and distinctive and their shared source of Babylon is not always apparent. We see step pyramids in Egypt, Mexico, Central and South America, as well as ziggurats in the Middle East and Africa

and pagodas in the Far East. All of these structures are modeled on the Tower of Babel and even share similar construction methods.[30] They are all structures which point to the sun and are a part of the religious beliefs and systems of the people that built them.

These pyramid-shaped objects have relatives known as obelisks: otherwise known as sun pillars, minarets and steeples. Sadly, these objects which trace directly back to sun worship are used today and litter the landscape of every major city in the world. While their modern day builders

may be ignorant of their original meaning, they are phallic symbols which derive from sun worship.

It saddens me whenever I view the landscape of modern day Jerusalem. Throughout the city you will see

obelisks, steeples, minarets and domes - all architectural styles used in sun worship.[31] This is a city dedicated to YHWH which looks more like a pagan capital as it was once renamed Aelia Capitolina by the Roman Emperor Hadrian in 135 CE and dedicated to the Roman god Jupiter.

According to mythology, Jupiter is the supreme god of the Roman pantheon, called dies pater, "shining

father." He is a god of light and sky, and protector of the state and its laws. He is a son of Saturn and brother of Neptune and Juno (who is also his wife). The Romans worshipped him especially as Jupiter Optimus Maximus (all-good, all-powerful). This name refers not only to his rulership over the universe, but also to his function as the god of the state who distributes laws, controls the realm and makes his will known through oracles.

Around 170 BCE the Seleucid King Antiochus IV dedicated an altar to Zeus on the Temple Mount, set up an image of Zeus, and slaughtered pigs on the altar. This could have been a fulfillment of the abomination which lays waste as prophesied by Daniel (see Daniel 9:27) although there would be another according to Mattityahu 24:15 and Mark 13:14. Zeus is the Greek god who is the same as the Roman god Jupiter - they are exactly alike, just named differently.[32] Interestingly, if you visit the Vatican

in Rome, Italy you will find a statue of Zeus/Jupiter on a throne which has been renamed Peter. Catholic Pilgrims line up to adore this image and kiss the foot of the Greco-Roman deity in the world headquarters of the Roman Catholic Church - most unwittingly paying homage to a pagan sun god.

The similarity between Roman and Greek mythology is a vivid example of the common roots of Babylonian worship that undergird and nourish many modern religious systems. The subject of pagan cultures and history is far too vast of a topic to fully address in one chapter, or even an entire book for that matter, so all we can do at this juncture is generalize.[33] As you begin to examine history with this understanding you will begin to "connect the dots" and see the common thread which traces back to Babylon.

After the scattering of Babel YHWH began to call out a people who would choose to love and obey Him. In

Beresheet 11 we read that Abram,[34] a descendent of Shem, was called out of the land of Ur, which is in southern Babylon, to Haran. Both of these regions were known to worship Sin, the moon god. Abram later moved

his family to the land of Canaan whose principal deities were Baal, El and Astarte. He lived his life surrounded by pagans and was the first person who was called a Hebrew. The word Hebrew is Ivri (עברי) and literally means:

"cross over." Abram, who was later renamed Abraham, was called a Hebrew because he crossed over the river - he was a sojourner who was different from those who lived in the lands that he traveled.

He and his household served and obeyed YHWH and he and his seed were directly identified with YHWH. In fact, YHWH is often described as the Elohim of Abraham, Isaac (Yitshaq)[35] and Jacob (Ya'akov).[36] It was through this lineage that YHWH would work His plan of Restoration through His covenants.

The seed of Abraham would become a set apart people who were to be a Kingdom of Priests that would shine as a light to all other nations which were not serving YHWH - thus the distinction between Israel, the seed of Abraham the Hebrew, and the Gentiles. Israel represented the Set Apart Assembly that served YHWH and the Gentiles referred to all of the other nations of the world that did not serve YHWH.

According to the Scriptures, Israel conquered the land of the Canaanites which was not only filled with giants, but also those who worshipped pagan deities. Israel was instructed not to worship the gods of the people they conquered. They were also commanded not to worship YHWH in the manner that their pagan neighbors worshipped their gods.

"*29 When YHWH your Elohim cuts off from before you the nations which you go to dispossess, and you displace them and dwell in their land, 30 take heed to yourself that you are not ensnared to follow them, after they are destroyed from before you, and that you do not inquire after their gods, saying, How did these nations serve their gods? I also will do likewise. 31 You shall not worship YHWH your Elohim in that way; for every*

*abomination to YHWH which He hates they have done to their
gods; for they burn even their sons and daughters in the fire to
their gods.* [32] *Whatever I command you, be careful to observe it;
you shall not add to it nor take away from it.*" Deuteronomy
(Devarim) 12:29-32.

We know that Israel continually strayed away
from YHWH and worshipped these pagan gods and as a
result, the Kingdom was divided after the death of Solomon
(Shlomo).[37] The Ten Northern Tribes, known as the
House of Israel split from the Kingdom and developed
their own polluted form of
worship. They established
two cities of worship and set
up golden calves to be
worshipped: one at Beth El
and one at Dan. They
established feast days which
were different than those
prescribed by YHWH.[38] They did this because Jerusalem
was located geographically within the territories of Judah
(Yahudah)[39] and Benjamin (Benyamin)[40] which were
known collectively as the Southern Kingdom or the House
of Yahudah

Jeroboam (Yaroboam)[41] the King of the House
of Israel did not want his people going to Jerusalem for
fear that he would lose his hold on power. Therefore he
established worship centers within the territories of the
tribes in his Kingdom. In doing so he committed the
same abomination which Israel committed when they left
Egypt only this time it was twice the abomination and it
was done within the land. This was a terrible reproach
to YHWH because the Northern tribes were committing

idolatry, which was spiritual adultery.

The House of Yahudah ended up falling into paganism as well, but in a different way. They built booths in the area of the House of YHWH and mixed the worship of false gods with the worship of YHWH. They turned the House of YHWH into a veritable Pantheon. The Prophets Ezekiel (Yehezqel)[42] and Yirmeyahu describe the abominations they committed which included erecting pagan statues and images, making cakes and burning incense to "The Queen of Heaven," pouring out drink offerings to pagan gods, "weeping for Tammuz" and praying to the sun. (Yehezqel 8, Yirmeyahu 7 and 44).

 As we read in the previous chapter, "Queen of Heaven" was the title taken on by Semiramis, also known as Ishtar in Babylon. This fertility goddess was known as Astarte in Canaan and Isis in Egypt. She was known as Venus by the Romans and Aphrodite by the Greeks. These are all the same goddess but again, she had different names in different cultures. Currently, we see the Catholic Church calling Mary "The Queen of Heaven" which is a tradition tracing directly back to Babylon.

As a result of the various abominations of Israel and Yahudah - both Houses were removed from the land and were scattered throughout the world  - not unlike what happened to the original Babylonians. Since they wanted to worship like pagans they were scattered amongst pagan cultures. YHWH was not going to allow them to commit these acts in His Land and in

His House just as no husband would knowingly allow his wife to commit adultery in their marital home or in their marriage bed. Instead of scattering them to spread their idolatry though, YHWH sent them into an idolatrous world so that He could later regather them and redeem them through His plan of Restoration.

We read in the Scriptures about some brief periods of restoration which Yahudah experienced but the land and the people who lived there would remain under the control of foreign nations for thousands of years. As a result of this foreign occupation, the land continued to be filled with pagans and pagan worship although the original Canaanite deities were replaced with other gods and goddesses bearing different names.

In the Fourth Century BCE, Alexander the Great conquered parts of the Mediterranean, the Middle East, Africa and India. One of the methods used by Alexander to pacify his conquered peoples and maintain peace and order throughout his kingdom was the process known as Hellenization. Hellenization was the process wherein Alexander spread the Greek language and aspects of Greek society throughout his empire. As he continued his  conquests, sometimes he would incorporate elements of conquered civilizations and spread them along with the Greek culture.

This developed into a fairly unified society which was also flexible enough to accommodate the unique religious and cultural practices of differing regions. What resulted was an expansive military and economic power which, as a society, was pagan at its core. Interestingly, Alexander died at a young age in Babylon, the city which he planned on making the capital of his new empire.

Despite his death the Hellenized Society which he created continued throughout the region under the control of the Roman Empire and that is why the term "Greco-Roman" is often used to describe the culture in this region and period of history. While the source of political power had changed, the polytheistic nature of these world religious systems had remained the same. Polytheism, which is the belief in many gods, was the norm.

Rarely would you find a person that did not acknowledge the gods in every aspect of life. This stood in stark contrast with those who followed the Holy One of Israel as the One and Only Elohim. Thus Israelites and later Christians were referred to as Atheists because they did not believe in the numerous gods of their culture, only One. That is what atheist means - one who does not believe in the gods or rather one "without the gods."

In modern times, the term "atheist" generally refers to one who does not believe in <u>any</u> god, but historically this is a fairly new concept. Belief in many gods was the custom throughout the world and it has only been since the spread of Judaism, Christianity and Islam that monotheistic belief has dominated the world religious scene. Thus Israelites were typically in the minority and seen as unbelievers since they did not believe in the popular gods. This is a good example of how language, perception and semantics can change over the centuries and the modern usage of a word can actually be the exact opposite of its original meaning.

Today we see countless religions, sects and

denominations whose adherents all believe they are worshipping according to the truth. In the beginning there were no religions - just the truth. Religions are man-made belief systems and I try to avoid the trappings of religion whenever possible. Interestingly, those in Western culture are not accustomed to identifying pagan behavior because many unknowingly participate in pagan activities and mimic pagan behavior which derives from the Greco-Roman source of their civilization.

I was once a Christian who, in many ways, acted like a pagan without even realizing it. I was a Christian and thought that I was automatically exempt from being labeled a pagan, heathen, sinner - you name it - while in reality some of my actions were no different than that of a pagan. This statement may appear to be an oxymoron and for it to make sense we must provide a definition for the word "pagan."

You can probably find numerous definitions for this very broad term, but generally a pagan is one who worships a god or gods in a fashion contrary to the worship found within the Scriptures. Without an understanding of paganism it will be impossible to understand some of the commandments of Elohim. They simply do not make sense unless you recognize that He was trying to keep His people away from pagan practices which He considered to be abominations.

A pagan is often defined as someone who does not belong to a major monotheistic religion and the word is often used interchangeably with the word heathen. In the context of this discussion I will use the word pagan in its "purest" sense to describe a person who is either actively or passively involved in idolatry, which is the recognition

and worship of false gods as identified within the context of the Scriptures. We could spend a lot of time refining and parsing these definitions, but I am more concerned with presenting the general concepts to the reader who can reexamine their definition of these terms as the discussion continues.

With that having been said, Ancient Israel was surrounded by pagans and many of the commandments given to them were intended to keep the followers of Elohim away from abominable practices and on the "straight and narrow" - which is the path of righteousness. So then, the purpose of the commandments was to instruct people how to live righteously before Elohim.

We have all likely read the examples given in Scriptures about Israel's repeated acts of idolatry. In fact, I remember as a boy reading the Scriptures and wondering how they could keep making the same mistake over and over. I also thought that I was immune from this sort of idolatry since I was "saved" and, after all, I did not worship little wooden or gold figurines.

I spent most of my life believing this lie, thinking I was a pretty good person - all the while living a life of idolatry in an idolatrous society. You see, it is hard for a person who grows up in an idolatrous nation to recognize that they are an idolater. This is why YHWH chose Israel to be a light to all of the nations that surrounded them. They were supposed to demonstrate the standard by which every other nation could measure up to - this way people could see how to serve the true Elohim and they would have a choice whether to remain in idolatry or follow the Holy One of Israel. The problem resulted when Israel became influenced by the idolatry of the surrounding

nations rather than the other way around.

Once that happened, Israel lost the blessings of obedience and fell subject to the curses associated with disobedience. They lost their primary purpose but even when they fell under the curse they were still an example to the nations. We see a pattern throughout history of their disobedience and restoration and the story is not over yet. For those who think that the saga of Israel ended when the "New Testament" was written they are in for a big surprise. Israel is still integral to YHWH's plan of restoration and they are still subject to the blessings and the curses promised by Elohim.

I grew up in Christianity, a religious system which often teaches that "God is finished with Israel" and is now focused on a new entity called "The Church." There is a common teaching that Israel was "under the Law" while the Church is "under grace" and as a result, Christians seem to believe that they are somehow immune from repeating the mistakes of Israel.

Ironically, Christianity has fallen into some of the same sins that plagued Israel over the centuries - they just do not recognize it. What I came to find out was that idolatry did not just involve bowing down to images, but it involved anything in my life which drew me away from the true and proper worship of the Creator of the Universe as prescribed by the Scriptures.

This is, in essence, paganism: the worship of false gods or the tainted worship of the Creator by mixing in pagan concepts or practices. When I speak of a false god I am referring to any god other than the One True Elohim, the Creator of the Universe, the Elohim of Abraham, Yitshaq and Ya'akov. A pagan is one who worships false

gods and an idolater is one who worships idols, although both acts can fall under the general definition of paganism.

To worship something has been defined to mean: "The reverent love and allegiance accorded a deity, idol, or sacred object or a set of ceremonies, prayers, or other religious forms by which this love is expressed."[43] While this definition may be accurate for some, I believe that it is overly broad and too generous because I do not believe that all people's worship is rooted in love. In fact, depending upon the religion, it could simply involve habit, tradition, fear, lust, selfishness, or even hate.

The reasons why people worship a god are varied and I will not attempt to define them all, suffice it to say that it is not always out of love. Therefore, when I speak of worship it will simply mean displaying reverence to either the Creator or to an idol or false god. I believe that the proper manner to worship the Creator is found in the Scriptures and any other form of worship will fall into the category of paganism or idolatry. These terms are often interchangeable and I may use them in such fashion throughout this book.

Over the years, I have heard a common anecdote repeated during sermons about recognizing counterfeit religions or doctrines. Basically, the story states that bank tellers are trained to discern counterfeit bills by only handling real bills. The moral of the story is that if you know how the real bills look, feel and smell then you will be able to tell a counterfeit when it comes along. I do not know if this is actually how tellers are trained but on the surface, it seems to make sense. It also seems to make sense that if we know correct doctrine, then we will not be deceived when false doctrine comes along.

The only problem with this example is that I discovered most of the preachers who used this example were involved in, or influenced by, paganism in one form or another. Probably most of them were ignorant of their pagan involvement, but nevertheless, it appeared to me that their example must be flawed - and it was. You see, for the example to work, one must be absolutely certain that the bills used during training are <u>all real</u>. If someone slipped a counterfeit bill into the training bills here and there throughout the years we would have tellers inadvertently believing that counterfeit bills were real.

I am sure that you can see how the problem could grow and perpetuate itself. It would not take long for the entire currency system to be flooded with counterfeit bills which the bank tellers <u>thought</u> were real. Every now and then the Secret Service, FBI or Treasury Department might spot the error and sound a warning to banks and the problem may be corrected, but if they do not completely get rid of all the counterfeit bills, pretty soon the cycle begins anew. As the Apostle Paul (Shaul)[44] states: "*A little leaven leavens the entire lump.*" Galatians 5:9.

This may really happen in the banking system, as I said I am not sure, but it makes for a good example and it shows that if we are not trained to recognize the real, as well as the counterfeit, we may end up being deceived because what we have originally been presented as truth may very well be a counterfeit religion. There are many religious systems and denominations that have either intentionally or inadvertently adopted false and counterfeit doctrines and beliefs which distract the True Believer from the straight path that Elohim has set before them. These lies and false doctrines have been perpetuated

and passed through the system, not unlike counterfeit bills being passed by untrained consumers - most of the time unwittingly.

Many times these counterfeit doctrines were learned from childhood and the person does not recognize the fact that it has been influenced by paganism over the centuries. Often these pagan-rooted beliefs have become so ingrained in tradition that the adherent would never even question the validity or propriety of the custom or belief.

As a child, I was taught and inherited false doctrines, through society and through my mainline Christian denomination, which I was told were the truth. As a result, I went through much of my life thinking certain fundamental beliefs were real when, in fact, they were actually counterfeit. At times the traditions which I was taught appeared to contradict the written Scriptures and it seemed that most of the time, tradition would triumph over the clear and unambiguous commandments found within the Scriptures.

While I could never quite understand this contradiction, it did not occur to me to question some of my core beliefs because they were ingrained so deeply within my being that I considered them to be absolute truth - even when they opposed the Scriptures. After all, how could so many people that lived before me believe these things if they were not true and who was I to question my predecessors? This is why I stated at the beginning of this book that you must be willing to re-examine your core beliefs. Everything we know or think we know to be truth must pass the scrutiny of the Scriptures.

Whenever I saw a disagreement between the

Scriptures and my traditional beliefs, I was often led to think that there was some spiritual answer that was not immediately apparent. In other words, there must be some explanation for this contradiction, even if I did not know what it was. With that justification, I would blithely continue in my ignorance and with blind faith I would continue to live and walk out my paradoxical faith - a walk which conflicted with the very Scriptures which were supposed to be the foundation of my faith. The fact that maybe the plain text of the Scriptures was correct and my traditional belief was wrong never really struck me as a viable solution to my dilemma.

In retrospect, I now realize that I had entrusted my entire belief system to men, many of whom were not even alive - people I had never even met. When I look back at how foolish this was, I simply shudder. My life is too important to assign to any mortal man and so is yours. We, as individuals, must endeavor upon our own quest to seek out and nurture a relationship with our Creator.

Of course, we can always benefit from the teaching, instruction and guidance of men, but ultimately you alone are responsible for what you believe. Some day you will appear before your Creator and give an account of your life and your deeds. No mortal Pastor, Priest, Rabbi, Imam or Cleric will be there with you explaining, defending or otherwise intervening between you and YHWH. This is why developing an intimate, individual and unique relationship with Him is so important. If you have that during this life, you will not dread judgment. Rather, you will look forward to that day when you can stand before Him and hear the words: *"Well done good and trustworthy servant."* (Matthew 25:23).

5

Patriarchs and Covenants

Having examined the influence of Babylon which created a false system of worship that has perpetuated itself through history, let us turn our attention to the righteous patriarchs who walked the straight path in the midst of the evil that surrounded them.

After man was expelled from the garden it is clear that he still knew what conduct pleased the Almighty. As we read through the Scriptures and look at the Ancestors in the faith we see that they knew the straight way and how to walk in it. For instance, Abel provided acceptable sacrifices which were pleasing to the Almighty while Cain did not. (Beresheet 4:4-5).[45]

The Scriptures record that Adam lived for 930 years and as the first man he surely would have continued to be an influence on mankind. In fact, it is quite evident that he was a High Priest for all of Creation. After his death it appears that things became very bad on the Earth. Apparently Noah was the only one on the planet who was walking upright because the Scriptures declare that: *"⁵ YHWH saw that the wickedness of man was great in the earth, and that every intent of the thoughts of his heart was only evil continually. ⁶ And YHWH was sorry that He had made man on the earth, and He was grieved in His heart. ⁷ So YHWH said, I*

will destroy man whom I have created from the face of the earth, both man and beast, creeping thing and birds of the air, for I am sorry that I have made them. ⁸ But Noah found favour in the eyes of YHWH." Beresheet 6:5-8.

The account of Noah continues by stating: "*Noah was a <u>just</u> man, <u>perfect</u> in his generations. Noah <u>walked</u> with Elohim.*" Beresheet 6:9. The Hebrew word translated as "just" is tzedek (צדיק) which means: "*straight or righteous.*" The Hebrew word translated as "perfect" is tamiyim (תמים) which means: "*clean or unblemished.*" The Hebrew word translated as "walked" is halak (הלך) which is where we get halakah - a word used to describe our walk with the Almighty. Our halakah is the way we live in a manner which is pleasing to Him - according to His instructions found within the Torah.

Therefore, Noah walked with the Almighty and was righteous which meant that he followed the instructions of YHWH and was obedient. Because of his walk, he found favor in the eyes of YHWH and he and his family were spared from the flood. Noah obviously knew the distinctions between right and wrong, righteousness and unrighteousness, clean and unclean - he was actually described as "clean" and "righteous."

We can see an example of this knowledge when He collected seven pairs of clean and one pair of unclean animals onto the Ark and when the flood waters receded he slaughtered only clean animals (Beresheet 7:2-4). I was always taught to believe that all of the animals entered the Ark "two by two" and that only two of every species were on the Ark. This is

a good example of an inherited tradition which has no basis in truth, but the tradition can actually become more powerful than truth.

There are numerous other traditions in Christianity which often take precedence over fact, some of which are described further in Chapter 15. Recognizing this fact is an important part of restoration but our response is the critical factor. Once we discover that we have inherited a tradition which conflicts with the Scriptures we must be willing to discard the tradition, change our thinking and get back to the truth contained in the Scriptures.

Noah obeyed the instructions of the Almighty and he and his entire family lived as a result. It was the rest of mankind choosing not to live righteously, that fell under judgment. After the flood we read that a covenant was made with the rest of mankind through Noah. Notice that the entire family of Noah was covered because of his conduct - not just Noah - and the covenant made with him included future generations. We see this as a common pattern in the covenants made between YHWH and man. A mediator is chosen to represent those that would benefit from the promises of the covenant.

Now many think of a covenant as a contract or an agreement but it has a much deeper meaning. In Hebrew the word for covenant is brit (ברית) and it literally means "cutting." This is why we see sacrifices as part of covenants. Typically, when making an ancient blood covenant the parties to the covenant would cut the sacrifice in two and then pass between the pieces – walking in the blood of the covenant.

This was intended to symbolize the consequences to anyone who broke the covenant: "may they be as the slaughtered animal" (Yirmeyahu 34:18). If you break a contract in most societies it is deemed a civil matter, and there are usually monetary damages assessed for the breach. When you break a blood covenant, someone is supposed to die - just as the sacrifice died when the covenant was formed.

Covenants are a wonderful example of the favour of YHWH - which is often mislabeled as grace. He did not have to enter into any covenants with man, but He did so as a gesture of His kindness and mercy and as part of His Plan to restore His creation. All of the covenants are specifically designed to bring about the Restoration of all things. Thanks to the mercy of the Almighty and the obedience of Noah we are all here today to participate in this process.

Noah and his righteous seed continued to act in the priestly role for mankind, just as Adam had once done. The righteous line of Noah descended through his son Shem and when Noah pronounced a blessing over Shem he called YHWH the Elohim of Shem and he prayed that Elohim would *"dwell in the Tents of Shem."* According to extra-Scriptural records Shem confronted Nimrod and Babylonian sun god worship. These ancient writings even refer to The Academy of Shem where he taught the ways of the Almighty to mankind. There are those who believe that he taught Abraham the ways after he left Ur and that Shem was actually Ha Melchi-tzedek - The Righteous King of Jerusalem to whom Abraham paid tithes. (Beresheet 14:18). It should be noted that Hebrews 7:3 indicates that Melchizedek was without geneology.

We know that Abraham obeyed the Torah because the Scriptures clearly tell us that he did. In Beresheet 26:4-5

we read: "⁴ YHWH *appeared to Yitshaq and said: in your seed all the nations of the earth shall be blessed;* ⁵ *because Abraham obeyed My voice and <u>kept My charge</u>, <u>My commandments</u>, <u>My statutes</u>, **and My Torah**.*"

The word shamar (שמר) is found in this passage as Abraham kept and guarded the Torah just as Adam was to keep and guard the Torah. Abraham guarded and protected the Torah - he lived a life exemplified by His faith which was made perfect through His obedience.

We see in the life of Abraham a covenant which was made between YHWH and a man, including the seed of the man. Unlike other covenants made between men, this covenant was different in that only YHWH passed between the pieces of the slaughtered animals. We read about it in Beresheet 15:9-11 when YHWH told Abram: "⁹ *Bring me a three year old heifer, a three year old female goat, a three year old ram, a turtledove and a young pigeon'.* ¹⁰ *Then he brought all of these to Him and cut them in two, down the middle, and placed each piece opposite the other, but he did not cut the birds in two.* ¹¹ *And when the vultures came down on the carcass, Abram drove them away.*"

Notice that he cut the three animals and did not cut the two birds. This provides for eight pieces through which the parties were to walk to confirm the covenant - <u>only that did not happen</u>. Interestingly vultures, which were unclean birds of prey, were attempting to take the clean animals that were part of the covenant process. Abram had to guard and protect the pieces until the covenant was executed.[46]

"¹² *Now when the sun was going down, a deep sleep fell upon Abram, and behold, dread and great darkness fell upon him.* ¹³ *Then He said to Abram know certainly that your*

descendants will be strangers in a land that is not theirs, and will serve them, and they will afflict them four hundred years. [14] And also the nation whom they serve I will judge, afterward they will come out with great possessions. [15] Now as for you, you shall go to your fathers in peace, you shall be buried at a good old age. [16] But in the fourth generation they shall return here, for the iniquity of the Amorites is not yet complete. [17] And it came to pass – then the sun went down and it was dark, that behold there appeared a smoking oven and a burning torch that passed between those pieces. [18] On the same day YHWH made a covenant with Abram saying: 'To your descendants I have given this land, from the river of Egypt to the great river, the River Euphrates - [19] the Kenites, the Kennizites, the Kadmonites, [20] the Hittites, the Perrizites, the Rephaim, the Amorites, the Canaanites, the Girgashites, and the Jebusites."[47]

All land between the Nile and Euphrates

There is one very important thing to point out: The covenant promise has never been completely fulfilled. This land grant is enormous - far greater than Ancient Israel or the Modern State of Israel ever experienced. It extends from Egypt through the Arabian Peninsula, Syria,

Lebanon, Jordan, Iraq and possibly other countries in the Middle East and Africa.

Another important point is that YHWH put Abram into what is described as a "deep sleep." Notice also that horror and great darkness fell upon him. This is a picture of death and the Hebrew word used here is tardemah (תרדמה) - which means more than just deep sleep. In fact, it means trance or stunned "like death."

This was the same word used in Beresheet 2:21 with Adam when Hawah was taken from his side. Interestingly woman came from man - the word for man is aish (איש) in Hebrew. Woman means "taken out of man" and the word for woman is aishah (אשה) in Hebrew. Notice that there is a Hebrew letter hey (ה) added to the word. The hey (ה) has changed over the centuries and in Ancient Hebrew script it symbolizes a man standing with arms raised (𐤄) and means: "behold." It is meant to announce something and also means: "to reveal." The hey (ה) also represents breath which is life - the Spirit of YHWH. In fact, we find the hey (ה) two times in YHWH (יהוה).

The reason I mention this is because there is something important going on and we are put on notice to behold and pay attention. Now we read in Beresheet 17:5 after YHWH entered into covenant with Abram, He changed his name to Abraham by adding a hey (ה) to his name. YHWH then details the covenant of circumcision (Beresheet 17:10 - 14). The covenant involved cutting his flesh and shedding his blood - not just the flesh and blood of the sacrificed animals. The fact that it was cut in the male organ is extremely significant.

In Beresheet 17:15 YHWH changed Sarai's name from Sarai to Sarah. He added a hey (ה) to her name also.

This reveals that the covenant would pass from the seed of Abraham through the cutting of Abraham into the womb of Sarah. Just as Hawah was a bride for Adam - YHWH is showing us that through Abraham and Sarah - He was preparing a Bride for Himself.

An important part of the execution of this covenant is the fact that Abraham did not pass through the cuttings. YHWH passed through the cuttings as a demonstration that He would bear the responsibility for both of the parties. All Abraham was responsible to do was carry the sign of the covenant in his flesh through circumcision and be perfect! Abraham was instructed to circumcise himself and <u>every male in His household</u> - not just his physical seed.

This is a very critical point to understand - Abraham had an enormous household that traveled with Him. They were not all his physical seed but they were part of his household and they dwelled within his tents. Therefore the covenant was made with him and included all of his household - just as the Rainbow was the sign of the covenant made previously with Noah and all of his household in perpetuity.

The significance of the circumcision was that Abraham's seed would pass through the cutting of the covenant and then the promises of the covenant would pass through with the seed. The child would then be circumcised on the eighth day and when that child grew up to become a man - his seed would in turn pass through the cutting of the covenant and so on - it was an everlasting covenant.

Notice the connection between the eight pieces of flesh that YHWH passes through and the eighth day circumcision when the flesh of the male child is cut. The number eight typically signifies new beginnings after the completion of the Scriptural cycle of sevens that began on the first day of creation. The number eight is the same as the letter het (ח) in Hebrew which means: "a fence" or "separation." This can be plainly seen in the Ancient Hebrew Script - "ﬡﬡ".

Therefore, from this covenant we can see that the seed of Abraham were to be set apart, surrounded by the hedge of the Torah as we saw in the Garden. This is very clear in the Scriptures. In fact, here is what the Almighty said about Abraham in Beresheet 18:19: *"For I have known him, in order that he may command his children and his household after him, that they* **keep** *the Way of YHWH, to do righteousness and justice, that YHWH may bring to Abraham what He has spoken to him."*

There is that word **shamar** (שמר) again which has been translated as "keep." Abraham watched and kept the hedge around his children and his entire household - all those who dwelled with him - and he instructed them all in the Way - which is the Torah.

This is a constant thread throughout the Scriptures although it is not always clearly recognized. Mankind knew the ways of the Almighty <u>before</u> they were given to Israel at Mount Sinai and those who obeyed were considered righteous. They had faith **and** they demonstrated that faith by the way they walked. This does not mean that they were perfect in every way. They all came up short but they placed their faith in the promises made to them by YHWH.

If you follow YHWH, then you serve the same Elohim of Abraham who was our example in the faith.

He obeyed YHWH and He worshipped YHWH in the midst of pagan peoples. It is well understood that he was an "evangelist" for YHWH. His tent was always open to the stranger and he was hospitable to all. He used these opportunities to share his Elohim and he developed an entourage with him which was his household. If you joined with Abraham and dwelled under his tents, then you would also join into the covenant by following the ways of the Elohim of Abraham.

6

Israel

If we take a giant leap forward through history we can follow the promises of Elohim through the seed of Abraham to Yitshaq and Ya'akov, who was later renamed Israel (Yisrael)[48] until finally we reach the children of Yisrael who had been enslaved in Egypt (Mitsrayim)[49] and were miraculously delivered under the leadership of Mosheh. Interestingly, Mosheh was raised in a pagan society and later lived in the land of Midian, who was a son of Abraham (Beresheet 25:2).

The Scriptures tell us that Mosheh married Zipporah who was the daughter of the priest of Midian - a man named Jethro (Yithro). The Midianites were known to worship Baal-Peor, Asherah and Hathor the Mitsrite goddess. Interestingly, there is evidence that at some point in history they worshipped YHWH and circumcised their males.[50] Could this have been the result of the influence Mosheh had on his father-in-law Yithro? We know that Yithro had a good relationship with Mosheh before and after the Exodus. It is possible that Yithro repented when he heard and saw the power of YHWH as He dwelled with Yisrael.

Besides Mosheh, the children of Yisrael had been immersed in a pagan culture for centuries and it was time for Elohim to deliver on His promises to Abraham, Yitshaq and Ya'akov. He plagued the Land of Mitsrayim, led the multitude out of Mitsrayim through divided waters and subsequently destroyed the army of Pharaoh. The Scriptures tell us that this was all done in such a dramatic fashion so that the entire world would know the Name of YHWH. Exodus (Shemot)[51] 9:16.

This is the concept that many people fail to recognize - it is His desire that the entire world knows Him. This was the reason why He chose to deliver Yisrael and make them a nation of priests. "Priests to what?" you might ask. Priests to YHWH and to the nations! It is all part of the plan of restoration.

After delivering the Children of Yisrael along with a mixed multitude of people in very dramatic fashion, Mosheh went up Mt. Sinai to meet with YHWH. While the instructions had been revealed to mankind from the beginning, something different happened at Mount Sinai - just like something different happened with Abraham. It was another step in the process of restoration. This time the Torah was written and incorporated into a covenant with a Nation of people called Yisrael.

YHWH had told Abraham that his descendants would be afflicted for 400 years. When the time was up - the promise was fulfilled through the seed of Abraham that passed through Yitshaq to Ya'akov - whose name was changed to Yisrael.

The primary difference with the Sinai covenant was that the Almighty was establishing a marriage covenant with Yisrael and included within that covenant

were those who dwelled with Yisrael. The Torah was still at the center of the covenant - like a Ketubah or a written marriage contract between a husband and a wife. The covenant was made between YHWH and Yisrael through Mosheh the Mediator.

It is important to reemphasize that along with the descendents of Yisrael - a mixed multitude of people were delivered from Mitsrayim. According to Shemot 12:37-38 "*37 The children of Yisrael journeyed from Rameses to Succoth, about six hundred thousand men on foot, besides children. *38* **A mixed multitude went up with them also**, and flocks and herds - a great deal of livestock.*"

You see, anybody could sojourn with Yisrael so long as they agreed to obey the Holy One of Yisrael - just like anyone could live with Abraham and enter into the covenant if they were circumcised and followed the Ways of YHWH. The Assembly of Yisrael always included non-native Yisraelites and the Torah was never considered to be the exclusive domain of those who had the right genes – i.e. full blooded offspring of the man named Yisrael.

The Torah was for all mankind, as it was from the beginning. Remember, Adam was not a Hebrew, a Yisraelite, a Jew or a Christian - he was a man created in the image of YHWH. After the sin of Adam and Hawah, it was then necessary to restore individuals and mankind back into a right relationship and standing before the Creator. YHWH was always concerned about the individual and when He established Yisrael as a nation it did not mean that He forgot about those who came prior to Yisrael nor does it mean that He was not concerned about the other nations that surrounded Yisrael. In fact, He established Yisrael to reveal Himself to the nations.

Therefore, anyone who wanted to enter into this covenant relationship with the Creator could do so provided that they observed the terms of the covenant - which was the Torah. This is specifically stated in Leviticus (Vayiqra)[52] 19:33-34: "*[33] And if a stranger dwells with you in your land, you shall not mistreat him. [34] The stranger who dwells among you <u>shall be to you as one born among you, and you shall love him as yourself</u>; for you were strangers in the land of Mitsrayim: I am YHWH your Elohim.*"

There were plenty of non-native Yisraelites who had joined with Yisrael and were redeemed from Mitsrayim. They were also with Yisrael when they became impatient with Mosheh and under Aaron's tutelage, crafted a golden calf and worshipped it as YHWH.

A casual observer might ask: Why on earth would they do such a thing? It seems absolutely absurd, until you realize that they were doing what was familiar to them. They were worshipping "god" the way that the gods had been worshipped in Mitsrayim.

You see, pagan societies such as Mitsrayim did not worship one god - they worshipped many gods. There were a multitude of gods and goddesses that symbolized different things on the earth and in the spirit realm. One of the major cults in Mitsrayim was the worship of Hathor. Hathor was one of the most  commonly worshipped goddesses in Ancient Mitsrayim who was originally considered to be the mother of Horus, the falcon god. That title eventually went to Isis and Hathor was in later times regarded as his wife. Hathor was associated with

love, fertility, sexuality, music, dance and alcohol. Who better to invite to a party - at least that is what the Yisraelites thought.

"She was sometimes represented entirely anthropomorphically, in the form of a cow, or as a woman with cow's ears. When in human form, her headdress could be one of cow's horns with a solar disc, or a falcon on a perch. She was also a sky goddess, and was regarded as a vast cow who straddled the heavens, with her four legs marking the four cardinal points."[53]

She was honored as the "Lady of Byblos", the source of the word "Bible."[54]

The Yisraelites declared a Feast to YHWH which was not a feast prescribed or ordained by YHWH. They

built an altar and made an idol in the manner that they had learned while in Mitsrayim. The golden calf was the child of Hathor and Apis. Thus we see another example of a pagan trinity - father, mother, child worship which is predominate in pagan systems and as we have already seen - derives from Babylon. They took what they were used to doing in a pagan society and

began doing it to YHWH. The only problem was that it was an abomination to YHWH. They were supposed to be a "holy" people which is qadosh (קָדֹשׁ) in Hebrew and means: "set apart."

They were not supposed to be doing pagan things and

saying that they were doing them to YHWH. They were mixing abominations in their worship which is strictly prohibited. Sadly, this error was continually repeated by Yisrael.

Interestingly, the very altar constructed by the Children of Yisrael at the base of Mount Sinai has been found in Saudi Arabia, although they will never find the golden calf, which was ground up and fed to the pagan practicing multitude.[55]

Not only has Mount Sinai been found but so has the split rock from which water poured out for the people and

livestock as they camped at the base of the Mountain. Most people are taught that these locations are found in the Sinai Peninsula which is nothing but a man-made tradition. Despite the fact that archaeology shows that the Red Sea crossing occurred at Nuweiba, Mitsrayim into Saudi Arabia[56] people tend to cling to traditions over truth.[57]

Now, it is important to remember that it was the Yisraelites along with a mixed multitude that left Mitsrayim. There is no reason to think that only the non-native Yisraelites worshipped false gods. In fact, their readiness to worship false gods only days after witnessing the miraculous deliverance from Mitsrayim only strengthens the position that many of the Yisraelites

had fallen into pagan worship while enslaved in Mitsrayim.

After all, they were surrounded by these gods and goddesses for centuries which pervaded every aspect of the Mitsrite culture.

These gods and goddesses had names, faces and temples where they could be worshipped. They had statues and idols which could be seen and touched - they appeared real to those who worshipped them. Yisrael likely forgot the Elohim of their father Abraham because He was invisible and without form.

This is why Elohim brought them out to the desert, to clean them up and straighten them out - to restore them. He wanted to reveal Himself to them and show them how to properly worship Him. If you read the Old Testament Scriptures (Tanak), you will see that time and again, Yisrael fell back into pagan worship. Their "backsliding" involved a variety of gods and goddesses from neighboring countries, some of which we will discuss further on in this book.

The cleaning up process which began in the wilderness has been continuing throughout the millennia. Elohim is still in the process of cleaning up His people and if you are a Believer, you are not excluded from this process. Throughout every generation He gleans those who have a heart for Him. He is looking for a people who will follow him wholeheartedly.

If you desire to follow the Elohim of Yisrael, then it is important to avoid any form of idolatry in your life. When reading the Scriptures it is easy to get the impression that the paganism which Yisrael experienced was old and does not exist anymore. As we will discover, the same paganism which Yisrael struggled with in the Scriptures is alive and well this very day. In fact, Christianity,

Catholicism and the entire world all have been tainted by the same elements which haunted Yisrael in years gone by.

Yisrael had to make a choice - whether they would follow the One True Elohim or whether they would chase after the false gods of the Gentiles. Yisrael consisted of anyone who wanted to follow the Elohim of Yisrael. It did not matter where you came from. If you were born a Gentile, you could join with Yisrael but if you wanted to dwell with the Redeemed people, you needed to live your life according to the instructions - the Torah. The Torah told Yisrael - the Bride - exactly what YHWH - the Husband - expected of her. It established boundaries for the marriage.

The Torah was, in essence, a wedding gift to Yisrael. It was never considered to be a burden by Yisrael; it was always understood to be a blessing and a privilege to be given the Torah. In fact, it showed them how to receive blessings and it warned them of how they could be cursed.

Many people wander through life wondering how to be blessed and wondering why they are not blessed or why they feel cursed. YHWH expressly told His Bride how to prosper and how to avoid problems. He showed her the path to abundance, blessings and life.

Who would not consider that to be a great gift? As a result, the assembly of Yisrael willingly agreed to obey the Torah; it was not forced upon them. In fact, the Almighty delivered them from slavery and freed them without any conditions other than to follow His instructions. This is so no one could **ever** state that they made a decision under duress.

Once the mixed multitude was delivered from slavery, they were <u>then</u> given the option to accept the Torah and their decision was unequivocal. After Mosheh told the people all of the words, they responded in Shemot 24:4: "*All the words that YHWH has commanded **we will do.***" They freely chose to live in a manner which allowed them to dwell in the presence of a Holy Elohim - the manner prescribed by the Torah.

According to Bemidbar 15:29 "*You shall have **one Torah** for him who sins unintentionally, for him who is native-born among the children of Yisrael and for the stranger who dwells among them.*" Again, your skin color did not matter; neither did the genes in your body. What mattered was what you believed and consequently what you obeyed. If you lived your life like many Christians do today, you would not be able to dwell with Yisrael and with YHWH because most Christians reject the Torah and do not obey the commandments.

Yisrael later rejected the promise of the covenant by refusing to enter the land. This demonstrated an utter lack of faith and trust in the promises of YHWH. This is remarkable because the Almighty had just recently delivered them from the most powerful nation on earth. They were about to receive the land which was promised to them but they were afraid, despite the miracles they had just witnessed. Their fear demonstrated that they did not trust YHWH and ultimately they did not love Him. If they loved Him, they would have done what He said even if it meant certain death. Sadly, YHWH was intent on blessing them and they still refused to obey. We should all meditate on this point because we too can miss the blessings if we fail to obey. There may come a time in the

future when we must make a similar choice. Our response must be to obey no matter what we see with our eyes.

As a result of the choice that Yisrael made, they were forced to wander in the wilderness for forty years until the next generation was raised up to enter into the land. This was very merciful of YHWH. He could have destroyed them all because of their disobedience but he let that generation live out the rest of their lives until only two from that generation remained.

An important fact to point out is that only two adults from the generation that left Mitsrayim in the Exodus actually crossed over into the Promised Land. Joshua (Yahshua)[58] and Caleb - two of the 12 who previously explored the land. They were the two who gave a good report to the people and encouraged them to enter into the land - despite the presence of giants. They also took the trouble to haul out an enormous cluster of grapes as proof of the bounty that awaited them. The reason why these two were different is specifically detailed in the Scripture: *"not one except Caleb son of Yephunneh the Kenizzite and Yahshua son of Nun, for they followed YHWH wholeheartedly."* Bemidbar 32:12.

Notice that Caleb was not a native Yisraelite. The Scriptures: record that his father was a Kenizzite yet they became part of Yisrael. Despite the fact that his father was from a foreign land, the Scriptures list Caleb as being part of the Tribe of Yahudah. This is how it

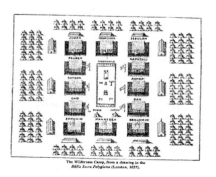

The Wilderness Camp, from a drawing in the
Biblia Sacra Polyglotta (London, 1657).

worked when Yisrael camped after the Exodus. They divided into tribes and they camped around the Tabernacle. There was no tribe of the Mixed Multitude - no tribe of the Gentiles. So Caleb's family joined Yisrael through the Tribe of Yahudah. Anyone that wanted to join with Yisrael was joined to a Tribe.

Now look at Yahshua son of Nun. His name was changed from Hoshea which means "salvation" to Yahshua which means "Yah is salvation." Yahshua was from the Tribe of Ephraim. The Tribe of Ephraim is extremely interesting because the name itself means: "doubly fruitful." Ephraim was the son of Joseph (Yoseph) and he was born in Mitsrayim along with his brother Manashah - unlike the other Children of Yisrael. His mother Asenath was a Mitsrite - the Daughter of a Pagan Priest - just like Mosheh's wife.

Ephraim was the youngest son of Joseph yet he received the blessing and birthright of a firstborn son. He was actually adopted by his grandfather Yisrael and elevated as a son. So we see this powerful picture of a child born into a pagan culture and Yisrael then adopting him into the family, making him a tribe and blessing Him - as a firstborn son! (Beresheet 48).

Therefore we have these two men - Caleb and Yahshua - representing Yahudah and Ephraim both of whom were adopted into Yisrael in different ways - these being the only two to enter into the land from their generation. How profound and encouraging for anyone born into paganism, finding themselves outside of the Covenant. Not to fret, there is room for everyone.

If you still are not convinced, then read on. Before this new generation entered into the Promised Land, the

Covenant was renewed at Moab. We read in Devarim 29:1 *"These are the terms of the covenant YHWH commanded Mosheh to make with the Yisraelites in Moab, in addition to the covenant he had made with them at Horeb."* All of Yisrael was assembled, including sojourners in the midst of the assembly, to hear the words of the renewed covenant.

"¹⁰ All of you are standing today in the presence of YHWH your Elohim - your leaders and chief men, your elders and officials, and all the other men of Yisrael, **¹¹together with your children and your wives, and the aliens living in your camps who chop your wood and carry your water.** *¹² You are standing here in order to enter into a covenant with YHWH your Elohim, a covenant YHWH is making with you this day and sealing with an oath, ¹³ to confirm you this day as his people, that he may be your Elohim as he promised you and as he swore to your fathers, Abraham, Yitshaq and Ya'akov.* **¹⁴ I am making this covenant, with its oath, not only with you ¹⁵ who are standing here with us today in the presence of YHWH our Elohim but also with those who are not here today."** Devarim 29:10-15.

The Covenant was renewed with that new generation as well as with those who were not there - a future people. This points to a future people who would enter into the same covenant - which would again be renewed. We have an example of this happening with Ruth who was, by no coincidence, a Moabite from the very land where this Covenant was renewed. We see from the story of Ruth a beautiful picture of a foreigner being grafted into Yisrael[59] and becoming an important part of the Messianic bloodline. Her famous words are the formula for becoming grafted in to Yisrael: *"For wherever you go, I will go; and wherever you lodge, I will lodge; Your people shall be my people, and your Elohim, my Elohim."* Ruth 1:16. Through this story

we see a vivid example of redemption.

We know also from the Scriptures that the generation that renewed the covenant at Moab - under leadership of Yahshua - crossed the Jordan (Yarden) River, which was a corporate baptism more accurately known as a mikvah.[60] They were circumcised and then celebrated the first Passover in the land. They then went on a campaign to conquer the land and drive out the giants which the previous generation had been afraid to confront.

The Children of Yisrael were specifically commanded not to worship false gods when they entered the land. *"You shall not bow down to their gods or serve them or do after their works; but you shall utterly overthrow them and break down their pillars and images."* Shemot 23:24. They were also instructed not to set up poles and pillars in order to worship false gods. *"[21] You shall not plant for yourself any tree, as a wooden image, near the altar which you build for yourself to YHWH your Elohim. [22] You shall not set up a sacred pillar, which YHWH your Elohim hates."* Devarim 16:21-22.

We read in the Scriptures how Yisrael settled into the Land but was regularly struggling with their leadership, their own inner turmoil, and the neighboring nations. Sadly, the marriage between YHWH and his people did not work out well because Yisrael was not a faithful bride. She kept going after foreign gods. The worship of these gods was idolatry - which is spiritual adultery.

There came a time when the people cried out for a King and Samuel (Shemuel) anointed Shaul although his reign did not last for long because he did not diligently obey the commandments. Here is what Shemuel told Shaul: *"[13] You have done foolishly. You have not kept the commandment of YHWH your Elohim, which He commanded you. For now*

YHWH would have established your kingdom over Yisrael forever. ¹⁴ But now your kingdom shall not continue. YHWH has sought for Himself a man after His own heart, and YHWH has commanded him to be commander over His people, because you have not kept what YHWH commanded you." 1 Shemuel 13:13-14.

Shaul failed just as Adam had failed. He did not keep, guard, watch over and protect (shamar) the commandments. Therefore, YHWH found a man like Yahshua and Caleb - a man who would follow Him with his WHOLE heart. David was a giant slayer as were Yahshua and Caleb. He trusted in his Elohim and we know from the Psalms (Tehillim) that he loved the Torah.⁶¹ The reign of King David is looked upon as the Golden years of Yisrael. He made mistakes but his heart for YHWH never wavered. After the reign of King David, things deteriorated very rapidly. His son, Solomon (Shlomo), built the House of YHWH and other great structures, he accrued incredible wealth, and was known for his great wisdom, but sadly he fell into serious idolatry at the end of his life.

Read how his heart turned away from YHWH:

"¹ But King Shlomo loved many foreign women, as well as the daughter of Pharaoh: women of the Moabites, Ammonites, Edomites, Sidonians, and Hittites - ² from the nations of whom YHWH had said to the children of Yisrael, 'You shall not intermarry with them, nor they with you. Surely they will turn away your hearts after their gods.' Shlomo clung to these in love. ³ And he had seven hundred wives, princesses, and three hundred concubines; and his wives turned away his heart. ⁴ For it was so, when Shlomo was old, that his wives turned his heart after other gods; and his heart was not loyal to YHWH his Elohim, as was

the heart of his father David. ⁵ For Shlomo went after Ashtoreth the goddess of the Sidonians, and after Milcom the abomination of the Ammonites. ⁶ <u>Shlomo did evil in the sight of YHWH, and did not fully follow YHWH, as did his father David</u>. ⁷ Then Shlomo built a high place for Chemosh the abomination of Moab, on the hill that is east of Jerusalem, and for Molech the abomination of the people of Ammon. ⁸ And he did likewise for all his foreign wives, who burned incense and sacrificed to their gods. ⁹ So YHWH became angry with Shlomo, because his heart had turned from YHWH Elohim of Yisrael, who had appeared to him twice, ¹⁰ and had commanded him concerning this thing, that he should not go after other gods; but he did not keep what YHWH had commanded. ¹¹ Therefore YHWH said to Shlomo, because you have done this, and have not kept My covenant and My statutes, which I have commanded you, I will surely tear the kingdom away from you and give it to your servant. ¹² Nevertheless I will not do it in your days, for the sake of your father David; I will tear it out of the hand of your son. ¹³ However I will not tear away the whole kingdom; I will give one tribe to your son for the sake of My servant David, and for the sake of Jerusalem which I have chosen." 1 Kings 11:1-13.

Despite the great blessings bestowed upon him, Shlomo disobeyed the commandment concerning taking foreign wives. He fell into serious sin and, as a result, the kingdom was taken away from his son - Rehoboam. The Northern tribes rebelled because of the heavy taxation imposed upon them by Rehoboam.

Thus, we see the House of Yisrael, often referred to as Ephraim in the Scriptures, separating from the House of Yahudah. Both houses strayed from YHWH and just as we previously saw Ephraim, represented by Yahshua, and Yahudah, represented by Caleb, enter in to the land because they followed YHWH wholeheartedly (Devarim 1:36) - both houses were eventually expelled because of their disobedience.

Over the centuries that followed, many prophets were sent to try to restore them to a right relationship with YHWH by pointing the way back to the Torah. This, after all, is the primary function of a prophet - Restoration. Many people think that a prophet is one who tells the future, like a soothsayer or a fortune teller, but the primary function of a prophet is to warn people and to point out the error of their way so that they can get back on the straight path, back into the fold, back behind the hedge of protection of the Torah.

There were different prophets sent to the different Kingdoms to warn them and they would often stand in the gap and encourage Yisrael (Ephraim) and Yahudah to get cleaned up and get right with their Creator. These prophets acted like marriage counselors but both Kingdoms failed to heed their warnings. They refused to give up their whoring and thus they remained separated from their Husband - YHWH. Read what YHWH spoke through the Prophet Hoshea:

"4 *What can I do with you, Ephraim? What can I do with you, Yahudah? Your love is like the morning mist, like the early dew that disappears.* 5 *Therefore I cut you in pieces with my prophets, I killed you with the words of my mouth; my judgments flashed like lightning upon you.* 6 *For I desire mercy, not sacrifice, and acknowledgment of Elohim rather than burnt offerings.* 7 *Like Adam, they have broken the covenant - they were unfaithful to me there.*" Hoshea 6:4-7.

Notice how he speaks to Ephraim and Yahudah separately and notice the connection with Adam. Adam

was supposed to commune with YHWH. Adam was literally and metaphorically split in two when Hawah was taken from his side - and both Adam and Hawah broke the Covenant. This was similar to what happened with Yisrael. The Kingdom was divided into Ephraim and Yahudah and both of them broke the covenant.

They all broke the covenant with YHWH by being unfaithful. They all disobeyed the Torah and what was needed was Restoration. This could only be accomplished through repentance - a change of heart followed by a renewal of vows - a renewal of the covenant that had been broken.

7

The Renewed Covenant

Restoration was the purpose of what is commonly called the New Covenant. Most Christians would readily admit that they rely upon the so-called New Covenant for their relationship with YHWH but many could not tell you what it is or where to find it.

The New Covenant was not created at the Last Supper as many believe. It had been prophesied centuries earlier and was anticipated by many. Interestingly, the terms of this "New" covenant are found in the "Old" Testament. I believe that it is a serious mistake to divide the Scriptures into "Old" and "New" because it gives the impression that the "Old" is not so relevant while the "New" is the really important stuff. This is what I was taught and I can assure you that this type of thinking wreaks doctrinal havoc.

I prefer to call the "Old" Testament the Tanak. Tanak is an acronym and stands for: **T**orah, **N**ebiim (Prophets), **K**ethubim (Writings) T-N-K – Tanak. The use of this acronym describes the contents but does not categorize them as "Old." Likewise, I generally refer to the "New" Testament manuscripts as the Messianic writings. This properly categorizes them without calling

them "New" and I refer to them collectively as "The Scriptures."

This is important because we need to realize that the Tanak is the foundation of our faith and is absolutely relevant and presently applicable to all who follow YHWH. While some of the things described in the Tanak occurred in the past - it may be old but it is not irrelevant. Likewise, most of the contents in the Messianic Scriptures occurred almost 2,000 years ago making it not such a "New" book. They are both important and they both contain prophetic writings which have yet to occur. As a result, there is absolutely no need to place Old/New labels on them. It only leads to problems and confusion.

Both the Tanak and the Messianic Writings fit together perfectly and there should be no division. It is the old/new false paradigm which has led to such misleading doctrines as Replacement Theology[62] and Dispensationalism.[63]

No one in their right mind would purchase a book and read it backwards or start in the middle and read a paragraph here and a paragraph there. For some reason, that is what many people do with their Bibles and some of this is due to the fact they do not understand the significance of the Tanak. You cannot possibly understand the plan of YHWH by doing such a thing but sadly, this is how Christianity has handled the Scriptures - particularly in the past decades. Get someone saved and give them a New Testament or a Gospel of John (Yahanan)[64] - that has become the recognized Christian formula for handling converts.

Again, this is backwards. It is difficult to fully understand the purpose and need for a Messiah without understanding the Torah, the Prophets and the Writings. Just as the Old/New dichotomy misrepresents the Scriptures, so it also misrepresents the covenants. The Abrahamic covenant, the Sinai covenant and the Renewed Covenant at Moab are often referred to as the Old Covenant while the covenant mediated by the Messiah is often called the New Covenant.

This gives the distinct impression that the New has replaced, or done away with, the Old or that the New makes the Old irrelevant. The proper Hebrew terminology for the "New" Covenant is Brit Hadashah. The word brit (ברית) means: "covenant" or "cutting." The word hadashah (חדשה) means: "renewed" or "refreshed." Therefore, it is more accurately described as The Renewed Covenant - just as the covenant was broken and renewed at Sinai and then renewed again with the next generation at Moab.

This is the pattern of renewal which we were given through the Scriptures. Again, using the word "new" gives the impression that it is something "brand new" which replaces the old. If this was the message intended then the Greek texts would have likely used the word neo (νεο). Instead, they use the word kainos (καηεενοσ) which means: "renewed" or "refreshed." Therefore, the term Renewed covenant provides that the former covenant is being refreshed, not replaced.

A good example of the renewal process can be seen in what is commonly called the new moon. The new moon is called rosh hodesh in Hebrew which literally means: "head of the month." Just as hadash in the Brit Hadashah refers to renewal so hodesh in rosh hodesh refers to a renewal of the moon. The words hodesh and

hadash share the same roots (h-d-sh) in Hebrew (חדש) and therefore have the shared meaning of "renewal." We are all familiar with the different phases of the moon but what most do not realize is that the Scriptural month actually begins with the sighting of the new moon when the first sliver is visible. As the moon progresses through its phases we see more and more until it is full. It then begins to wane until it disappears altogether usually for two or three days. When we see it disappear we know that we need to watch.

We watch because when we sight that first sliver it is Rosh Hodesh - the Renewed Moon and the beginning of the next month - a traditional time to celebrate. Now, when we sight the renewed moon we know that it is the same moon that we saw only days prior - it is not a <u>brand</u> <u>new</u> moon, but a renewal of the former moon. Likewise, the Brit Hadashah is not a <u>brand</u> <u>new</u> covenant but a renewal of the former covenant.

We were even given a vivid example at Sinai how the covenant would be renewed. When Mosheh went up the mountain the first time, YHWH carved out tablets of stone and wrote His covenant on those tablets. When Mosheh brought the tablets down from the mountain, he observed Yisrael committing idolatry by worshipping foreign gods.

They had broken the covenant and thus Mosheh

broke the tablets. After His anger subsided, YHWH agreed to renew the covenant with Yisrael - only this time Mosheh had to carve out the stone tablets himself and carry them up the mountain where man, through Mosheh the mediator, presented the tablets to YHWH, Who then wrote His covenant upon tablets presented by man.

It was the same covenant that was written on the first tablets only it was written on different tablets brought by man. The covenant was renewed - the same terms, the same Torah - just renewed on different tablets after the first ones were broken. The same pattern applies to the Renewed Covenant only now we see the Messiah acting as the Mediator of the Renewed Covenant.

The promise of how this renewal would come about is found in Yirmeyahu 31:31-33: "*31 Behold, the days are coming, says YHWH, when I will make a renewed covenant with the house of Yisrael and with the house of Yahudah - 32 not according to the covenant that I made with their fathers in the day that I took them by the hand to lead them out of the land of Mitsrayim, My covenant which they broke, though I was a husband to them, says YHWH. 33 But this is the covenant that I will make with the house of Yisrael after those days, says YHWH: I will put My Torah in their minds, and write it on their hearts; and I will be their Elohim, and they shall be My people.*"

Notice that the renewed covenant is made with the House of Yisrael and the House of Yahudah, <u>not</u> some new religion called Christianity or some new entity called "The Church." Also, recognize that the Torah is at the heart of this renewed covenant.

Now read how the renewed covenant is performed: "*17 I will <u>gather you from the peoples</u>, <u>assemble you from the</u>*

countries where you have been scattered, and I will give you the land of Yisrael. *¹⁸ And they will go there, and they will take away all its detestable things and all its abominations from there. ¹⁹ Then <u>I will give them one heart, and I will put a renewed spirit within them,</u> and take the stony heart out of their flesh, and give them a heart of flesh, ²⁰ **that they may walk in My statutes and keep My judgments and do them**; and they shall be <u>My people,</u> and I will be <u>their Elohim.</u>"* Yehezqel 11:17-20.

This, of course, is what the Almighty always wanted through the original covenant - for His people to keep (shamar) His commandments and do them. So the renewed covenant is made with the divided kingdom of Yisrael - with both the House of Yisrael (Ephraim) and the House of Yahudah. YHWH will regather all of His people by restoring the Kingdom. He will also write His Torah on the hearts and on the minds of His people instead of tablets of stone.

Like the first tablets presented by YHWH - He presented His Son as the Torah in the flesh. Just as the first tablets were broken because of the sin of Yisrael, so the Messiah was broken because the covenant was broken. As foretold through the Abrahamic Covenant, YHWH paid the price for the covenant being broken. As YHWH renewed the covenant by writing the covenant on the second set of tablets presented by man, so now YHWH writes His covenant upon the tablets (heart and mind) of those who present themselves to Him - those who love and obey Him. This is how the Renewed Covenant with the Messiah as the Mediator was implemented.

The terms of the covenant are not new, rather it is renewed and refreshed through a different Mediator. Look back to Devarim 10:12-16: *"¹² And now, Yisrael, what does YHWH your Elohim require of you, but to fear YHWH your Elohim, to walk in all His ways and to love Him, to serve YHWH your Elohim with all your heart and with all your soul, [13] and to keep the commandments of YHWH and His statutes which I command you today for your good? [14] Indeed heaven and the highest heavens belong to YHWH your Elohim, also the earth with all that is in it. [15] YHWH delighted only in your fathers, to love them; and He chose their descendants after them, you above all peoples, as it is this day. [16] Therefore circumcise the foreskin of your heart, and be stiff-necked no longer."*

The covenants are the same - the purpose of the Renewed Covenant was to circumcise our hearts - not just our flesh. Through this process, by His Spirit, He would write the Torah on our hearts and in our minds so that we can keep (shamar) His commandments and do the instructions and walk with Him.

Here is the promise when we obey: *"[5] Now therefore, if you will indeed obey My voice and keep My covenant, then you shall be a special treasure to Me above all people; for all the earth is Mine. [6] And you shall be to Me a kingdom of priests and a holy nation. These are the words which you shall speak to the children of Yisrael."* Shemot 19:5-6.

Notice the promises to Yisrael - they will be a special treasure, a kingdom of priests and a holy Nation. This sounds like something we read about in the Messianic Scriptures. In fact, we read in 1 Peter (Kepha) 2:9-10: *"[9] But you are a chosen generation, a royal priesthood, a holy nation, His own special people, that you may proclaim the praises of Him who called you out of darkness into His marvelous light; [10] who once were not a people but are now the people of Elohim, who had not obtained mercy but now have obtained mercy."*

It sounds an awful lot alike because they are

referring to the same people - the people of Elohim - those who once were not a people but are now the people of Elohim. A people who had not obtained mercy but now have obtained mercy. For those familiar with the prophets, this is a direct reference to the prophecy given through Hoshea to the House of Yisrael - Ephraim.

"2 YHWH said to Hoshea: Go, take yourself a wife of harlotry and children of harlotry, for the land has committed great harlotry by departing from YHWH 3 So he went and took Gomer the daughter of Diblaim, and she conceived and bore him a son. 4 Then YHWH said to him: Call his name Yizreel, for in a little while I will avenge the bloodshed of Yizreel on the house of Yehu, and bring an end to the kingdom of the house of Yisrael. 5 It shall come to pass in that day that I will break the bow of Yisrael in the Valley of Yizreel. 6 And she conceived again and bore a daughter. Then Elohim said to him: Call her name Lo-Ruhamah, for I will no longer have mercy on the House of Yisrael, but I will utterly take them away.7 Yet I will have mercy on the house of Yahudah, will save them by YHWH their Elohim, and will not save them by bow, nor by sword or battle, by horses or horsemen. 8 Now when she had weaned Lo-Ruhamah, she conceived and bore a son.9 Then Elohim said: Call his name Lo-Ammi, for you are not My people, and I will not be your Elohim. 10 Yet the number of the Children of Yisrael shall be as the sand of the sea, which cannot be measured or numbered. And it shall come to pass in the

*place where it was said to them, <u>You are not My</u>
<u>people, there it shall be said to them, You are</u>
<u>sons of the living Elohim</u>.* " Then the Children
of Yahudah and the Children of Yisrael shall
be gathered together, and appoint for themselves
one head; and they shall come up out of the land,
for great will be the day of Yizreel!" Hoshea
1:2-2:1

Therefore, Hoshea prophesied the following
concerning the House of Yisrael: 1) They would be brought
to an end; 2) YHWH would not have mercy on them and
would scatter them; 3) They would not be His people and
He would not be their Elohim; 4) In the end the House
of Yisrael would be restored with the House of Yahudah
under One Head and be called "Sons of the Living El."

These are the people to whom Peter (Kepha)[65]
was writing. Notice how he addressed his letter: "*¹ To the
pilgrims of the Dispersion in Pontus, Galatia, Cappadocia, Asia,
and Bithynia, ² elect according to the foreknowledge of Elohim
the Father . . .*" 1 Kepha 1:1-2.

He is writing to people who had been dispersed -
scattered throughout the world and in exile - the Lost Sheep
of the House of Yisrael. He is reminding them about the
promises in the Tanak and telling them about the Good
News that Messiah has come to restore the Kingdom.

The House of Yisrael was rejected and forgotten
because of what they did with the Torah. The Prophet
Hoshea further declared: "*my people are destroyed from lack
of knowledge. Because you have rejected knowledge, I also reject
you as my priests; because you have ignored the Torah of your
Elohim, I also will ignore your children.*" Hoshea 4:6

If we want to be priests we need to act like priests

and obey the Torah. Kepha is not making up anything new - again it is all about the Torah. This is not something brand new, it is simply the renewal promised by Mosheh.

In Devarim 30:5-6 he stated: "⁵ *Then YHWH your Elohim will bring you to the land which your fathers possessed, and you shall possess it. He will prosper you and multiply you more than your fathers.* ⁶ *And YHWH your Elohim will* **circumcise your heart and the heart of your descendants,** *to love YHWH your Elohim* <u>*with all your heart and with all your soul,*</u> <u>*that you may live.*</u>"

As Mosheh was the Mediator of the Sinai Covenant he foretold that there would be another - like him. We read in Devarim 18:18-19: "¹⁸ **I will raise up for them a Prophet like you** *from among their brethren, and will put My words in His mouth, and He shall speak to them all that I command Him.* ¹⁹ *And it shall be that whoever will not hear My words, which He speaks in My name, I will require it of him.*" This points to the Messiah Who was the Mediator of the Renewed covenant.

8

Hellenism

Before we can fully understand the ministry and teaching of the Messiah and His disciples, it is important to understand the world in which He walked and taught. The land of Yisrael had been conquered and repeatedly found itself under the rule of various empires which was a direct result of Yisrael's failure to obey the Torah.

Alexander the Great, the Macedonian military ruler, had a profound influence upon the Mediterranean region of the world and beyond from 330 BCE through 30 BCE, a period known as the Hellenistic Age. From 30 BCE until 330 CE, the Roman Empire greatly influenced this

The Empire of Alexander the Great

same geographic area. Alexander was primarily responsible for the spread of Hellenistic culture throughout this region which was called Hellenization. When he conquered a city or civilization he would proceed to

Hellenize that culture by permeating Greek ideas, style, architecture, philosophy, religion and culture into that particular society. This was done while preserving the essence of the defeated culture and maintaining the basic political structure which is a process called peaceful syncretism.

Thus, Hellenization involved a blending of Grecian culture with other civilizations in the region of the world referred to as the middle and near east. A large part of the Grecian culture which was spread involved their pagan worship system and it was  through this syncretism that the Canaanite god Baal, the Egyptian god Amon, and the Persian god Ahura Mazda became identified with the Greek sun god Zeus and later the Roman sun god Jupiter.

Likewise, the Canaanite goddess Astarte (also known as Easter) and the Persian goddess Anahita (also  known as Anaitis) became identified with the Greek goddess Aphrodite and later the Roman goddess Venus. Through this blending process many similarities developed between the gods and goddesses of the pagan cultures - parallels developed which led to continuity and consistency. What developed was a religious melting pot with tolerance and general acceptance of all gods.

"Alexander himself had a passion for Homer. The invasion of Asia Minor was recounted as another Trojan

War, and the first thing Alexander did at Troy was to pay an act of homage to Achilles, who was initially his heroic prototype. Later, Heracles, a hero who became a god in virtue of his achievements, filled this role. Alexander was  also connected to Dionysus, whom the Greeks believed came from Asia and who became "the god" of the Greek expansion into the Middle East, receiving the greatest amount of personal devotion in the Hellenistic kingdoms. Alexander held a Dionysiac celebration at Nysa where, according to tradition, Dionysus was born. This religious emphasis was characteristic of Alexander. He gave his own adhesion to Zeus, and religious acts . . . were not antiquarian features for him."[66]

Dionysus is an interesting pagan god because of the similarities which can be seen between him and the Jesus of modern Christianity. Dionysus is the Greek name for the Roman god Bacchus. "Dionysus was a savior god who, like Jesus, died and rose from the dead. The Dionysians believed in rewards in Heaven and punishments in Hell. They believed in salvation through repentance and baptism for the remission of sins. They practiced the rituals of communion and baptism."[67]  An ancient engraving has been found which shows Dionysus being crucified on a cross which could easily be confused with Christian crucifixion relics. It is important to note that the Dionysian religion was flourishing in the land of Yisrael two hundred years before the birth of the Messiah.

The gods that pervaded the Greco-Roman era formed a divine society which revolved around Zeus (Jupiter) on Mount Olympus. Zeus was considered to be the father of gods and men and was the sky and weather god. The book of Acts describes an interesting event involving those who believed in Zeus. "*8 And in Lystra a certain man without strength in his feet was sitting, a cripple from his mother's womb, who had never walked.9 This man heard Paul (Shaul) speaking. Shaul, observing him intently and seeing that he had faith to be healed,10 said with a loud voice, 'Stand up straight on your feet!' And he leaped and walked.11 Now when the people saw what Shaul had done, they raised their voices, saying in the Lycaonian language, 'The gods have come down to us in the likeness of men!' 12 And Barnabas they called Zeus, and Shaul, Hermes, because he was the chief speaker.13 Then the priest of Zeus, whose temple was in front of their city, brought oxen and garlands to the gates, intending to sacrifice with the multitudes. 14 But when the apostles Barnabas and Shaul heard this, they tore their clothes and ran in among the multitude, crying out 15 and saying, 'Men, why are you doing these things? We also are men with the same nature as you, and preach to you that you should turn from these useless things to the living Elohim, who made the heaven, the earth, the sea, and all things that are in them,16 who in bygone generations allowed all nations to walk in their own ways.17 Nevertheless He did not leave Himself without witness, in that He did good, gave us rain from heaven and fruitful seasons, filling our hearts with food and gladness.18 And with these sayings they could scarcely restrain the multitudes from sacrificing to them." Acts 14:8-18.*

The people in the region of Lystra were familiar with mythical tales of the gods appearing in human form so their natural inclination was to assume that Shaul and

Barnabas were gods appearing in human form. Since Shaul was the one who spoke primarily, the people called him Hermes, which was the Greek name for the Roman god known as Mercury, the messenger of the gods. Notice how the people immediately fit what they saw into their own religious paradigms - it was the only way that they knew how to explain what they saw. Their initial response was to make a sacrifice to their god when they witnessed and heard of the miracle performed through Shaul. Even after Shaul and Barnabas explained that they were mere men, not Zeus and  Hermes, the people still desired to make sacrifice as they were accustomed.

This is a pattern that we see repeatedly throughout history. Mankind is continually falling into patterns, customs and beliefs which miss the truth or exclude the Creator all together. This is the terrible effect that paganism has upon men - it clouds their perception of reality. These pagans witnessed a miracle from the Creator and their immediate impulse was to give credit to their pagan deities. This is the environment within which the Messiah taught, it was heavily steeped in Hellenism - which is nothing short of rampant paganism.

During the ministry of Shaul, Athens was the center of Greek culture and the Scriptures clearly record that it was a pagan culture. *"16 Now while Shaul waited for them at Athens, his spirit was provoked*

*within him when he saw that **the city was given over to idols.***[17] *Therefore he reasoned in the synagogue with the Yahudim and with the Gentile worshipers, and in the marketplace daily with those who happened to be there.*[18] *Then certain Epicurean and Stoic philosophers encountered him. And some said, What does this babbler want to say?"* Acts 17:16-18.

Greece was a pagan society with a variety of gods who all had various personalities and "specialties" if you will. In typical pagan fashion, these gods represented different aspects of the spiritual and the physical realm and had various strengths and powers, as well as weaknesses. Greek mythology is one big mythological soap opera involving love affairs, wars, feasts, triumph and tragedy all acted out by an array of gods, goddesses and some select human participants. Temples, altars and shrines were littered throughout the Greco-Roman territories.

The typical Hellenized community would consist of an array of temples dedicated to the worship of different gods or goddesses. They also would include a gymnasium which literally means to exercise naked. The whole point of being in a gymnasium was to be in the nude and it would therefore become very apparent who was an uncircumcised Gentile and who was a circumcised Yisraelite. The gymnasiums were directly linked to the temple worship which normally involved fornication, sacrifices and meals. Therefore, the temples became the center of most social activity.

Athletics and the gymnasium were closely associated with the Hellenistic culture. The Olympics are rooted in paganism and their very core was religious in nature. They were held every four years, beginning on the second or third full moon after the summer solstice, not unlike those held in modern times. They were actually a religious festival held at major sacred sites and they derive their name from the most famous, Olympia.

The activities would all occur in and around pagan temples and shrines and the various athletic contests were intermixed with sacrifices and ceremonies honoring Zeus, the Roman sun god and Pelops, the hero and mythical king of Olympia. All of the athletes trained and competed naked, offering their bodies to the glory of Zeus. Before  the games began a priest would sacrifice a bull in front of all of the participants who took an oath to Zeus.

 The most honored and oftentimes bloody events occurred before a 30 foot altar made entirely from the ashes of sacrificed animals. Winners of events were awarded a kotinos, which was a garland of wild olive from a sacred tree which grew at the site. The branch was cut by a boy whose parents were still living which derives from an ancient fertility rite. The first recorded celebration of the games in Olympia was in 776 B.C.E and they reached their apex in the sixth and fifth  centuries BCE. The Olympic Games gradually diminished in importance as the Roman Empire expanded and broadened its power in Greece. Eventually, Emperor Theodosius outlawed the Olympics in 393 CE.

These games were so pervasive that they even affected the Temple service in Jerusalem. There came a time when many Yisraelites became enamored by the Grecian lifestyle to such an extent that they learned the Greek language and took on the Greek attire. These Yisraelites were called Hellenists and they grew in power until in 175 BCE they took over the office of the High Priest.

One particular Hellenized Yisraelite named Jason became High Priest from 146 BCE to 145 BCE*. "He transformed Jerusalem into a Greek City, with Greek schools and gymnasiums where traditionally young athletes exercised nude (a Greek athletic practice). Even some of the young priests at Jerusalem took up the Greek language, athletic sports, and manner of dress: ' . . . he {Jason} founded a gymnasium right under the citadel, and he induced the noblest of the young men to wear the Greek hat. There was . . . an extreme of Hellenization and increase in the adoption of foreign ways . . .' (2 Maccabees 4:12-13 RSV).

At the apex of Greek influence, the priests of the Jerusalem temple would sometimes leave the sacrifices half-burned on the altar to rush off to a stadium to compete in the Greek games: ' . . . the priests were no longer intent upon their service at the altar. Despising the sanctuary and neglecting the sacrifices, they hastened to take part in the unlawful proceedings in the wrestling arena after the call to the discus, disdaining the honors prized by their fathers and putting the highest value upon Greek forms of prestige.' (2 Maccabees 4:14-15 RSV)."[68]

Jason went so far as to send money to Antiochus to offer sacrifices to the Greek god Hercules in the city of

Tyre. At that time, Hercules was a popular Greek deity in the Land. Hercules was considered to be a demi-god who was the result of the union between the god Zeus and the mortal woman Alcmene. After his death, the legends teach that Hercules became a god.

It is hard to believe that priests called to the highest service in the House of YHWH in Jerusalem would act in such a manner. Sadly, this is the danger of the impact that a pagan culture has upon those who desire to follow Elohim. If you take your eyes off of YHWH and His Torah, you may find yourself being influenced by your pagan surroundings. This will result in the dilution of your faith and a compromise of the truth.

If this occurs, you will no longer be walking in the light - on the straight path - but rather your way has become diverted by lies. This is not unlike the condition in which many find themselves today. They leave their priestly duties unfinished in order to watch the Super Bowl, the Masters, the NBA Finals, March Madness, the World Series or _____ - you fill in the blank. Society has innumerable attractions to distract and divert the attention of the Believer.

"Menelaus, an extreme Hellenist supplanted Jason by offering Antiochus IV more money for the position of high priest. Menelaus' original name was Onias, but, like Jason, because of his love for the Greek culture changed his name to Menelaus. Menalaus and the sons of Tobias went to King Antiochus. According to Josephus, they told the king that 'they were desirous to leave the laws of their country [the Torah], and their [Yisraelite] way of living, and to follow the king's laws {i.e. the religion of Dionysus}, and the Greek way of living {i.e. Greek philosophy}.' Antiochus made Menelaus the high priest . . . while Antiochus was campaigning in [Mitsrayim], Jason heard a false rumor that Antiochus had died and thus he attempted to regain by force his former position of the high priest. Jason and his supporters conquered Jerusalem, with the exception of the citadel, and murdered many supporters of his rival, the high priest Menelaus: 'When a false rumor arose that Antiochus was dead, Jason took no less than a thousand men and suddenly made an assault upon the city. When the troops upon the wall had been forced back and at last the city was being taken, Menelaus took refuge in the citadel.' (2 Maccabees 5:5 RSV). In response to this riot, when Antiochus came back from Egypt . . . he took Jerusalem by storm and proceeded to enforce the Hellenization of the [Yahudim]. He forcefully established the religion of Dionysus: ' . . . king Antiochus wrote to his whole kingdom, that all should be one people, and every one [Yahudee] should leave his laws [Torah] . . . many . . . of the [Yisraelites] consented to his religion . . . For the king had sent letters by messengers to Jerusalem and the cities of [Yahudah] that they should . . . forbid burnt offerings, and sacrifice [to Elohim]. . . set up altars, and groves, and chapels of {Dionysian} idols, and sacrifice swine's flesh, and unclean beasts: That they should also leave their children uncircumcised . . . forget the law [Torah], and change all the {religious} ordinances . . . And he appointed inspectors over all the people and commanded the cities of [Yahudah] to offer sacrifices, city by city. Many of the people, everyone who forsook the law, joined them . . .' (1 Maccabees 1:41-49, 51-51 RSV)

Many people forsook the law of Moses [Torah] and joined the mysteries of Dionysus."[69]

Josephus wrote: ". . . there were many Jews who complied with the king's commands, either voluntarily, or out of fear of the penalty that was announced." According to the First Book of Maccabees ". . . some of the people eagerly went to the king. He authorized them to observe the ordinances of the Gentiles. So they built a gymnasium in Jerusalem, according to Gentile custom, and removed the marks of circumcision, and abandoned the holy covenant. They joined with the Gentiles . . ." (1 Maccabees 1:13-15 RSV).

It was this joining with the Gentiles and abandonment of the Torah which set the stage for the coming of the Messiah. After both Houses were ejected from the land there was no common ruler, there was no unified kingdom or permanent priesthood. Despite temporary periods of restoration the Kingdom of Yisrael would never again experience a time as was seen under the rule of King David. The Maccabean revolt offered a brief reprieve after Antiochus went so far as to profane the Altar of YHWH by offering swine upon it and setting up idols in the House. Sadly, this period did not last and the people longed for a leader.

This was the hope that many had inside of them - a Messiah who would rule as David had once ruled. Without a properly operating priesthood or an anointed leader, Yisraelites found themselves divided into different sects including, but not limited to the Pharisees, the Sadducees, the Essenes and the Zealots. They were a conquered and divided people living under the control of the Roman Empire and in the midst of a pagan culture.

Many Yisraelites had been led astray by their pagan occupiers while others held on to their faith longing for the promised restoration of the Kingdom. This was the complex and highly charged environment into which the Messiah came to fulfill the promises provided in the Scriptures.

9

The Messiah

The previous chapter was meant to provide some background for the political and religious climate in which the Messiah lived and taught. It was also the world within which the early disciples lived, taught and traveled as they fulfilled the Great Commission by spreading the Good News.

While most people correlate the faith and teaching of the Messiah and His disciples with Christianity - none of them were Christians. In fact, there was no such thing as a religion called Christianity nor was there even a religion called Judaism. While there were Yisraelites present in the land who were generally referred to as Yahudee, this was not a term used in the Scriptures except for the Book of Esther. The word "Yahudee" was a very loose label for Yisraelites that has developed into the word "Jew." Etymologically speaking "Jew" is not a Hebrew word nor is it even accurate although there is a strong tradition surrounding the term so that it has become quite common.

In the strictest sense, a "Jew" or Yahudee was simply someone who was a member of the Tribe of Yahudah. After the division of the Kingdom, we see the

Tribes of Yahudah, Benyamin and much of Levi being grouped together as the House of Yahudah within the geographical tribal boundaries of Yahudah and Benyamin known collectively as Judea (Yudea). Therefore, the term Yahudee could be used to refer to someone from the House of Yahudah and it could also refer to someone who lived geographically within the boundaries of Yudea.

Over time, after the House of Yisrael was exiled, they were mixed with the nations and lost their identity just as Hoshea had prophesied. While the House of Yahudah was exiled, they were later allowed to return and never lost their identity. As a result, the term Yahudee, and later Jew, became a general label given to any Yisraelite - regardless of what tribe they were from because the Yahudee were the only recognizable Yisraelites in existence.

In the Scriptural sense, a person became a Yisraelite by being born into a tribe or by joining with a tribe - as we saw with Caleb and his family. In modern times, the term has another meaning - it now refers to someone who is an adherent to the religion of Judaism. Therefore, whenever you see the term "Jew" it is important to understand how the word developed and the context in which it is used.

Neither Christianity nor Judaism existed when Messiah ministered on the Earth. He and His disciples were all Yisraelites who obeyed the instructions of YHWH - the Torah. Messiah was from the tribe of Yahudah but interestingly he did not live in the region of Yudea - rather He lived in the Galilee and spent most of His time in the region of Naftali. Neither He nor His disciples created, taught or converted to the religion of Christianity.

Now this statement may sound quite radical to a Christian who believes that Jesus or Paul started the

Christian religion, but it is absolutely true. The Christian religion was started hundreds of years after the death and resurrection of Messiah, a subject which will be discussed further in this book. The reason why this may sound preposterous to some is because they fail to understand the ministry of Messiah and the history of the religions of Judaism and Christianity that followed His death and resurrection.

A fundamental teaching in the Christian religion is that Jesus was the Messiah as promised in the Tanak. Most Jews[70] are awaiting a Messiah and while they know about the Christian Jesus they generally reject Him as the Messiah because of the way that He has been presented to them and due to their expectations of what the Messiah will accomplish.

In their eyes, Jesus does not qualify as the Messiah because He has not restored the divided kingdom according to the prophecies. He also does not qualify on a very fundamental level because of his name. It is clear that the English name Jesus would never be the Name of the Hebrew Messiah - it is philologically impossible.

You see, Jesus is the English version of the Hellenized Greek name Iesous, spelled Iesus in Latin. Some say that this name has no specific meaning, while others indicate that it refers to different pagan deities. One thing is for certain, Jesus was not a Hebrew name nor is it a translation of the true Name of the Hebrew Messiah as some might contend. An important thing to realize is that you do not translate a name - you transliterate names, which means that you pronounce them the same in different languages.

Regardless of this fact, the English name Jesus is

not even a transliteration of the Greek or Latin spellings because it starts with a "J" sound. The Messiah was definitely not called Jesus nor was that name ever spoken while He walked the Earth. There was and is no letter "J" in either the Hebrew or Aramaic languages, nor was there a letter "J" in the Greek alphabet. None of these languages even contain the "J" sound in their vocabulary.

Any time you see a "J" in an English translation of a Hebrew or Aramaic transcript it should be given the "Y" sound and any time you see a "J" in an English translation of a Greek manuscript it should be given an "I" sound. In fact, the letter "J" with the unique and specific "J" sound did not exist in any language until the 15th Century. It is a fairly new addition to the linguistic world - yet it has been littered throughout ancient Scriptural translations erroneously perverting the names of Prophets, Sages, the Messiah, YHWH and even the City where He places His Name - Jerusalem (ירושלם) which is more accurately transliterated as Yahrushalaim.

Since there was no letter "J" in the Hebrew language it does not even make sense to call the Messiah Jesus. The name Jesus has only been in existence since the year 1559 A.D. As a result, it is important to look deeper into the origin of the name Jesus to see how the name and nature of the Savior was changed. There is no authoritative source which claims that the name Jesus or Iesous is the original name of the Hebrew Messiah. To the contrary, they all validate the fact that it derives from the name of the Hebrew patriarch commonly called Joshua.

While the traditional English, Greek and Latin names for the Messiah bear little resemblance to His correct Hebrew Name there are striking similarities to

the names of pagan deities. In fact, some claim that they are directly related to the name Iaso, also spelled Ieso, who was the Greek goddess of healing - directly related to sun god worship. According to Greek mythology, the father of Ieso was Asclepius - the deity of healing. His father was the sun god Apollo. "Iaso is Ieso in the Ionic dialect of the Greeks, Iesous being the contracted genitive form. In David Kravitz's, *Dictionary of Greek and Roman Mythology*, we find a similar form, namely Iasus. There are four different Greek deities with the name Iasus, one of them being the Son of Rhea."[71]

There is significant proof that Iesous is linked to the mystery cult of the pagan god Dionysus, whose father was Zeus, the Greek sun god. According to mythology, Zeus also had sons named Iasus, Iasion and Iasius, all who were considered to be "sons of god."

There is also a relationship to the Egyptian goddess Isis and her son Isu. "According to Reallexikon der Agpyptischen Religionsgeschichte, the name of Isis appears in hieroglyphic inscriptions as ESU or ES. Isu and

Esu sound exactly like "Jesu" that the Savior is called in the translated Scriptures of many languages. Esus was a Gallic deity comparable to the Scandinavian Odin. The Greek abbreviation for Iesous is IHS, which is found on many inscriptions made by the "Church" during the Middle Ages. IHS was the mystery name for Bacchus (Tammuz) [Dionysus] another sun-deity."[72]

I remember as a child seeing IHS adorned on various furniture and religious items in the Church that I attended. I never knew what it meant and I doubt that anybody in the congregation knew that it was related to pagan sun worship. Therefore, we see Christianity  directly identifying their Savior with mythical sun deities. It is out in the open for anybody to see, but nobody recognizes the connection because these are simply inherited traditions whose true meaning has been obscured through time, ignorance and misinformation.

On that note, Bacchus was also known as Ichthus, the Fish which is the source of the fish symbol commonly used in Christianity. Sadly, the fish symbol was a pagan religious icon long before it was adopted by Christianity. In fact, in many cultures it  represented the outline of the vulva of the great mother goddess. Some have attempted to legitimize the use of the fish symbol by creating an anagram from the word ichthus as "Iesous CHristos Theo Uiou Soter" or rather "Iesous Christos God Son Savior." This sounds noble, but why would anyone want to use a name or title associated with pagan sun worship? In doing so, we see Christianity identifying their Savior with Bacchus and Dionysus.

Now that we have shown how Christianity does not use the correct name for the Hebrew Messiah we are still left with the question: What is the real Name of the Messiah? I have already mentioned that it is the same name as the patriarch commonly called Joshua and interestingly we are given specific clues in the Tanak concerning the Name.

There are several prophecies that refer to the Messiah as "The Branch" (Isaiah (Yeshayahu)[73] 4:2, 11:1; Zecharyah 3:8, 6:12). There are various words in Hebrew which have been translated as branch. In Yeshayahu 4:2 we see tsemach (צמח) which literally means: "sprout, growth or shoot" and in Yeshayahu 11:1 we see netser (נצר) which can also mean: "sprout or shoot" but also means "descendant."

In Tehillim the word "branch" and "son" are even mixed in certain translations because the meaning is so clear. For instance, look at how The Amplified Version translates Tehillim 80:15: "*[Protect and maintain] the stock which Your right hand planted, and the branch (the son) that You have reared and made strong for Yourself.*" In the Hebrew text we find the word ben (בן), translated as "branch," which refers to the "seed continuing." Thus in Tehillim it clearly refers to The Branch as the Seed or Son of Elohim - which is the Messiah.

Once we understand that the Messiah is referred to as "The Branch", we then can look to the prophecies of Yirmeyahu which direct us to the Name of the Branch. "*5 Behold, the days are coming, says YHWH, that I will raise to David a Branch of righteousness; a King shall reign and prosper, and execute judgment and righteousness in the earth. 6 In His days Yahudah will be saved, and Yisrael will dwell safely; Now this is His Name by which He will be called: YHWH Our Righteousness.*" Yirmeyahu 23:5-6 (see also 33:16).

In Hebrew this Name is: YHWH Tsidqeenu (יהוה צדקנו). This does not mean that the full Name of the Messiah will actually be "YHWH Tsidqeenu." Rather

it provides a hint of His character. The Hebrew name that means "YHWH our righteousness" is Yahutzedek (יהוצדק).

This is an important link to the Name of the Messiah. In many modern English translations they incorrectly transliterate this name as Jehozadak but remember, there is no "J" sound in Hebrew. We are now ready for the final piece in the puzzle which is provided by the Prophet Zecharyah. *"¹¹ Take the silver and gold and make a crown, and set it on the head of the high priest, Yahushua son of Yahutzedek (יהוצדק). ¹² Tell him this is what YHWH of Hosts says: '**Here is the man whose name is the Branch**, and He will branch out from his place and build the temple of YHWH. ¹³ It is He who will build the House of YHWH, and He will be clothed with majesty and will sit and rule on his throne. And He will be a priest on his throne. And there will be harmony between the two."* Zecharyah 6:11-14.

This prophecy is profound because it not only provides a key to the Name of the Messiah but it also describes what the Messiah will do: He will build the House of YHWH and sit as King and High Priest. This is the Melechtzedek - Melech (King) Tzedek (Righteous) - that we read of in the Torah when Abram paid tithes (Beresheet 14:17-20) and Zecharyah tells us prophetically that His Name will be Yahushua son of Yahutzedek (יהוצדק) or literally "Yahushua the son of YHWH our righteousness."

So then - as we have already seen - the Name of the Messiah is the same name as Joshua, the commander of Yisrael who began as a servant and later led the children of Yisrael across the Jordan River as a symbolic mikvah so that they could celebrate their first Passover in the Land –

the same one who circumcised them and who led them into battle as they conquered their enemies. How appropriate that the Messiah of Yisrael would bear the same Name as this great patriarch. The proper transliteration for His Name is Yahushua or Yahshua.[74]

So when you tell a Jew[75] that their Messiah is named Jesus - it does not fit for them, but when you tell them that His Name is Yahushua - that will make much more sense because we have the pattern of Yahshua and Mosheh and we have the prophecies which provide this Name as the Name of the Branch.

When we present the Messiah Yahushua - healing the lame, the blind, the lepers and raising the dead it all starts to fit into place for a Jew who knows the Scriptures because the House of Yaakov - which often represents Yisrael in exile - was described as lame, blind, lepers and dead. Yahushua's actions were specifically intended to fulfill prophecy and point to the Restoration and healing of Yisrael.

By the way, there is no dispute on this issue. Both secular and believing Bible scholars agree on the fact that Jesus is not the name of the Messiah and that His Hebrew Name is Yahushua – although some spell it differently. The problem is that tradition has become so strong it often overwhelms the truth and people actually are more comfortable following a false tradition with pagan roots than they are following truth - even when they know it is wrong!

This is not only a problem for Christians but also for those who need to hear the Good News of the Messiah and His work because the Scriptures clearly state: *"To Him all the prophets witness that, through His Name, whoever*

believes in Him will receive remission of sins." Acts 10:43. Also we are told: *"Nor is there salvation in any other, for there is no other Name under heaven given among men by which we must be saved."* Acts 4:12.

Besides the issue of the name, many Jews have a problem accepting that Jesus is the Messiah because they have been told that Jesus fulfilled the Law and thus did away with the Torah. This claim makes no sense to most Jews because there is nothing in the Scriptures which would ever foretell or allow such a thing to happen. In fact, we are told that the reason the Houses of Yisrael and Yahudah were exiled was because of their failure to obey the Torah. Further, the prophecies tell that the Renewed Covenant will involve the Torah being written on our hearts and in our minds and that the Messiah will rule according to the Torah and teach us the Torah from Zion. Yeshayahu 2:1-4; Micah (Michayahu)[76] 4:1-5.

Accordingly, the typical representation given by Christians that Jesus was the Messiah and came to abolish the Torah utterly contradicts their expectations concerning their Messiah. When Christians proceed to talk about some fictitious entity called the Church replacing Yisrael instead of restoring Yisrael - most Jews will probably lose all interest in the conversation. If that were not enough - the icing on the cake is when they describe how Christians no longer celebrate the Scriptural Appointed Times (Vayiqra 23) but instead they celebrate pagan holidays such as Easter and Christmas.

At that point, there is typically no hope of converting the Jew to a religion that looks to be completely pagan and opposed to some of the most fundamental principles contained in the Scriptures. We will discuss this further

in the book, but for now I would like to stay focused on Yahushua and the ministry of the Messiah which should help put things into perspective.

The Messianic Writings provide us with an account of the life and ministry of Yahushua beginning with the Book of Matthew (Mattityahu)[77] so we will look there first to see how Yahushua handled the Torah. But before we go there I want to mention the Prophecy of Malachi which in most modern Bibles is the last book in the Tanak and immediately precedes the Good News according to Mattityahu.

Interestingly, the final words recorded by the Prophet are as follows: "[4] *Remember the Torah of Mosheh My servant which I commanded unto him in Horeb for all Yisrael, with the statutes and judgments.* [5] *Behold I will send you Elijah the prophet before the coming of the great and dreadful day of YHWH* [6] *And he shall turn the heart of the fathers to the children and the heart of the children to their fathers, lest I come and smite the earth with a curse.*" Malachi 4:4-6.

After this unambiguous statement to **remember the Torah** we then turn the page to the Messianic Scriptures where most of Christianity does the exact opposite – they forget the Torah. Part of the problem is the dividing page that separates the Tanak from the Messianic Writings that says: NEW TESTAMENT. In my opinion you would do well to tear it out - I can assure you that it was not inspired by YHWH. We then turn to Mattityahu and we read about the birth of Messiah and in Chapter 3 we read the words of John the Baptist who was Elijah (Eliyahu)[78] according to the Messiah.

John, whose Hebrew Name was Yahanan,[79] was making the way straight which is all about preaching the

Torah. His message was clear in Mathew 3:3: *"Repent, for the Kingdom of Heaven is at hand!"* In Chapter 4:13 we read that Yahushua preached the same exact message: *"Repent for the Kingdom of Heaven is at Hand!"*

This message of the Kingdom often gets overlooked but both were proclaiming the Kingdom preceded by repentance. Repentance is the act of acknowledging that one has sinned - which means a transgression of the commandments - the Torah. After acknowledging that you have disobeyed the Torah you then need to correct your behavior. Traditionally, this act of repentance would include immersion in a mikvah which symbolically washed away the sins. As was already mentioned, repentance in the Hebrew language has the same meaning as restoration - returning to the way that things used to be or were meant to be - getting rid of the filth and returning to a right relationship with YHWH. In a very basic sense it involves a reconnection - getting plugged into YHWH.

So then right from the start of His ministry - Yahushua is focusing on the Torah and the restoration of the Kingdom. The Messianic Writings refer continually to the Good News of the Kingdom, but just what was the Good News of the Kingdom that the Yisraelites were waiting to hear?

Quite simply - the Good News was that Messiah had come to gather the Lost Sheep and restore the divided Kingdom through the Renewed Covenant. On different occasions, Yahushua stated that He came for the Lost Sheep of the House of Yisrael. (Mattityahu 10:6, 15:24). This is a much different message than what Christianity has been proclaiming and it does not even make sense to many because they have been taught that He came to build

His Church.

When you read the promise of the Renewed Covenant in Yirmeyahu and recognize that it was made with the House of Yisrael and the House of Yahudah, you start to see the work of Restoration that was being accomplished by the Messiah. After the Kingdom was divided, some from the House of Yahudah had been returned but the House of Yisrael had been scattered - like **lost sheep** throughout the world. That is why Yahushua referred to Himself as the Good Shepherd (Yahanan 10). When He was speaking to the Pharisees who were of the House of Yahudah, He specifically stated: "*And other sheep I have which are not of this fold; them also I must bring, and they will hear My voice; and there will be one flock and one Shepherd.*" Yahanan 10:15-16.

The sheep that were not of the fold to which the Pharisees belonged were the House of Yisrael. So then the work of restoration that the Messiah was setting in motion was the regathering of the lost sheep of Yisrael, just as we read in Ezekiel 11:17 earlier and we are given a vivid picture in Yehezqel 36 and 37.

In Yehezqel 36:24-27 we read: "*24 For I will take you out of the nations; I will gather you from all the countries and bring you back into your own land. 25 I will throw clean water on you, and you will be clean; I will cleanse you from all your impurities and from all your idols. 26 I will give you a new heart and put a new spirit in you; I will remove from you your heart of stone and give you a heart of flesh. 27 And I will put my Spirit in you and move you to follow my decrees and be careful to keep my Torah.*"

In Yehezqel 37:1-23 we read:
"*37:1 The hand of YHWH was upon me, and He*

brought me out by the Spirit of YHWH and set me in the middle of a valley; it was full of bones. [2] He led me back and forth among them, and I saw a great many bones on the floor of the valley, bones that were very dry. [3] He asked me, Son of man, can these bones live? I said, O Sovereign YHWH, you alone know. [4] Then He said to me, Prophesy to these bones and say to them, Dry bones, hear the word of YHWH! [5] This is what the Sovereign YHWH says to these bones: I will make breath enter you, and you will come to life. [6] I will attach tendons to you and make flesh come upon you and cover you with skin; I will put breath in you, and you will come to life. Then you will know that I am YHWH. [7] So I prophesied as I was commanded. And as I was prophesying, there was a noise, a rattling sound, and the bones came together, bone to bone. [8] I looked, and tendons and flesh appeared on them and skin covered them, but there was no breath in them. [9] Then he said to me, Prophesy to the breath; prophesy, son of man, and say to it, This is what the Sovereign YHWH says: Come from the four winds, O breath, and breathe into these slain, that they may live. [10] So I prophesied as he commanded me, and breath entered them; they came to life and stood up on their feet - a vast army. [11] Then he said to me: Son of man, these bones are the whole House of Yisrael. They say, Our bones are dried up and our hope is gone; we are cut off. [12] Therefore prophesy and say to them: This is what the Sovereign

YHWH says: O my people, I am going to open your graves and bring you up from them; I will bring you back to the land of Yisrael. [13] Then you, my people, will know that I am YHWH, when I open your graves and bring you up from them. [14] <u>I will put my Spirit in you and you will live, and I will settle you in your own land.</u> Then you will know that I YHWH have spoken, and I have done it, declares YHWH. [15] The word of YHWH came to me: [16] Son of man, <u>take a stick of wood and write on it, Belonging to Yahudah and the Yisraelites associated with him. Then take another stick of wood, and write on it, Ephraim's stick, belonging to Yoseph and all the House of Yisrael associated with him.</u> [17] <u>Join them together into one stick so that they will become one in your hand.</u> [18] When your countrymen ask you, Won't you tell us what you mean by this? [19] say to them, This is what the Sovereign YHWH says: <u>I am going to take the stick of Yoseph - which is in Ephraim's hand - and of the Yisraelite tribes associated with him, and join it to Yahudah's stick, making them a single stick of wood, and they will become one in my hand.</u> [20] Hold before their eyes the sticks you have written on [21] and say to them, This is what the Sovereign YHWH says: <u>I will take the Yisraelites out of the nations where they have gone. I will gather them from all around and bring them back into their own land.</u> [22] <u>I will make them one nation in the land, on the mountains of Yisrael. There will be one king</u>

*over all of them and they will never again be two
nations or be divided into two kingdoms. ²³ They
will no longer defile themselves with their idols
and vile images or with any of their offenses, for
I will save them from all their sinful backsliding,
and I will cleanse them. They will be my people,
and I will be their Elohim."*

The Hebrew word for "stick" is ets (עץ) and it is
the same word as "tree". Therefore this prophecy is the
same teaching given by Shaul in Romans 11 regarding
the olive tree. The olive tree represents the Assembly of
Yisrael - "the planted of El." The two sticks being joined
together represent the restoration of the Kingdom.

Many people have problems processing this Good
News of the Kingdom because they believe that the Church
replaced Yisrael when, in fact, the Kingdom is being
restored by the joining of the two sticks or trees - The
Native Tree Branch - Yahudah which was not completely
cut off and the Wild Tree Branch - Yisrael which was
completely cut off but is being restored.

The confusion rests in large part because of our
language. Throughout the Tanak, the commonwealth of
Yisrael was often referred to as the **qahal** (קהל) in Hebrew
which means: "the set apart assembly or congregation."
The problem with most modern English Bibles is that they
have the word Yisrael in them when the text refers to the
set apart assembly - the qahal - in the Tanak, but they use
the word "church" when it refers to the set apart assembly
in the "New Testament." This gives the reader the distinct
impression that the Church is something newly formed
by the Messiah and definitely different from Yisrael.

Since the word church is never seen in the Tanak

- readers often get confused. This confusion reinforces the notion that the Church must have been the objective of the "New Covenant" since it is something **new**, never seen before in the "Old Testament." The word church is never found in the Hebrew or Greek manuscripts because it is a fabricated word which was inserted into the King James English edition of the Bible in the 1600's.

It was inserted in place of the Greek word <u>ekklesia</u> (εκκλησια) which means the same thing as <u>qahal</u> (קהל) - a set apart assembly or congregation. Let me state that another way - the Hebrew word qahal means: "Set apart assembly, congregation" and the Greek word ekklesia means: "Set apart assembly, congregation."

Therefore, when you see the word "church" in the English translations it is most likely replacing ekklesia in the Greek. It is typically referring to the Assembly in a particular geographical area or the entire assembly throughout the world - not some new concept or entity created by the Messiah.

This is reinforced by the Hebrew version of Mattityahu[80] which clearly uses more authentic terms than most modern English translations that insert the word "church." In the translation of the Hebrew Mattityahu 16:18 we read: *"And I tell you that you are Kepha, and on this rock I will build my <u>House of Prayer</u>, and the gates of Gehenna will not overcome it."* In Matthew 18:17 we read: *"If he refuses to listen to them, tell it to the <u>Assembly</u>; and if he refuses to listen even to the <u>Assembly</u>, treat him as you would a pagan or a tax collector."*

Even in the Septuagint,[81] which is the Greek translation of the Tanak, we read about the ekklesia when it refers to Yisrael - which is the set apart assembly.

Therefore in either case the Scriptures are talking about "the congregation or assembly" or "the citizens of the Kingdom." There is no such thing as a church which has replaced Yisrael - there is only One Assembly.

It may be helpful to look further into the word "church" to see just how improper it is to describe the set apart assembly. The word "church" derives from the Greek word kuriakee (κυριακεε) which means "house of the lord." It is a word which passed to the Gothic tongue; the Goths being the first of the northern hordes convert- ed to Christianity. They adopted the word from the Greek Christians of Constantinople, and so it came to us Anglo-Saxons.  It derives from circus, from whence kirk, a circle, because the oldest temples, as the Druid ones, were circular in form.[82]

Any dictionary which provides etymology will indicate that the word derives from the old English word  "circe." Circe was the goddess-daughter of Helios, the sun-deity. Therefore, the word which many Christians use to describe their buildings and their believing community as a whole, ultimately derives from the name of a pagan goddess and the term used to describe pagan temples. The word church was inserted into the English translations whenever the word ekklesia was used, thus instead of properly

translating ekklesia as the set apart assembly so that the connection with Yisrael could be made - it was replaced with a pagan reference to appear to be something different from Yisrael.

Qahal in the "Old Testament" and Ekklesia in the "New Testament" never meant the building or house of assembly, because "church" buildings were built long after the apostolic age. The true Assembly consists of those people who trust in the promises of Elohim, believe in His promised Messiah and obey His commandments. With this understanding, you can see how Abraham and Mosheh belong to this Assembly just as easily as the early Disciples, Shaul, you or I.

It seems that man, in his "finite" wisdom, has attempted to separate the plan of Elohim into a pre-Messianic age and a post-Messianic age as if Mosheh will somehow be treated different from Shaul because he died before the Messiah was sacrificed. This is not true: The blood of Messiah is powerful enough to reach back and claim all of His Assembly (Sheep) from the beginning of time until the end of days. It is important to understand that when He rose from the dead He stepped out of time, where YHWH resides and His blood atoned for all who believe from the beginning to the end of time since He was *"the beginning and the end."* (Revelation 22:13). Therefore, the Assembly, whether those before or after the crucifixion, will all be judged when He returns and those who are counted worthy will be called, "Sons of Elohim."

Now the use of the very different words Yisrael and Church has driven a wedge where one does not belong - it is the same wedge which divides the Old and New Testaments as well as the Old and New Covenants.

YHWH declares He is one - Echad (אחד) Devarim 6:4. In the most basic sense echad means: "unity." His assembly is not fractured nor is His Body and He does not rule over a divided kingdom - He is the Elohim of unity.

Yahushua specifically stated in Yahanan 10:16 that there is: *"One Flock and One Shepherd."* He is the Good Shepherd gathering His sheep, His people, His qahal, His ekklesia, His assembly Yisrael which consists of a mixed multitude from every nation tribe and tongue - A people who willingly choose to love and obey YHWH.

This is where the Torah comes in. The Torah is the Constitution of the Kingdom, the law of the land, a sort of constitution - if you will. It is very important to understand this aspect of the Kingdom because otherwise you may fall into doctrines which set aside the Torah.

In Devarim 18:18 YHWH states: *"I will raise up for them a Prophet **like you** from among their brethren, and will put My words in His mouth, and He shall speak to them all that I command Him."* Maimonides, a highly regarded Sage in Judaism, is noted for stating that the meaning of this commandment is that we are *"to heed the call of every prophet in each generation, provided that he neither adds to, nor takes away from the Torah."* Still other commentaries provide that if any prophet comes to alter the Torah we know that he is a false prophet.[83] We know that the Yisraelites were anticipating this Prophet because they speculated whether  Yahanan the Baptist (Immerser) and Yahushua were "The Prophet" and we read about this in Mark 6:15 and Yahanan 1:21.

Interestingly, in His first recorded message

commonly known as the Sermon on the Mount, Yahushua taught the Torah and specifically addressed the issue of adding to and taking away from the Torah. In Mattityahu 5:17-19 He stated: "*17 Do not think that I came to destroy the Torah or the Prophets. I did not come to destroy but to fulfill. 18 For assuredly, I say to you, till heaven and earth pass away, one jot or one tittle will by no means pass from the Torah till all is fulfilled. 19 Whoever therefore breaks one of the least of these commandments, and teaches men so, shall be called **least in the kingdom of heaven**; but whoever does and teaches them, he shall be called **great in the kingdom of heaven.**"

Many try to interpret His fulfillment of the Torah as if He abolished the Torah. This interpretation is wrong by just looking at the plain meaning of the text because He specifically said He did not come to destroy the Torah. If you look at the Greek it becomes clearer.

The Greek word translated as "fulfill" is PLEROSAI (πληρωσαι) which means: "to fill up, to fully preach, to make full, to make complete." It does not mean: "destroy, dissolve or demolish" which is KATALOOSAI (καταλυσαι) in the Greek. In fact - these two words mean the exact opposite.

Also, He said "*until heaven and earth pass away*" not the smallest portion of the Torah will pass away. I believe that we can all observe that heaven and earth have not passed away. The fulfillment spoken of here is not a doing away with but rather - it filled the Torah with meaning. Through the life and teaching of Yahushua we were able to see how the Torah was meant to be lived.

In the Shem Tov commentary of the Hebrew version of Mattityaha the intent is even clearer. It states that He did not come to add or to take away from the

Torah. This is completely consistent with the Hebrew expectation of The Prophet.[84]

On the other hand, the common Christian teaching that Yahushua, by fulfilling the Torah, did away with the Torah has no foundation in the Scriptures. The notion that Yahushua, by fulfilling the Torah, meant that people no longer have to obey the Torah is the same thing as saying that people no longer need to live righteously. It simply does not make sense especially since the necessity for His ministry was the result of mankind's disobedience to the Torah which required forgiveness and cleansing.

Because He fulfilled the Torah can we now murder, steal, lie, cheat, commit adultery, gossip or commit any other conduct prohibited in the Torah? Of course not! Yahushua fulfilled the Torah by living out the Torah as all mankind was intended! As the Son of Adam he did what Adam failed to do. Where Adam failed in the Garden of Eden Yahushua stepped in and broke the cycle in another Garden.

Right before the death of Yahushua we see Him keeping vigil in the Garden of Gethsemane as He is about to complete His mission. While He stays awake and prays - His disciples kept falling asleep. In the Hebrew Mattityahu we get a vivid picture of His instructions as He tells His disciples the same thing that the Creator  instructed Adam - He tells them to <u>watch</u> and He gives them something <u>to do</u>.

In Mattityahu 26:38 He says: "*Support me and **watch** with me*." The word for watch is **shamar**. In Mattityahu

26:40 He asks: "*So you are unable to* **watch** *with me one hour?*" Again the word is **shamar**. In Mattityahu 26:41 He states: "**Watch** *and pray – lest you fall into temptation.*" Again we see the word **shamar**. In each case this presents the picture of a watchman keeping guard. And notice the connection - **Watch and pray lest you fall into temptation.**

Adam failed in his duty to watch, just as the disciples did, and as a result both he and the woman fell into temptation. Yahushua the Messiah stayed awake and watched - like a watchman over Yisrael just as was written: "*He who watches (shamar) over Yisrael will neither sleep nor slumber.*" Tehillim 121:4.

The purpose of His watching is to preserve, protect and guard our souls - our very lives - we read this in Tehillim 121:7-8. Again to watch over (shamar) our souls is to keep and to protect us. He also instructs <u>us</u> to watch and an important part of our watching involves the Torah. Over and over again we are instructed to **keep** the commandments and to **watch** the commandments and **to guard** the commandments. This is the same word **shamar** and we are given this instruction so that we stay within the hedge of protection provided by the Torah - **so that we don't fall into temptation - so that we are kept from evil.**

The purpose of a hedge is to make a separation between those things on one side and those things on the other side. The Torah provides us with distinctions and draws a line for us to understand <u>right from wrong</u>, <u>clean from unclean</u>, <u>righteous</u> conduct from <u>abominable</u> conduct. **On that foundation the Kingdom is established and it will only be populated with those who will also OBEY.**

The subsequent death and resurrection of the Messiah had nothing to do with abolishing the Torah

and everything to do with establishing the Torah. People misunderstand the notion of His fulfilling the Torah because they misunderstand the ministry of the Messiah. Sadly, He could not have made it any clearer when He stated that the person who obeys and teaches others to obey the Torah shall be called **"Great in the Kingdom"** while the one who disobeys and teaches others to disobey the Torah shall be called **"Least in the Kingdom."**

Obviously, if you love the instructions of the Kingdom and abide by them you will do well. On the other hand, it is difficult to excel in a Kingdom when you despise or disregard the rules of the King. Yahushua spent most of His time teaching the Torah - which is all about the Kingdom of Heaven. Once it is understood that Yahushua affirmed the Torah and its' continuing validity *"until all is fulfilled and as long as Heaven and Earth remain"* we can then begin to see that all of His teachings were in absolute agreement with the Torah.

The reason that He made the proclamation at the Sermon on the Mount was because the religious leaders had added to and subtracted from the Torah through their "oral Torah." They taught that there were certain words spoken to Mosheh but not written down which meant that there was an oral Torah that was handed down and ultimately written down in the Talmud and other writings. There is no such thing as an oral Torah - the Scriptures are clear on this. *"³ So Mosheh came and told the people <u>all the words of YHWH</u> and all the judgments. And all the people answered with one voice and said, All the words which YHWH has said we will do. ⁴ And <u>Mosheh wrote all the words of YHWH</u>."* Shemot 24:3-4.

The laws and traditions which constitute the oral

Torah of Judaism are specifically known as the takanot (תקנות) and ma'asim (מעשׂים). The word takanot means "enactments" and refers to the laws enacted by the Pharisees. Ma'asim literally means "works or deeds" and refers to the precedents of the Rabbis that provide the source for Pharisaic rulings along with subsequent rulings based on those precedents.[85]

Over the centuries, these enactments and precedents developed into a powerful set of rules and regulations that have operated to define and control the religion now known as Judaism, which is quite different from the faith of ancient Yisrael. These enactments and precedents established by the Rabbis, the successors of the Pharisees, were given the same, if not greater weight, than the Torah.[86]

Yahushua came to restore the Torah to its' rightful place and part of His mission involved confronting the self-imposed authority of the Pharisees and their Oral Torah. This was the underlying controversy concerning most, if not all, of their exchanges.

At times, we read about the Messiah doing some rather peculiar things which do not necessarily make sense because we do not always understand this underlying conflict. As part of His ministry, He confronted the religious leadership and intentionally violated their man made laws. By doing so, He was knocking down the fence that they had build around the Torah.

On one particular occasion, using saliva, Yahushua made clay and placed it into a man's eyes to heal him which was in direct contradiction to the man-made laws regarding what could be done on the Sabbath. We can read about it in Yahanan 9:6-7: "⁶ *Having said this, he spit on the*

ground, made some mud with the saliva, and put it on the man's eyes. ⁷Go, he told him, wash in the Pool of Siloam. So the man went and washed, and came home seeing."

According to tradition, it was a violation to make anything on the Sabbath and, believe it or not, it was prohibited to put saliva in a person's eyes to heal them on the Sabbath. There were also those who considered it a violation to heal on the Sabbath. Therefore, in this one instance He violated three of the man-made laws, but none of the Torah commandments. (Yahanan 9:1).

Notice that he sent the man to the Pool of Siloam which means "Sent" - thus the Pool of the Sent one. This is where the water was taken once a year and poured on the Altar during the Feast of Succot.[87] For years, the exact location of the Pool was unknown, but recently it was excavated near the City of David in Jerusalem.

Yahushua provided another wonderful example of breaking the laws of men when he healed the man with the withered hand on the Sabbath. (Mattityahu 12:9-13). According to the Pharisees, such conduct was not permitted on the Sabbath. This, of course, is absurd because nowhere in the Torah does it ever put any prohibitions on healing, especially on the Sabbath. There are very few commandments concerning the Sabbath in the Torah, but the Pharisees had developed hundreds.[88]

Again, it is apparent that Yahushua calculated His actions to challenge the authority of the Pharisees and their takanot, although He always observed the Torah.

Yahushua clearly instructed people to obey the Torah and He may have instructed His disciples and others to disobey the takanot intentionally so that He could point out the error of the Pharisees.

A good example of this fact is when the disciples were walking through grain fields on the Sabbath (Luke 6:1-2). As they walked they plucked heads of grain, rubbed them in their hands and ate them. Seeing this, some of the Pharisees asked Yahushua why they were doing something which was not permitted on the Sabbath.[89] Again, you can search the Torah high and low and you will not find any commandment prohibiting such conduct on the Sabbath, although it was prohibited by the traditions of men.

In another instance of healing, Yahushua told a paralyzed man waiting by the pool at the Sheep Gate called Beit Zatha: "[8] . . . 'Rise, take up your bed and walk.' [9] And immediately the man was made well, took up his bed, and walked. And that day was the Sabbath. [10] The Yahudim therefore said to him who was cured, 'It is the Sabbath; it is not lawful for you to carry your bed.'" Yahanan 5:8-10. The Greek word translated as "bed" most likely refers to a mattress or a mat so we are not talking about a large piece of furniture as we think of a bed in the Western culture. Therefore, instead of focusing on the miraculous healing, the religious leaders criticized the man because it was a violation of their takanot to carry anything substantial on the Sabbath.

These are just a few examples, but armed with this knowledge it now makes His conduct much easier to understand. Many of His actions were a direct affront to the laws of the religious leaders and unless you understand the dynamics of what was going on you will miss much of the flavor of His ministry. The religious leaders had hidden the Torah from most people and Yahushua came to reveal the Torah and expose the Pharisees - He was right in their face.

In Mattityahu 23:27-28 we read: "*27 Woe to you, scribes and Pharisees, hypocrites! For you are like whitewashed tombs which indeed appear beautiful outwardly, but inside are full of dead men's bones and all uncleanness. 28 Even so you also outwardly appear righteous to men, but inside you are full of hypocrisy and lawlessness.*"

The word lawlessness comes from the Greek word "anomia" which specifically means: "**without the instructions or without Torah.**" Therefore, the very people who were supposed to be teaching the Torah are accused of not having the Torah in them. Through their takanot and ma'asim they **added to** and **took away** from the Torah.

They placed heavy burdens upon men which was the exact opposite of what the Torah was intended to do. The Torah was given to a redeemed people who were former slaves and Yahushua specifically stated that His yoke - which is the Torah - is "light and easy." (Mattityahu 11:30).

Yahushua taught the pure Torah. For instance, in Mattityahu 22:36 when asked "*which is the great commandment in the Torah?*" Yahushua said to him, "*37 You shall love YHWH your Elohim with all your heart, with all your soul, and with all your mind. 38 This is the first and great commandment. 39 And the second is like it: You shall love your neighbor as yourself. 40 On these two commandments hang all the Torah and the Prophets.*"

The Great Command - "*Love YHWH with all you heart, with all your soul and with all your mind*" is straight out of the Torah although it was not the first commandment in the Ten Commandments. It is called the Shema and is found in Devarim 6:4. It sums up the way we worship Elohim - the first four of the 10 commandments.

He stated the Second was - "*You shall love your neighbor as yourself.*" This is not the second commandment in the Ten Commandments - rather it is found in Vayiqra 19:18. It sums up the way we treat our fellow man - the last six commandments.

Therefore, when asked what was the most important commandment Yahushua summed up the Torah and the Prophets by citing two commandments that were <u>not even</u> in the Ten Commandments, although they were in the Torah and they did, in fact, summarize the Ten Commandments.

Neither of these were **new commandments** - again they were always part of the Torah. Messiah was not starting something new - rather He was restoring, renewing, refreshing and fulfilling that which already existed. Throughout His ministry He was telling people what was expected of those who would be part of the Kingdom of Heaven. He was refocusing people to the heart of the Torah.

Yahushua aptly demonstrated this point to the Pharisees in an account recorded in Mattityahu 23:23 as follows: "*Woe to you, Scribes and Pharisees, hypocrites! For you pay tithe of mint and anise and cummin, and have neglected <u>the weightier matters of the Torah</u>: justice and mercy and faith. These you ought to have done, without leaving the others undone.*"

To properly understand this statement it is important to understand the tithe. For the purposes of this discussion we will look at one of the primary passages in the Torah concerning the tithe found in Sefer Devarim. *"You shall truly tithe all the increase of your grain that the field produces year by year.* And you shall eat before YHWH your Elohim, in the place where He chooses to make His Name abide, *the tithe of your grain and your new wine and your oil, of the firstborn of your herds and your flocks,* that you may learn to fear YHWH your Elohim always." Devarim 14:22-23.

The tithe revolved around the Scriptural Appointed Times described in Vayiqra 23 which are intimately connected to the major harvests in the land.[90] The object was that after the harvest, people would bring their

offerings up to the place where YHWH designated and enjoy a celebration. For a long time it was located at Shiloh and later, under the reign of King David, it was moved to Yahrushalayim. The tithe was on the increase and the Scriptures refer to the first fruits of grain, grapes, olives and flocks. There is no mention of herbs or the need to tithe herbs although if you want to, you are free to tithe them.

The point that Yahushua was making was that the Pharisees did things which were not even specifically prescribed in the Torah - yet at the same time - they missed the most important things that they were supposed to learn: justice, mercy and faith. In a similar passage in Luke 11:42 it refers to *"justice and the love of Elohim."* These are the important lessons that we are supposed to be learning through the Torah and these are the things that Yahushua came to teach us about the Kingdom.

The Kingdom of YHWH is here and now and if you are in it, you need to understand and obey the Torah. If you reject the Torah, then you reject Messiah, you reject His teachings and you reject His Kingdom. This is why it is imperative to get this issue straight. Yahushua specifically instructed people to obey the Torah and He told the man that He healed to go and sin no more. (Yahanan 5:14).

When He saved the woman accused of adultery from being stoned He told her to: *"go and sin no more."* (Yahanan 8:11). He was willing to deliver them from sickness and death but His underlying message was to **stop transgressing the Torah so that they could walk in the blessing and life which was available to them.**

Sadly, many people completely miss the purpose of His ministry and believe that the Torah - which was the underlying message of His entire ministry - somehow does not apply to them. His ministry from the beginning to end was about the restoration of the Kingdom and the Torah which is the blueprint for our lives and the rule of the Kingdom of YHWH.

You must understand the Torah to understand the Restoration of the Kingdom. The Messiah proclaimed: *"I have not come to destroy the Torah AND the Prophets"* because He was THE PROPHET foretold by Mosheh. (Mattityahu 5:17)

He was like Mosheh, but not the same as Mosheh. Just as the Almighty gave tablets of stone to Mosheh upon which He wrote His Torah (Shemot 24:12) so He gave us His Son Who was the Torah in the flesh. Just as those tablets of stone were broken because of the peoples' sin, so the Messiah was broken because of our sin. Just as

Mosheh **cut** two tablets **like the first two** and presented them before the Almighty Who wrote the same Torah as the first, so the Messiah cuts or circumcises our hearts and writes His Torah on the tablets of our hearts and minds. Remember that the Hebrew word for covenant is brit (ברית) which means: "cutting." There must be a cutting to be a covenant.

The same Torah that was given to Yisrael on the first set of tablets is the same Torah that was written on the second set of tablets. It is the same Torah that was made flesh in the Messiah and it is the same Torah written on our hearts and minds. The Torah never changed - only how and where it was written.

Like Mosheh told Yisrael in Devarim 6:5-6: *"You shall love YHWH your Elohim with all your heart, with all your soul, and with all your strength. And these words which I command you today shall be in your heart."* So Yahushua stated that this was the greatest command and He gave us His Spirit so that we could truly love Him with all our heart with all our soul and with all our strength by placing the Torah on our hearts and in our minds. Mosheh gave us the written Torah and Yahushua showed us the *Heart of the Torah* and wrote it on our hearts and minds.

Consistent with this, in Mattityahu 5:21-22 He taught: *"You have heard that it was said to those of old, 'You shall not murder, and whoever murders will be in danger of the judgment.' But I say to you that whoever is angry with his brother without a cause shall be in danger of the judgment."* Again in Mattityahu we read 5:27-28: *"You have heard that it was said to those of old, 'You shall not commit adultery.' But I say to you that whoever looks at a woman to lust for her has already committed adultery with her in his heart."*

Yahushua was getting to the heart of the Torah because that is what He wants from us - our hearts. He did not say that it was now permissible to commit murder or adultery - He took it to another level. While Mosheh mediated the marriage covenant with a Bride who was unfaithful from the start, Yahushua mediated the renewed marriage covenant with a Bride who loves and obeys from the heart. The Torah was a wedding gift which was given to Yisrael and likewise the Spirit writing the Torah on our hearts and minds is the gift that Messiah gives His Bride.

The Scriptures extol the Torah and I would encourage you to read Tehillim 119 to see what King David had to say about the Torah. He loved the Torah because He knew that it was pleasing to YHWH. He had incredible insight into the Messiah. Read what He said about the coming Messiah: "*17 Let Your hand be upon the man of Your right hand, upon the Son of Man (Adam) whom You made strong for Yourself.*18 Then we will not turn back from You; revive us, and we will call upon Your Name.*19 Restore us, O YHWH Elohim of hosts; cause Your face to shine, and we shall be saved!*" Tehillim 80:1-19. King David expected the Messiah, who he referred to as the Son of Man which is more properly the Son of Adam. King David expected the Son of Adam to revive us - to wake us up, so that we will call upon The Name of YHWH and then restore us so that we might be saved. Notice the direct link between restoration and salvation.

The Prophet Daniel also described the Son of Adam: "*13 I was watching in the night visions, and behold, one like the Son of Adam, coming with the clouds of heaven! He came to the Ancient of Days, and they brought Him near before Him.*14 Then to Him was given dominion and glory and a kingdom,

that all peoples, nations, and languages should serve Him. His dominion is an everlasting dominion, which shall not pass away, and His kingdom the one which shall not be destroyed." Daniel 7:13-14.

The Messiah will reign over the Kingdom and the rule of the Kingdom is the Torah. According to Tehillim 119:142, the Torah is "*truth.*" According to Proverbs 6:23, the Torah is "*the way and the light*" and according to Proverbs 12:28, "*In the way of Righteousness is life*" - the way of righteousness is the Torah.

Therefore, according to the Tanak - **The Torah is the Way, the Truth, the Light and the Life**. These are the very same words used by Yahushua to describe Himself - The Way, the Truth, The Life (Yahanan 14:6) and The Light (Yahanan 8:12). Thus Yahushua clearly identifies Himself with the Torah, and rightly so because He was the Torah in the Flesh according to Yahanan 1:14.

Yahushua said: "*if you have seen Me you have seen the Father.*" (Yahanan 14:9). He also said that "*I and the Father are One*" - Echad (Yahanan 10:30). As a result of these statements we can conclude that the Torah is the very Image of YHWH. And as we allow Him to fill us with His Spirit and the Torah becomes part of us then we begin to be restored into the Image of YHWH - just as Adam was made in the Image of YHWH. We then can become living Tabernacles that make up the House of YHWH. This is the restoration that we all need and is now available through the work of the Messiah - this is the Good News of the Kingdom.

Yahushua stated that He came for the lost sheep of the House of Yisrael - that was His mission. We know that the House of Yisrael had been scattered throughout

the world, that they had been divorced from their Husband YHWH yet there were also many prophecies indicating that they would be restored.

According to the Prophet Yirmeyahu: "¹⁴ . . . *the days are coming, says YHWH, that it shall no more be said, YHWH lives who brought up the children of Yisrael from the land of Mitsrayim, ¹⁵ but, YHWH lives who brought up the children of Yisrael from the land of the north and from all the lands where He had driven them. For I will bring them back into their land which I gave to their fathers. ¹⁶ Behold, I will send for many fishermen, says YHWH, and they shall fish them; and afterward I will send for many hunters, and they shall hunt them from every mountain and every hill, and out of the holes of the rocks.*" Yirmeyahu 16:14-16.

From this prophecy we can learn a number of things. First, we know that there will be a regathering and deliverance greater that the one out of Mitsrayim. Instead of delivering Yisrael out of Mitsrayim with a mighty hand, the next deliverance and regathering will be from the entire planet. We can also safely assume that it will be more dramatic than the parting of the Red Sea - so much more dramatic that we will no longer speak about the deliverance from Mitsrayim. This has obviously not happened yet.

Next, we are told that He will send many fishermen to fish them. It could not be any clearer that this was an integral part of the first coming of Messiah. He clearly told His disciples that He would make them *"fishers of men."* (Mattityahu 4:19; Mark 1:17). Not only did Yahushua begin His ministry with this theme, but He also ended His ministry with the same message.

In Yahanan 21 we read how some of the disciples

had returned to the Galilee after the death and resurrection of Messiah. They went fishing but they did not catch anything. The reason for this is because they were supposed to be fishing for men - not for fish.

"*4 But when the morning had now come, Yahushua stood on the shore; yet the disciples did not know that it was Yahushua. 5 Then Yahushua said to them, Children, have you any food? They answered Him, No. 6 And He said to them, Cast the net on the right side of the boat, and you will find some. So they cast, and now they were not able to draw it in because of the multitude of fish. 7 Therefore that disciple whom Yahushua loved said to Kepha, It is the Master! Now when Shimon Kepha heard that it was the Master, he put on his outer garment (for he had removed it), and plunged into the sea. 8 But the other disciples came in the little boat (for they were not far from land, but about two hundred cubits), dragging the net with fish. 9 Then, as soon as they had come to land, they saw a fire of coals there, and fish laid on it, and bread. 10 Yahushua said to them, Bring some of the fish which you have just caught. 11 Shimon Kepha went up and dragged the net to land, full of large fish, **one hundred and fifty-three**; and although there were so many, the net was not broken.*" Yahanan 21:4-11.*

Anyone reading this passage should immediately ask: Why are we told that there are 153 fish? The reason is not so obvious unless you are familiar with the Hebrew language and the Hebrew Prophets.

There is a wonderful mystery surrounding this passage which can only be discovered through gematria (the study of numbers) in the original Hebrew. If you only rely upon English translations, you will miss an enormous amount of information in both the Tanak and the Messianic Texts. In the Hebrew language every letter also has a numeric value - they do not have a separate set of numerals as we do in the English language. Likewise, words and phrases also have a corresponding numeric value.

A significant phrase in the Scriptures which calculates to 153 is "Sons of Elohim." Sons of Elohim in Hebrew is Beni Ha-Elohim (בני האלהים). The gematria calculation for Beni Ha-Elohim goes as follows: (ב = 2) (נ= 50) (י= 10) (ה = 5) (א = 1) (ל = 30) (ה= 5) (י = 10) (ם = 40). Therefore the phrase is calculated as follows: 2+50+10+5+1+30+5+10+40 = 153.

The number 153 was not just selected at random. It was intended to be clearly understood by all who read the passage that Messiah was telling them to go fishing for the "Sons of Elohim." (Yirmeyahu 16:16). Now when we link this passage to the prophecy in Hoshea we see that the Messiah was telling His disciples to cast the net throughout the world and start to regather the "lost sheep of the House of Yisrael" who would be called the "sons of the living Elohim." (Hoshea 1:10-11).

This is the prophesied restoration of the Kingdom and this is a mystery that Christianity often misses because they have forsaken the Hebrew Scriptures for English translations which can never fully, completely and adequately translate the meaning of the Hebrew text. There is a fundamental difference between Eastern Semitic languages such as Hebrew and Western languages such as Greek and English.

While Hebrew is an active language, Greek and English are passive languages. Translating from Hebrew to Greek or English does not necessarily involve a word for word translation but rather concepts to words. It requires an understanding of the thought process of one language and then reinterpreting that thought by using the available word or words in the new language which most closely relate the intended thought or concept from the original language. It is not an easy task and an important part of this type of translation is understanding the culture and mindset of the people who wrote the original text. Because of these difficulties we find many Scripture passages where the meaning has been lost or even changed because of translation errors.

This is why it is so important for us to examine the Hebrew roots of our faith so we can recognize and repent from false traditions that we have inherited. The ultimate plan of Elohim is to restore His creation and join those who believe in Him, the Sons of Elohim, consisting of both "Jews" and Gentiles - Yahudah and Ephraim. *"This is what YHWH Almighty says: In those days ten men from all languages and nations will take firm hold of one Jew by the hem of his robe and say, Let us go with you, because we have heard that Elohim is with you."* Zecharyah 8:23.

The word for "Jew" in the Hebrew text is Yahudee (יהודי) which means either a descendent of the Tribe of Yahudah or one from the House of Yahudah. In other words, ten Gentiles will grab a hold of one from the House of Yahudah and walk together with him to seek The Elohim of Yisrael. These ten men represent the ten tribes from the House of Yisrael who once were not the people of Elohim but heard the voice of their Shepherd and are now trying to figure out, not only their own identity, but the identity of the One they serve.

This verse provides a beautiful picture of the restorative work of Elohim and it is a direct reference to the

Prophecy in Yehezqel which details the restoration of the House of Yisrael and the House of Yahudah. (Yehezqel 37:18-22).

The hem that the people will be taking hold of is the same hem that the Messiah wore on His garment. It is the hem that anyone who is living in obedience to the Scriptures will be wearing. This hem is known as the tzitzit and is to be worn to remind the wearer of the commandments of YHWH.

The tzitzit are commanded in the Torah in two separate occasions. In Devarim 22:12 YHWH commands: *"Make tzitzit on the four corners of the garment with which you cover yourself."* According to 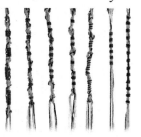 Bemidbar 15:37-41: *"37 YHWH spoke to Mosheh, saying, '38 Speak to the children of Yisrael, and you shall say to them to make tzitziyot on the corners of their garments throughout their generations, and to put a blue cord in the tzitzit of the corners. 39 And it shall be to you for a tzitzit, and you shall see it, and shall remember all the commands of YHWH and shall do them, and not search after your own heart and your own eyes after which you went whoring, 40 so that you remember, and shall do all my commands, and be set apart unto your Elohim. 41 I am YHWH your Elohim, who brought you out of the land of Mitsrayim, to be your Elohim. I am YHWH your Elohim."*

A prophecy in the Tanak speaks of the Messiah as follows: *"The Sun of Righteousness shall arise with healing in His wings."* Malachi 4:2 NKJV. These "wings" are kanaph (כָּנָף) in Hebrew and refer to the edge of a garment, which is the tzitzit.

We read in the Good News according to Luke:

"*43 Now a woman, having a flow of blood for twelve years, who had spent all her livelihood on physicians and could not be healed by any, 44 came from behind and touched the border of His garment. And immediately her flow of blood stopped.*" Luke 8:43-44 NKJV. The Greek word used to describe a border is kraspedon (κρασπεδον) which means a fringe or tassel. In other words, she grabbed His tzitzit which He was wearing in obedience to the Torah and He came with healing in His tzitzit just as was foretold by the Prophet Malachi.

Also, in Mattityahu 14:35-36 we read: "*35 And when the men of that place (Gennesar) recognized Him, they sent out into all that surrounding country, and brought to Him all who were sick, 36 and begged Him to let them only touch the tzitzit of His garment. And as many as touched it were completely healed.*" We see in these passages not only a beautiful fulfillment of prophecy, but also an example of the Torah observance of Yahushua which has been obscured due to translation inconsistencies and ignorance on the part of Gentile translators.

Yahushua made it abundantly clear what His mission was all about - teaching the Torah and the restoration of the House of Yahudah and the House of Yisrael through the Renewed Covenant. This is the Good News of the Kingdom.

10

Christianity and Judaism

After the death and resurrection of Yahushua we know that the early assembly consisted, almost exclusively, of native Yisraelites who were no different than their other Yisraelite brethren but for the fact that they believed in Messiah and followed His teachings. They no longer submitted to the authority of the Pharisees although they still fellowshipped and lived with their fellow Yisraelites for a time. They continued to go to the Synagogue and the House of YHWH and they continued to observe the Torah as taught by the Living Torah - Messiah.

Over the centuries, things changed dramatically to the point where today we see two religions, Christianity and Judaism which both claim to worship the same "Elohim" but they have little else in common. What we now call Judaism traces back directly to the Pharisee sect that Yahushua confronted so often during His ministry. Interestingly, there were Pharisees who followed the teachings of Yahushua and still considered themselves to be Pharisees - including Shaul. (Acts 23:6).

There is not necessarily anything wrong with being a Pharisee so long as you are not a hypocrite and your heart is pure and so long as you do not subscribe to what was referred to as *"the leaven of the Pharisees."* (Mattityahu 16:6, 11; Mark 8:15). The problem was that there were many of the Pharisaic sect that did not believe in Messiah. After the House of YHWH was destroyed in 70 C.E., they seized control of the faith. They reached an agreement with the Romans and were permitted to establish their headquarters at Yavneh.[91] Yahrushalaim was sacked and with no Temple the Sadducees practically disappeared. The Essenes, the Natzrim and the Zealots were scattered by the Romans leaving the Pharisees as the only significant identifiable sect of Yisraelites remaining. This was the beginning of Rabbinic Judaism where the Rabbis assumed authority over interpreting the Scriptures and over the people.[92]

While Judaism has ancient roots, contrary to popular belief, Judaism is not what Mosheh taught in the Torah but rather it is a religion developed by Rabbis. Much of modern Judaism is based upon Talmudic Law rather than strictly Elohim's Torah. This is an error and it is the same reason why Yahushua rebuked the Pharisees by asking: *"Why do you also transgress the commandment of Elohim because of your tradition?"* Mattityahu 15:3. You see the Pharisees had been teaching their traditions as if they carried the same or more weight than the commandments. At the same time, they were neglecting the commands of Elohim. This became increasingly more prevalent once they moved to Yavneh.[93]

Judaism now claims to represent Yisrael of old, but it does not. It is actually the continuation of the Pharisaic Sect of Yisrael which we read about in the Messianic Scriptures. In fact, it has changed drastically since the destruction of the Temple. The religion of Judaism as we see it today is not Yisrael nor is the religion of Christianity. You do not have to convert to Judaism or Christianity to become part of Yisrael because currently, neither of these religions accurately represent the Assembly of Yisrael - both have been at odds for centuries.

We read in the Book of Acts how Shaul was given authority by the religious leaders to hunt, persecute and even kill followers of Yahushua - known as Natzrim. The Natzrim were not Christians, as Christianity would not become an actual religion for hundreds of years. The Natzrim were a sect of Yisraelites who believed that Yahushua was the Messiah but over time the divisions between the sects grew wider. One thing which led to the division was the Birkat ha-Minim which translates to "The Heretic Benediction." It is the Twelfth Benediction of the set daily prayer commonly referred to as the Shemoneh Esreh (the Eighteen Benedictions) or Amidah.

The Twelfth Benediction of the Genizah text reads: "For meshumaddim [apostates] let there be no hope, and the dominion of arrogance do Thou speedily root out in our days; and let the Natzrim and minim perish in a moment, let them be blotted out of the book of the living and let them not be written with the righteous." This was not a blessing as is the purpose of a benediction. Thus many have considered this to be a malediction or curse.[94]

The Shemoneh Esreh is one of the most important rabbinic prayers and is to be recited three times every day. Obviously, if you were a Natzrim - follower of Yahushua - you would not say this prayer and it would be awfully hard to fellowship with people who were cursing you three times a day.

Another clear point of contention between the

sects came with the Bar Kokhba revolt which occurred between 132-135 CE. The revolt started from Emperor Hadrian constructing a pagan temple in Yahrushalaim on the site where once stood the House of YHWH, renaming Yahrushalaim "Aelia Capitolina," and forbidding Torah observance. Rabbi Akiva (alternatively Akiba) convinced the Sanhedrin to support the impending revolt, and regarded the chosen commander Simon Bar Kokhba to be the Messiah, according to the verse from Numbers 24:17: "There shall come a star out of Jacob" ("Bar Kokhba" means "son of a star" in the Aramaic language).[95]

Sadly Akiba changed this would be messiah's name to fit within these prophecies. His original name was Bar Kosiba which can mean "son of a lie" which was really quite apropos. A close examination reveals that much of what Akiba did to contrive the messiahship of Kokhba was a distortion of the truth.

At the time of the revolt, the Natzrim were still a minor sect of Yisrael, and most historians believe that it was this messianic claim in favor of Bar Kokhba that alienated many Natzrim, who believed that the true Messiah was Yahushua. Because the people rallied around not only their faith, but also a false messiah, the Natzrim were prohibited from joining the revolt. They were thus viewed with disdain and disloyalty which further separated them from their Yisraelite brethren.

This was particularly a problem for the native Yisraelites. The Gentile Converts did not necessarily share any of the loyalties of their native Yisraelite brethren. Thus we can see that there was also inner turmoil within the Natzrim community between the Native Yisraelites and the Gentile Converts who flooded into the Assembly and soon overwhelmed the native Yisraelites.

So what began as an assembly of Yisraelites who believed that Yahushua was their promised Messiah eventually became a religion separate and distinct from Yisrael to the point where the Natzrim of the First Century would not even recognize the religion called Christianity, which bears little resemblance to the original faith.

The religion of Christianity was actually created hundreds of years later and incorporated many of the pagan elements from the environment which it developed, namely, the Roman Empire. There was no such religion as Christianity when Yahushua walked the earth, nor did He create a new religion after His death and resurrection. Likewise, the Christian religion did not exist during the lives of the original disciples nor was it created by Shaul. These early disciples were all Yisraelites and they never converted to any new religion - they always maintained their original faith.

Most students of the Christian religion are taught that Roman Emperor Constantine converted to Christianity and from that point on Christianity became the official state religion of the Roman Empire. What most are not taught is that Constantine was a Mithra worshipper until the day he died. He had his wife and child  murdered after his "so-called" conversion and he had a mother who used sorcery and divination to locate most, if not all, of the Christian Holy Places. Constantine did not convert to Christianity – he created the religion as we now know it!

A closer analysis of history reveals that it was that period of time when the original faith was repackaged into a new religion. This new religion birthed the Roman Catholic Church and was littered with heresy from the very beginning. It turns out that the "conversion" of Constantine was a political tactic to save his declining Empire and it actually worked for a time. Read what M. Turretin, wrote in describing the state of Christianity in the 4th century, saying, "that it was not so much the [Roman] Empire that was brought over to the Faith, as the Faith was brought over to the Empire; not the Pagans who were converted to Christianity, but Christianity that was converted to Paganism."[96]

Emperor Constantine was responsible for salvaging the faltering Roman Empire through reconstruction, including making Christianity the official state religion of the Roman Empire - most notably through The Council of Nicaea in 325 C.E. The official state religion created by Constantine is what  we now know as the Roman Catholic Church. Despite his claims of conversion, it is doubtful that his change of faith was anything but a political maneuver or an act of syncretism which the Catholic Church has been renowned for throughout its existence (i.e. the blending of pagan faiths with the Christian or Catholic doctrine). We know this because he actually had a coin minted which depicts himself on one side and Mithra on the other side with the statement: SOLI INVICTO COMITI - Committed to

the Invincible Sun.

After this not so illustrious beginning, centuries later we see that the Christian religion - having splintered into countless denominations - has remained a repository for paganism and various cultic beliefs. It is not the same assembly that received the outpouring of the Holy Spirit at the Appointed Time in Yahrushalaim, popularly known as Pentecost, after the Resurrection of the Messiah. While Christianity often claims to have picked up where Yisrael left off, this is a false doctrine called Replacement Theology. Yisrael is still the community of faith and the Christian "Church" has not replaced Yisrael.

Thus we see two religions, Christianity and Judaism, both laying claim to the same Elohim, stumbling through the centuries to this point in history where they find their destinies converging like the two sticks becoming one as prophesied in Ezekiel 37:19. Although these two religions have shared common roots, and even common Scriptures, they have also been divided by a seeming un-crossable chasm.

The problem is that you cannot both serve the same Elohim in two separate fashions. As the Apostle Shaul aptly states: "⁴ *There is one body and one Spirit, just as you were called in one hope of your calling;* ⁵ *one Master, one faith, one baptism;* ⁶ *one Elohim and Father of all, who is above all, and through all, and in you all.*" Ephesians 4:3-6.

He further states that: "*For there is one Elohim and one Mediator between Elohim and men . . .*" (1 Timothy 2:5) and "¹³ *. . . by one Spirit we were all baptized into one body - whether Jews or Greeks, whether slaves or free -- and have all been made to drink into one Spirit.* ¹⁴ *For in fact the body is not one member but many.*" (1 Corinthians 12:12-14 NKJV).

We are further exhorted by Shaul to *"stand fast in one spirit, with one mind"* and to be *"of one accord and one mind."* (Philippians 1:27; 2:2).

The Messiah Himself stated: *"20 I do not pray for these alone, but also for those who will believe in Me through their word; 21 that they all may be one, as You, Father, are in Me, and I in You; that they also may be one in Us, that the world may believe that You sent Me.22 And the glory which You gave Me I have given them, that they may be one just as We are one: 23 I in them, and You in Me; that they may be made perfect in one, and that the world may know that You have sent Me, and have loved them as You have loved Me."* Yahanan 17:20-23 NKJV. He also stated: *"And other sheep I have which are not of this fold; them also I must bring, and they will hear My voice; and there will be* one *flock and* one *shepherd."* Yahanan 10:16 NKJV.

This oneness is seen throughout the Scriptures. The people of Elohim were never meant to remain divided into different religions or denominations. This is evident from the command given to Yisrael that *"one Torah shall be for the native-born and for the stranger who dwells among you."* Shemot 12:49. **"14 *And if a stranger dwells with you, or whoever is among you throughout your generations, and would present an offering made by fire, a sweet aroma to YHWH, just as you do, so shall he do.15 one ordinance shall be for you of the assembly and for the stranger who dwells with you, an ordinance forever throughout your generations; as you are, so shall the stranger be before YHWH.16 one law and one custom shall be for you and for the stranger who dwells with you."* Bemidbar 15:14-16.

In other words, anyone who wanted to worship the Elohim of Yisrael and dwell in the Kingdom was subject to the same Torah as a native-born Yisraelite. There was

no distinction made in the Torah concerning how people worshipped Elohim, they all had to do it in the same way - His way.

Today if a Gentile tells a Rabbi that he wants to obey the Torah he or she will probably be met with a puzzled look. Next the Rabbi would probably ask why and gently tell the person that they do not have to obey the Torah, only Jews need to obey the Torah because the Torah was a gift to the Jews from Elohim. This is absolutely false and if you buy into this thinking you will have missed the entire plan of Restoration which YHWH is accomplishing.

It was not to select a special people and treat them special for no apparent reason and then punish the day lights out of them. No, instead, it was to select a people through which He could demonstrate His love for all of His Creation. This people called Yisrael were called to establish a Kingdom which would shine as a light for the rest of humanity. They were supposed to show the world how to live for Elohim. Instead they ended up being influenced by the world and they were punished. Elohim is not finished with Yisrael, and His plan is still operating through the covenants that He made with them. The point is that Elohim did not intend for just the genetic descendants of Ya'akov to obey Him. His plan is to restore His entire Creation to Him.

Notice that Elohim did not say that all native born Yisraelites must obey the Torah while all foreigners need only obey the seven Noahic Laws. This is a false idea being propagated by some in Judaism who try to promote the idea that Elohim treats natural born "Jews" different from Gentiles. It basically promotes the idea that Jews are expected to live a more set apart life than the Gentiles - while Elohim wants the Jews to obey the Torah He only expects the Gentiles to obey the "Seven Noahic Laws."

Those who expound this teaching will tell you that Elohim does not look on Gentiles as inferior and they will be considered righteous if they just obey "The Seven Noahic Laws." Therefore, why would you want to obey the Torah which is much harder. Just be happy that you are a Gentile and obey the Seven Laws - leave the Torah to the Jews.

The so-called, Seven Noahic Laws are gleaned from Beresheet 9 as follows: 1) not to commit idolatry; 2) not to commit blasphemy; 3) not to commit murder; 4) not to commit incest and adultery; 5) not to commit theft; 6) not to eat flesh from a living animal; and 7) establish courts of justice to punish violators of the other six laws.

If you look at Beresheet Chapter 9, you will find that Elohim gave some general instructions for Noah and his offspring and He established His covenant with all of creation. He did not establish rules for Gentiles and later establish separate rules for just the descendents of Ya'akov, who was renamed Yisrael. Here is a typical quote from a Jewish source: "The Torah maintains that the righteous Gentiles of all nations (those observing the Seven Laws of Noah, listed below) have a place in the world to come."[97]

This is simply not true - the Torah does not say that - it is the Rabbis that say it and it is completely contrary to the Scriptures. Are these people trying to tell me that there is some type of atonement provided in these "Noahic Laws" for Gentiles? There is none - YHWH was pointing out some fundamentals as we saw done with Adam and it is clear that He is addressing issues which ultimately led to the judgment of the planet. Teaching Gentiles that they do not need to obey the instructions of the Almighty is a grave mistake and it is in direct opposition to the mission of Yisrael.

The fact that Yisrael was chosen does not mean that they were greater or better than the other Nations. In fact, YHWH makes a special point to let them know that is not the case. "*YHWH did not set His love on you nor choose you because you were more in number than any other people, for you were the least of all peoples . . .*" Devarim 7:7. In fact, at one point YHWH declared to Mosheh: "*⁹ I have seen this people, and indeed it is a stiff-necked people! ¹⁰ Now therefore, let Me alone, that My wrath may burn hot against them and I may consume them. And I will make of you a great nation.*" Shemot 32:9-10.

The point is that YHWH did not choose Yisrael because they were better than the other people - He chose them because He loved their fathers - their fathers who were allegedly only subject to the Seven Noahic Laws. That really makes no sense - the Scriptures make it clear that Abraham observed the Torah but according to Rabbinic tradition he was only subject to the Seven Noahic Laws. Would they dare say that Noah, Shem, and Abraham were Righteous Gentiles! Absolutely not - that term is an oxymoron because they mean the opposite. Our Patriarchs of the faith followed the Instructions of YHWH and are part of the set apart Assembly.

Yisrael was chosen for a <u>purpose</u>. The purpose being to shine as a light to all humanity - to draw them to YHWH and teach the Nations the ways of YHWH - not to try to exclude the rest of the world from the blessings that come from serving and obeying Elohim. This type of

teaching is divisive and elitist.

The Scriptures do not support this divisive teaching, but rather they support the notion that Elohim is searching for a set apart people to follow and obey all of His commandments, to serve Him, to Worship Him, to love Him, and to dwell with Him in His Eternal Kingdom. These are a people who will follow the One Way which He has provided.

The Prophet Yirmeyahu speaks of the one way provided under the renewed covenant. "*37 Behold, I will gather them out of all countries where I have driven them in My anger, in My fury, and in great wrath; I will bring them back to this place, and I will cause them to dwell safely.38 They shall be My people, and I will be their Elohim; 39 **then I will give them one heart and one way,** that they may fear Me forever, for the good of them and their children after them.40 **And I will make an everlasting covenant with them, that I will not turn away from doing them good; but I will put My fear in their hearts so that they will not depart from Me.**41 Yes, I will rejoice over them to do them good, and I will assuredly plant them in this land, with all My heart and with all My soul.*" Yirmeyahu 32:37-41.

This prophecy is speaking of a future event, a time when the renewed covenant will be established between Elohim and His people - Yisrael. Both Judaism and Christianity are wrestling over this covenant, but the Scriptures clearly record that the covenant will be with Yisrael - not the modern State of Israel or a particular religious denomination, or a political entity. Yisrael is simply the set apart people who obey Elohim who have taken hold of His covenant.

While Christians and Jews (in this sense meaning adherents to Judaism) may not realize it, their destinies lie with each other through the Messiah. The Christians believe in the Hebrew Scriptures although they have added to and taken away from the Torah. They believe in the Messiah prophesied in the Scriptures and they believe that He is the one called Jesus - The Christ. Christians believe that The Messiah has already come and will come again at the end.

While Christians accept some of the teachings found in the Hebrew Scriptures, especially the prophecies concerning the Messiah, they have lost many other critical elements of the original faith - the one taught by the Messiah, not the one in Rome. As a result, Christianity has adopted pagan customs and beliefs.

The Jews, on the other hand, have preserved the Word to some extent, but have also added their own customs, traditions, and interpretations which have clouded the purity of the Torah, and sometimes supersede the Torah. They too believe in the Messiah, but they believe that He has yet to come. They have also inherited paganism. There are numerous archaeological sites of ancient synagogues which revealed pagan symbols and designs.[98] I think the Synagogue in Hamath Tiberias is an excellent example as it contains a beautiful depiction of the Temple and its implements right along side a pagan zodiac with the sun

god Helios in the middle. You will find a similar mosaic, although much less sophisticated, at the ancient Synagogue

in Bet Alpha. These are examples of the mixing or acceptance of pagan concepts that occurred within Judaism.

These two groups, Christianity and Judaism, are so close yet, at the same time, they are so far apart. Judaism, in many respects, tries to exclude non-native Jews from their faith while Christians believe that they have, in essence, replaced the Jews. They are like a couple of children vying for the rights of a firstborn. In many ways, this looks like a repeat of the sibling rivalry, jealousies, and maneuvering that we read about all throughout the Scriptures. Each has something that is needed by the other and they both need to get cleaned up and get into right standing before their Creator.

II

Division

At present there are relatively few people of "Jewish" decent who believe that Yahushua is the Messiah of Yisrael because so far they have only been presented with a Hellenized Lawless Christ named Jesus. Further still, they have generally not seen the love of their Messiah from Christians who claim that Jesus is the Messiah. Based upon recorded history, most Jews have an underlying suspicion and distrust of Christians. This is perfectly understandable and is it any wonder that this distrust continues when Christians hold large evangelistic events seeking converts called **Crusades**!

No Jew in his or her right mind would ever willingly go to something called a Crusade. The history of the Crusades invokes memories of anti-Semitism, hate,

 torture, death, suffering, bloodshed, and forced conversions where both Christians and Moslems wreaked havoc upon the Jews and the Promised Land. If you ever want to drive a Jew away from the Messiah, go ahead and invite them to a Crusade. I doubt that many will accept your

invitation and with good cause. It should have about the same effect as if you invited them to a Hamas recruitment meeting. This type of insensitivity within the Christian realm is part of the cause for the division between the two faiths, although we will see many more throughout this book.

Read how many Jews perceive Christianity and their messiah based upon history and in particular what happened during World War II: "Instead of bringing redemption to the Jews, the false Christian messiah has brought down on us base libels and expulsions, oppressive restrictions and burning [our] holy books, devastations and destructions. Christianity, which professes to infuse the sick world with love and compassion, has fixed a course directly opposed to this lofty rhetoric. The voice of the blood of millions of our brothers cries out to us from the ground: No! Christianity is not a religion of love but a religion of unfathomable hate! All history, from ancient times to our own day, is one continuous proof of the total bankruptcy of this religion in all its segments."[99]

Now read another quote from Michael Brown in his powerful book *Our Hands are Stained with Blood*: "Rabbi Ephraim Oshry, one of the few Lithuanian rabbis who survived the Holocaust, wrote: Another shocking surprise for us was the position taken by the Lithuanian populace - our 'good' Christian neighbors. There was literally not one gentile among the Christians of Slobodka who openly defended a Jew at a time when Slobodka's ten thousand Jews, with whom they had lived together all their lives, were threatened with the most horrible pogrom imaginable. On the evening of June 25, 1941, the Lithuanian fascists began going from house to house, from apartment to apartment, murdering people by the most horrible deaths - men, women, and children - old and young. They hacked off heads, sawed people through like lumber, prolonging the agony of their victims as long as possible. Finding the Rabbi of Slobodka studying Talmud in his home, they bound him to a chair, put his head on his open [Talmud volume] and sawed his head off - before slaughtering the rest of his family. Yet while the crazed Lithuanians raised their weapons to destroy the Jews, the 'Christian' Lithuanians hardly raised a finger to defend them. Professor Eugene Borowitz explains: 'We might be more inclined to give Christian claims some credence had we seen Christians through the ages behave as models of a redeemed humanity. Looking through the window of history we have found them in as much need of saving as the rest of humankind. If anything, their social failings are especially discrediting of their doctrine for they claim to be uniquely free of human sinfulness and freshly inspired by their faith to bring the world to a realm of love and peace . . . Until sinfulness ceases and well-being prevails, Jews know that the Messiah has not come.' The fact that a leading Jewish thinker like Eliezer Berkovits could speak of 'the moral bankruptcy of Christian civilization and the spiritual bankruptcy of Christian religion' should cut us to the heart. Berkovits goes on to say: 'After nineteen centuries of Christianity, the extermination of six million Jews, among them one-and-a-half million children, carried out in cold blood in the very heart of Christian Europe, encouraged by the criminal silence of virtually all Christendom, including that of an infallible Holy Father in Rome, was the natural culmination of this bankruptcy. A straight line leads from the first act of oppression

against the Jews and Judaism in the fourth century to the holocaust in the twentieth.'"[100]

Were it not for the intervention of the United States of America, one can only imagine the extent of the killing. Sadly, it was not so much the desire to save the persecuted Jews that led America into World War II as it was the attack by the Japanese at Pearl Harbor. As an American, I would like to think that this "Christian Nation" went willingly to the aid of the persecuted Jews, but this is simply not the case. Rather, this country was manipulated and ultimately pushed into the fray, which eventually led to an end of the killing.

As a result of this undeniable historical passivity demonstrated by the Christian world populace, the Jews have a deep distrust toward Christians and their perceived "bankrupt" religion, and rightly so. This wall must be shattered and this chasm must be bridged. Only when this occurs and Jews and Christians shed themselves of their unscriptural customs and traditions and join the Body of Messiah will they form the One Renewed Being, as Shaul described in the following passage:

> *[11] Therefore, remember that formerly you who are Gentiles by birth and called 'uncircumcised' by those who call themselves 'the circumcision' (that done in the body by the hands of men) - [12] remember that at that time you were separate from Messiah, excluded from citizenship in Yisrael and foreigners to the covenants of the promise, without hope and without Elohim in the world. [13] But now in Messiah Yahushua you who once were far away have been brought near through the blood of Messiah. [14] For He Himself*

is our peace, who has made the two one and has destroyed the barrier, the dividing wall of hostility, ¹⁵ *by abolishing in His flesh the enmity - The Torah of commands in dogma - so as to create in Himself one renewed being out of the two, thus making peace,* ¹⁶ *and in this one body to completely restore to favour both of them to Elohim through the stake, having destroyed the enmity by it.* ¹⁷ *He came and preached peace to you who were far away and peace to those who were near.* ¹⁸ *For through Him we both have access to the Father by one Spirit.* ¹⁹ *Consequently, you are no longer foreigners and aliens, but fellow citizens with Elohim's people and members of Elohim's household,* ²⁰ *built on the foundation of the emissaries and prophets, with Messiah Yahushua Himself as the Chief capstone.* ²¹ *In him the whole building is joined together and rises to become a set apart Dwelling Place in YHWH.* ²² *And in Him you too are being built together to become a dwelling of Elohim in the Spirit.* Ephesians 2:11-22.

This passage is a good example of a text which has traditionally been poorly translated to mean something far different than the original intent of the author. The text of verse 15 was gleaned from The Scriptures, a translation published by The Institute for Scripture Research. The corrected translation helps to demonstrate that the division between the two was not the Law or The Torah as is often taught - it is the enmity of the dogma which was abolished - not the commandments.

Only when this "dividing wall of hostility" is

destroyed will the Body be complete and the Bride ready for her Bridegroom. That day will never come until both Christianity and Judaism experience true Scriptural restoration. This does not involve Jews converting to Christianity, nor does it involve Christians converting to Judaism. Rather, it requires both of these religions, shedding all of their man-made trimmings and trappings and becoming One Nation - which is the Kingdom of Elohim.

The Jews, I believe, have preserved a key which Christianity has been missing for hundreds of years: The Torah. Sadly, the purity of the Torah has been obscured by a myriad of customs, traditions and interpretations which have driven Christians away from the simplicity and truth contained therein. On the other hand, I believe that Christianity has preserved a key which Judaism has been missing for almost two thousand years: The Messiah. Regrettably, the Messiah has been obscured by layers of paganism and tradition and other clear errors which have distracted the Jews from the true identity of their Messiah. Both groups hold a key to the restoration of the true worship of the Creator yet there exists a barrier between the two which seemingly cannot be bridged.

This barrier originated thousands of years ago, and was literally a wall of separation in the Temple court which prohibited Gentiles from passing "under penalty of death." The Gentiles were not permitted to enter in as far as the Yisraelites which, in essence, kept them away from the Elohim of Yisrael. It sent a clear and resounding message to the Gentiles that they were "unclean" and not as privileged in the eyes of Elohim. They were treated as second class, which is absolutely contrary to the teaching

of the Torah. The primary reason why Yisrael was "chosen" was to shine as a light to the Gentiles and draw all men to Elohim. Sadly, those Gentiles who were drawn to Elohim and His Temple, were then treated as inferior to the Yisraelites and were prohibited from approaching and worshipping Elohim in the same fashion as the Yisraelites - under penalty of death.

This was one of the primary issues that the early disciples of Yahushua had to contend with. It is important to remember that the entire Bible was written by Yisraelites and most, if not all, of the early disciples were Native Yisraelites. It was not until Kepha met with the House of Cornelius and when Shaul set out on his mission trips that large numbers of Gentiles began converting - not into Christianity but into a sect of Yisrael. This was quite a shock to some because for a pagan to convert and walk in accordance with the Torah was a big change.

On the other hand, it was probably quite natural for a Yisraelite to believe that Yahushua was the Messiah and it was likely a simple transition once his or her eyes were opened to the truth. A practicing Yisraelite would have been steeped in the Torah so they should have already been walking and seeking after righteousness. Yahushua was considered to be a teacher and He taught the purity and essence of the Torah. Those Yisraelites who heard His teaching would have understood Elohim's

commandments, His calendar, His Feasts, His prophets, His language, etc.

If the Yisraelites were able to see Yahushua as The Prophet, the fulfillment of the Torah - the Messiah whose blood would provide the final atonement for the transgressions of mankind - it could be a very smooth transition becoming a follower of Yahushua. This is why the early assembly consisted of Yisraelites who accepted Yahushua as Messiah. Many had spent their lives waiting for that revelation.

For Gentiles - it was an entirely different matter. Gentiles were heathens - they lived like pagans and their lifestyles were generally an abomination. This is why some Yisraelites spoke of them as "dogs" and refused to socialize with them. Now this was not an appropriate attitude, but it certainly reflects the division that existed between Yisraelites and Gentiles.[101]

As a result of these differences, the early Assembly went through many struggles and divisions. One of the primary points of contention hinged upon how the Torah was treated, understood, and applied to the Gentile converts. Now notice that I say Gentile "converts" because they were former pagans who converted to the True Way which means they were no longer Gentiles - they were grafted into the Assembly of Yisrael.[102]

The problem is that many did not immediately forget their pagan heritage. Conversion was a process for most people and it took some time to get them cleaned up. You can imagine what happened when thousands of rag tag pagan practicing Gentiles flooded into the congregation of faith during Shaul's ministry. You had the Native Yisraelites who were used to living Torah

observant lives steeped in their tradition and culture and separated from other cultures. This was met head on by a flood of Gentile converts who spent their lives steeped in the filth and perversion of paganism.

I am sure that there were many difficulties trying to assimilate these two groups. The pagan practicing Gentile converts were no doubt a shocking addition to the Assembly. They were people who had spent their lives worshipping false gods, fornicating in the temples, slaughtering and eating unclean animals as part of their pagan rituals, committing all sorts of unthinkable abominations - suddenly thrust into an Assembly which was passionate about the righteous instructions found within the Torah. The Gentile converts had lived lives in contradiction to Torah and surely brought with them a lot of baggage.

In Acts 15 we read how the early disciples of Yahushua attempted to deal with the situation at the Council of Yahrushalaim. The elders gave them some basic Torah essentials which must be obeyed immediately so they could join into the Congregation. They were then instructed to go to the assembly each Sabbath where the Torah was read. This was a brilliant solution. The pagan converts needed to, at the very least, avoid the pagan temple system which involved eating unclean things, fornication and idolatry.

This was the essence of the necessities prescribed by the Council. The converts then needed to start hearing and learning the Torah so that they could get fully restored. Due to the time and expense involved in preparing a Torah Scroll, most people did not have their own personal copy to read and study. Therefore, the place to go and hear the

Torah was the local synagogue and the synagogue was the place where early disciples of Yahushua used to meet - not a church building.[103]

Sadly, as a result of the multifaceted differences between the groups, divisions crept in between the Gentile converts and their Native Yisraelite brethren. This continued over the centuries and once the original disciples had passed away, things were ripe for wolves to step in and try to kill the sheep, just as the Messiah (Mattityahu 7:15) and Shaul had predicted. (Acts 20:29).

As more and more Gentile converts flooded into the Assembly, the original Natzrim who adhered to the Torah, were ultimately overrun and swept aside due to a number of reasons. Amazingly, these Natzrim were not only persecuted by their Yisraelite brethren as previously described - they were eventually even persecuted by the very people who owed their new found faith to their evangelism and missionary efforts. This led to the near extinction of the original Natzrim and the continued increase and influence of the converted Gentiles.

With the development of The Shemoneh Esreh, the Natzrim were no longer welcome in the synagogues so they had to establish new and different meeting places which was a major factor in the division that occurred between the Natzrim and their Yisraelite brethren. Ultimately, this led to the Synagogue/Church dichotomy and the formation of Christianity as a separate and distinct religion which was eventually birthed as the Roman Catholic Church.

This is a very condensed version of facts which are readily available to any student of history. The point I am trying to get across to the reader is that the religion

that is currently called Christianity is not the original belief system taught by the Messiah, the disciples, and the Natzrim, but rather an augmentation of that faith.

By the time the Fourth Century rolled around, there were many pagan influences within this new religion called Christianity. In 313 C.E., through the Edict of Milan, Constantine announced toleration for the Christian religion, which had previously been subject to persecution, and he also removed penalties for professing Christianity. Emperor Constantine convened the Council of Nicaea in 325 C.E. which played a significant role in shaping Christianity which would soon become the official religion of the pagan Roman Empire. Constantine incorporated his own blend of Mithraic sun god worship and performed many acts to strip the faith of any traces of Hebrew roots.

He changed the day of worship from the Sabbath to Sun Day which was very natural for the pagans who worshipped the sun god Mithra on Sun Day. On the contrary, this was an unthinkable act for Torah observant Yisraelites. He also continued a policy of persecution of the Yisraelites which had been quite prevalent since the Judean Revolt against Rome in 135 C.E.

Since the Natzrim were still native Yisraelites they were included in the persecution by the Christian Roman Empire. Because of their alienation from Gentile converts and the Constantinian version of Christianity, they were persecuted by the state sponsored "Church." Also, because the Natzrim refused to join in the revolt against Rome, they were persecuted by their fellow Yisraelites. Likewise, Rabbinic Judaism was on the rise which did not accept Yahushua as the Messiah. They, too, began persecuting the Natzrim and made a concerted effort to destroy their Messianic texts.[104]

So what we see is the early Assembly, which originally consisted almost exclusively of native Yisraelites, having become inundated by Gentile converts who eventually assumed control over the faith. The remaining Natzrim had no where to turn, they were persecuted on all sides and decimated into near extinction. The enemy clearly wanted to destroy the early Assembly of those who followed the true path and his plan included the persecution of the Natzrim and the deception of the Gentile converts.

He did a pretty good job of destroying the Natzrim and today there is very little recorded history of their existence or influence outside of the New Testament texts. It is as if the first three centuries of religious history prior to the establishment of the Roman Church vanished and was rewritten. The typical history that we are presented is that Peter (Kepha) was the first in an unbroken lineage of Popes and that the Roman Catholic Church was the first and only Assembly of Believers until the Reformation occurred when the Protestants "protested" against the Catholic Church and became a new branch of Christianity.

This, of course, was the intention of some Church historians - those who propagated a false faith would like to erase the history of the early Assembly because that would raise too many questions - namely: Why don't modern Christians worship the same way as the Messiah, His disciples and the early Assembly?

There is no acceptable answer to that question so it is easier to get rid of the evidence that there was once a direct link between Native Yisraelites and Gentile converts who shared the same faith and worshipped together in the same fashion. Most of that evidence has been destroyed and replaced with pagan practices and false doctrines.

One of the favorite methods used to separate the two has been anti-Semitism - especially from within the Christian Church. While both Christianity and Judaism have had their fair share of arrogance and elitism, there is no question that the Christian religion has either caused or advocated tremendous persecution against the Jews who have suffered over the centuries. This has led to a major chasm between Christians and Jews. The Church over the centuries has been plagued with anti-Semitism and the Jews have generally seen the Church as nothing but an instrument of persecution.

In their defense, most Christians would be shocked at some of the anti-Semitic statements and attitudes of early church leaders, Bishops, and Popes including among others St. John Chrysostom, St. Augustine, Peter the Venerable up through Protestant reformation leaders such as Martin Luther and John Calvin, as well as modern Christian preachers and writers who, among other things, are promoting Replacement Theology.

We can read these anti-Semitic views from prominent "Church Fathers" beginning within a mere century from the death and resurrection of the Messiah. According to Justin Martyr, in his dialogue with Trypho he writes: "We too, would observe

your circumcision of the flesh, your Sabbath days, and in a word, all your festivals, if we were not aware of the reason why they were imposed upon you, namely, because of your sins and the hardness of your heart. The custom of circumcising the flesh, handed down from Abraham, was given to you as a distinguishing mark, to set you off from other nations and from us Christians. The purpose of this was that you and only you might suffer the afflictions that are now justly yours; that only your land be desolated, and your cities ruined by fire, that the fruits of your land be eaten by strangers before your very eyes; that not one of you be permitted to enter your city Jerusalem. Your circumcision of the flesh is the only mark by which you can certainly be distinguished from other men . . . as I stated before it was by reason of your sins and the sins of your fathers that, among other precepts, God imposed upon you the observance of Sabbath as a mark."[105]

Notice the divisive, condescending, and disdainful tone presented by this supposed pillar of the Christian Church as He speaks, not only of the Chosen people of YHWH, but also His covenant and His commandments - The Torah.

Here is another quote from another highly esteemed "Early Church Father" named Origen which demonstrates the anti-Semitic attitudes which pervaded early Christianity.  "We may thus assert in utter confidence that the Jews will not return to their earlier situation, for they have committed the most abominable of crimes, in forming this conspiracy against the Savior of the human race . . . hence the city where Jesus suffered was necessarily

destroyed, the Jewish nation was driven from its country, and another people was called by God to the blessed election."[106] Here Origen clearly asserts the premise of Replacement Theology.

According to John Chrysostom: "The synagogue is worse than a brothel . . . it is the den of scoundrels and the repair of wild beasts . . . the temple of demons devoted to idolatrous cults . . . the refuge of brigands and dabauchees, and the cavern of devils. It is a criminal assembly of Jews . . . a place of meeting for the assassins of Christ . . . a house worse than a drinking shop . . . a den of thieves, a house of ill fame, a dwelling of iniquity, the refuge of devils, a gulf and an abyss of perdition . . . I would say the same things  about their souls . . . As for me, I hate the synagogue . . . I hate the Jews for the same reason."[107]

Chrysostom was called "The Golden Mouth" and considered to be the greatest preacher in the early church because of his eloquence and rhetoric. He held numerous positions of authority in the early church and he is noted for eight of his sermons which played a considerable part in the history of Christian anti-Semitism, and were extensively used by the Nazis in their ideological campaign against the Jews.[108]

St. Augustine, another revered individual in the early church spoke negatively toward Jews. "How hateful to me are the enemies of your Scripture! How I wish that you would slay them (the Jews) with your two-edged sword, so that there should be none to oppose your word! Gladly would I have

them die to themselves and live to you!"[109]

Here is what Peter the Venerable had to say about the Jews: "Yes, you Jews. I say, do I address you; you, who till this very day, deny the Son of God. How long, poor wretches, will ye not believe the truth? Truly I doubt whether a Jew can be really human . . . I lead out from its den a monstrous animal, and show it as a laughing stock in the amphitheater of the world, in the sight of all the people. I bring thee forward, thou Jew, thou brute beast, in the sight of all men."[110]

The following are quotes concerning Jews from arguably the most famous reformer in Church History - Martin Luther:

> So it came apparent that they were a defiled bride, yes, an incorrigible whore and an evil slut . . . a disobedient, evil people and as the vilest whore, although they boasted so much of the law of Moses, or circumcision, and of their ancestry . . . However wicked they may be, they presume to be the noblest lords over against us Gentiles, just by virtue of their lineage and law. Yet the law rebukes them as the vilest whores and rogues under the sun . . . they are full of malice, greed, envy, hatred toward one another, pride, usury, conceit, and curses against us Gentiles. Therefore, a Jew would have to have very sharp eyes to recognize a pious Jew. Speaking to them about it is much the same as preaching the gospel to a sow. They cannot know what God's commandment

really is, much less do they know how to keep it . . . Be on your guard against the Jews, knowing that wherever they have their synagogues, nothing is found but a den of devils . . . they know they are steeped in manifest vices, just as the devils themselves do. And wherever you see or hear a Jew teaching, remember that you are hearing nothing but a venomous basilisk who poisons and kills people . . . The devil with all his angels has taken possession of this people . . . Jews, Turks, papists, radicals abound everywhere. All of them claim to be the church and God's people in accord with their conceit and boast, regardless of  the one true faith . . . Therefore, dear Christian, be advised and do not doubt that nest to the devil, you have no more bitter, venomous, and vehement foe than a real Jew . . . the history books often accuse them of contaminating wells, of kidnapping and piercing children . . . I do know that they do not lack the complete, full, and ready will to do such things either secretly or openly where possible . . . If they weren't so stone-blind, their own vile external life would indeed convince them of the true nature of the pentinence. For it abounds with witchcraft, conjuring signs, figures, and the Tetragrammaton of the name, that is, with idolatry, envy, and conceit. Moreover, they are nothing but thieves and robbers who daily eat no morsel and wear no thread of clothing which they have not stolen and pilfered from us . . . Alas, it cannot be anything but the terrible wrath of God which permits anyone to sink into such abysmal, devilish, hellish, insane baseness, and arrogance. If I were to avenge myself on the devil himself I should be unable to wish him such evil and misfortune as God's wrath inflicts on the Jews . . . [111]

Martin Luther continues by asking:

What then shall we Christians do with this damned, rejected race of Jews? Since they live among us and we know about their lying and blasphemy and cursing, we can not tolerate them if we do not wish to share in their lies, curses, and blasphemy. In this way we cannot quench the inextinguishable fire of divine rage nor convert the Jews. We must prayerfully and reverentially practice a merciful severity. Perhaps we may save a few from the fire and flames [of hell]. We must not seek vengeance. They are surely being punished a thousand times more than we might wish them. Let me give you my honest advice.
    First, their synagogues should be

set on fire, and whatever does not burn up should be covered or spread over with dirt so that no one may ever be able to see a cinder or stone of it. And this ought to be done for the honor of God and of Christianity in order that God may see that we are Christians, and that we have not wittingly tolerated or approved of such public lying, cursing, and blaspheming of His Son and His Christians.

Secondly, their homes should likewise be broken down and destroyed. For they perpetrate the same things there that they do in their synagogues. For this reason they ought to be put under one roof or in a stable, like gypsies, in order that they may realize that they are not masters in our land, as they boast, but miserable captives, as they complain of incessantly before God with bitter wailing.

Thirdly, they should be deprived of their prayer-books and Talmuds in which such idolatry, lies, cursing, and blasphemy are taught.

Fourthly, their rabbis must be forbidden under threat of death to teach any more . . .

Fifthly, passport and traveling privileges should be absolutely forbidden to the Jews. For they have no business in the rural districts since they are not nobles, nor officials, nor merchants, nor the like.

Let them stay at home . . . If you princes and nobles do not close the road legally to such exploiters, then some troop ought to ride against them, for they will learn from this pamphlet what the Jews are and how to handle them and that they ought not to be protected. You ought not, you cannot protect them, unless in the eyes of God you want to share all their abomination . . .

To sum up, dear princes and nobles who have Jews in your domains, if this advice of mine does not suit you, then find a better one so that you and we may all be free of this insufferable devilish burden - the Jews . . .

Let the government deal with them in this respect, as I have suggested. But whether the government acts or not, let everyone at least be guided by his own conscience and form for himself a definition or image of a Jew. When you lay eyes on or think of a Jew you must say to yourself: Alas, that mouth which I there behold has cursed and execrated and maligned every Saturday my dear Lord Jesus Christ, who has redeemed me with his precious blood; in addition, it prayed and pleaded before God that I, my wife and children, and all Christians might be stabbed to death and perish miserably. And he himself would gladly do this if he were able, in order to appropriate our goods . . .

Such a desperate, thoroughly evil, poisonous, and devilish lot are these Jews, who for these fourteen hundred years have been and still are our plague, our pestilence, and our misfortune.

I have read and heard many stories about the Jews which agree with this judgment of Christ, namely, how they have poisoned wells, made assassinations, kidnapped children, as related before. I have heard that one Jew sent another Jew, and this by means of a Christian, a pot of blood, together with a barrel of wine, in which when drunk empty, a dead Jew was found. There are many other similar stories. For their kidnapping of children they have often been burned at the stake or banished (as we already heard). I am well aware that they deny all of this. However, it all coincides with the judgment of Christ which declares that they are venomous, bitter, vindictive, tricky serpents, assassins, and children of the devil, who sting and work harm stealthily wherever they cannot do it openly. For this reason, I would like to see them where there are no Christians. The Turks and other heathen do not tolerate what we Christians endure from these venomous serpents and young devils . . . next to the devil, a Christian has no more bitter and galling foe than a Jew. There is no other to whom we accord as many benefactions and from whom we suffer as much as we do from these base children of the devil, this brood of vipers.[112]

Here is another quote from Martin Luther concerning the Jews.

> But your [God's] judgment is right, justus es Dominie. Yes, so shall Jews, but no one else be punished, who held your word and miracles in contempt and ridiculed, insulted and damned it for such a long time without interruption, so that they will not fall, like other humans, heathens and all the others, into sin and death, not up in Hell, nor in the middle of Hell but in the pit of Hell, as one cannot fall deeper . . . Even if they were punished in the most gruesome manner that the streets ran with their blood, that their dead would be counted, not in the hundred thousands, but in the millions, as happened under Vespasian in Jerusalem and for evil under Hadrian, still they must insist on being right even if after these 1,500 years they were in misery another 1,500 years, still God must be a liar and they must be correct. In sum, they are the devil's children, damned to Hell . . . The Jews too got what they deserved. They had been called and elected to be God's mouth as Jeremiah says . . . Open your mouth wide and I will fill it; they however, kept tightly closed their muzzles, eyes, ears, nose,

whole heart and all senses, so he polluted and squirted them so full that it oozes from them in all places and devil's filth comes from them. Yes, that tastes good to them, into their hearts, they smack their lips like swine. That is how they want it. Call more: 'Crucify him, crucify him.' Scream more: 'His blood come upon us and our children.' (Matthew 27:25) I mean it came and found you . . . Perhaps, one of the merciful Saints among us Christians may think I am behaving too crude and disdainfully against the poor, miserable Jews in that I deal with them so sarcastically and insulting. But, good God, I am much too mild in insulting such devils . . . [113]

This is by no means a comprehensive list of hateful quotes made by the great protestant reformer, there are many more. I believe that the reader should be able to sufficiently gauge the spirit that was working within Mr. Luther. Now read what John Calvin, the  highly revered Protestant reformer had to say about the Jews: "Their [the Jews] rotten and unbending stiffneckedness deserves that they be oppressed unendingly and without measure or end and that they die in their misery without the pity of anyone."[114]

John Calvin was also responsible for the death of his theological arch enemy, Michael Servetus, who disputed certain doctrinal issues with Calvin. Calvin had him arrested as a heretic, convicted, and burned to death.[115] Prior to his death, Servetus was tortured in the most inhuman fashion. A wreath strewn with sulfur was placed upon his head and ignited. He continued in agony for over a half hour as the half green stake burned slowly until he finally died.[116] "Only two counts, significantly, was Servetus condemned – namely, anti-Trinitarianism and anti-paedobaptism."[117]

I hope that it is now plain to see that early Church fathers and many great Protestant Reformers have contained a seed of hatred toward the Jews throughout the centuries. Although it is a topic too grand to address in this brief overview of Christian attitudes toward the Jews, the history of the Catholic Church is, likewise, riddled with anti-Semitism.

Although there were periods of reprieve and moderation, the general trend of the Catholic Church has been contempt and persecution toward the Jews. The very fact that a recent Pope fawned over a well known deceased terrorist who has much Israeli blood  on his hands is consistent with the historical attitude of the Catholic Church toward the Jews. It would require an entire book to detail the Catholic Church's historical treatment of the Jews and there are books on this subject, but for now I will provide information concerning one edict that was issued by Pope Pius VI in the late 1700's which became "the blueprint followed by Pius's successors well into the nineteenth century:

"'Among the pastoral solicitudes that

occupy the soul of the Holiness of our Lord [ie., the Pope] at the outset of his Pontificate,' the edict began, 'the foremost priority is that which guards the Catholic religion from corruption among the Faithful. Considering, therefore, the need to protect the Faithful from the danger of subversion that can result from excessive familiarity with the Jews, the exact  observance of the measures taken by [the Pope's] predecessors is absolutely necessary.' Here Pius VI skipped his immediate predecessor to cite earlier examples of proper rigor directed at the Jews. Having conferred with the cardinal inquisitors of the Holy Office, the Pope announced, he was issuing this new edict and ordering its rigorous enforcement throughout the Papal States. The task of overseeing the Jews was to be returned to the inquisitors. Jews had to be kept in social quarantine so as not to infect the Christian population. The ghetto, designed for this purpose, was over two centuries old at the time Pius VI took office. Before Pope Paul IV came to power in 1555, the Jews of the Papal States had been free to live where they wanted. But the new Pope, who had formerly headed the newly created Holy

Office of the Inquisition, had strong feelings about how to deal with the Jews. One of his first acts as pope was to issue a bull that rescinded all of the Jews previous privileges, forbade them from engaging in any occupation other than selling rags, or from owning any land or any houses, and ordered that they be confined to a ghetto. Following the Pope's edict, ghettoes were set up in those towns of the Papal States where Jews resided, forcing them to live in cramped quarters surrounded by walls that closed them off from the Christian population, with gates that locked them in at night. Rome's ghetto was located in a particularly unhygienic, flood-prone part of the city along the banks of the Tiber."[118]

The location of Rome's ghetto was most likely selected to naturally kill off as much of the population as possible without the need for the energies of The Inquisition which, of course, is responsible for the murder of countless Jews.

With this type of treatment and hate speech being spewed by Catholic Popes and prominent Protestant Christian leaders throughout the centuries, it is easy to see how hatred of the Jews extended throughout the world along with the spread of Christianity. There is not much difference between the attitudes and treatment of the Jews by organized religion and the treatment of the Jews by Adolf Hitler and his Third Reich.

In fact, Hitler actually developed some of his ideas and methods from the Church. History also records the

silence of the German Christian community as well as the Pope, and the world Christian Church as masses of Jews were exterminated by the Nazi regime. There were a few voices such as Dietrich Bonhoffer and, of course, there were Christians who helped some Jews, but they were far too few and their collective voices amounted to deafening silence.

It is not just the blood of the Jews that has been spilled by the Church over the centuries. The Crusades that were called by various Popes promised remission of all sins, an expiation of penances and an assured place in Heaven for all of those who fought to vanquish heathens from the land. History notes that when a Crusader asked a representative of the Pope how to distinguish heretics from true Believers the response was: "Kill them all. God will recognize his own." That type of bloodlust in the name of religion has now transferred itself into the Muslim religion.

The Catholic religion, aside from the Crusades has been infested with false doctrines, corruption, scandals and the notorious Inquisition which terrorized and tortured tens of thousands of people compelling false confessions and forced conversions. Protestants, like it or not, share this same heritage and the Reformation  was not a true Restoration from the former misdeeds of the Church. Much of the same leaven existed from the Catholic system and has found its way back into the hundreds of hybrid denominations that were spawned from that era.

The religion that is now called Christianity is a far cry from the set apart Assembly described in the Book of Acts and it does not accurately represent the teachings of the Messiah. It has become a socio-political organization with a history of hatred, bloodshed, and hypocrisy.

As it now exists, the "Church" has become a grouping of organized, Nicolaitan systems[119] which have spent decades and sometimes centuries, as well as billions of dollars, building earthly kingdoms instead of the Kingdom of Heaven. Men have created artificial church governments, denominations, corporations and organizatons which completely lack Scriptural support and are more effective at building, promoting and perpetuating their systems or the personalities of their figureheads than they are at making disciples of the Messiah. In short, it is a pagan religion which claims to be founded upon truth, but was actually grounded in lies from its inception.

12

Pagan Christianity

As was indicated previously - the Messiah was not the founder of Christianity. He came to restore the Kingdom and seek out the Lost Sheep of the House of Yisrael. The Christian religion was established by the Roman Emperor Constantine and its world headquarters is in Rome. Christianity often takes solace in the fact that the Emperor of Rome became a Christian and soon thereafter the Roman Empire converted to Christianity, but this was primarily a politically motivated illusion.

Emperor Constantine did worship a christ, although it was not the Hebrew Messiah. He was a worshipper of the sun god Mithras and remained one after his alleged conversion to Christianity. All you have to do is look at his works to see which god he worshiped. Anybody can make a profession of faith - men have been calling themselves Christians for ages if they thought it was advantageous - but it is what they do which demonstrates their real faith.

It would seem fairly strange that a newly converted Emperor would establish Christianity as the official state religion of Rome and, at the same time, continue to practice and promote paganism. Constantine called Mithras the "Unconquered Sun, my companion." He issued coins proclaiming "Sol Invictus" The Unconquered Sun and in

331 C.E. he issued a coin to commemorate the founding of Rome by none other than Romulus and Remus, the mythical twin brothers who were the sons of the pagan god Mars and the Vestal Virgin. The coin displays the she-wolf that allegedly suckled the twins when they were children on one side and the goddess Roma on the other side. This sounds like something a pagan would do - not someone who worshipped the Elohim of Yisrael.

This is where the confusion lies - most people make the assumption that Christianity is a pure and unadulterated faith but it was, in essence, founded by a pagan. The term Christian even derives from paganism. The pagans called every one of their deities a "christ" which is commonly translated as "anointed." While Yahushua was indeed "anointed" He was not a christ in the pagan sense - He was The Messiah. The fact that early disciples were called Christians at Antioch (Acts 11:26), which was a profoundly pagan culture, is by no means an endorsement of the term.

While Constantine supposedly made a profession with his mouth that he was a Christian, his actions demonstrated how he defined the term Christian. This is exactly why James (Ya'akov)[120] said "show me your works" because your actions reveal what you really believe.

> "[14] What does it profit, my brethren, if someone says he has faith but does not have works? Can faith save him? [15] If a brother or sister is naked and destitute of daily food, [16] and one of you says to them, Depart in peace, be warmed and filled,

but you do not give them the things which are needed for the body, what does it profit?[17] *Thus also faith by itself, if it does not have works, is dead.*[18] *But someone will say, You have faith, and I have works. Show me your faith without your works, and I will show you my faith by my works.*[19] *You believe that there is one Elohim. You do well. Even the demons believe - and tremble!* [20] *But do you want to know, O foolish man, that faith without works is dead?* [21] *Was not Abraham our father justified by works when he offered Yitshaq his son on the altar?* [22] *Do you see that faith was working together with his works, and by works faith was made perfect?* [23] *And the Scripture was fulfilled which says, Abraham believed Elohim, and it was accounted to him for righteousness. And he was called the friend of Elohim.* [24] *You see then that a man is justified by works, and not by faith only.* [25] *Likewise, was not Rahab the harlot also justified by works when she received the messengers and sent them out another way?* [26] *For as the body without the spirit is dead, so faith without works is dead also.*" Ya'akov 2:14-26.

History is clear that the Christian religion had  tremendous pagan influences from its inception. With this type of beginning is it any wonder that we currently see the Roman Catholic Church filled with relics, idols, as well as pagan customs, symbols, and beliefs. From the concept of the Pope, to the very headpiece that the Pope wears called a Mitre - which is styled after what the priests of Dagon, the Philistine fish god, used to wear. The exaltation of Mary as "The Mother of God" and "The Queen of Heaven" comes straight out of Babylon and the practice of praying to the dead (saints) is all contrary to the Scriptures. (Devarim 18:9-14).

The engraved images which fill Catholic Cathedrals and schools are all a violation of the commandments of Elohim. (Shemot 20:4, Vayiqra 26:1, Devarim 4:15-25, 4:8-10, 27:15). The use of rosary prayer beads is directly linked to other pagan religions including Islam, Hinduism, and Buddhism. "Every one knows how thoroughly Romanist is the use of the rosary;

and how the devotees of Rome mechanically tell their prayers upon their beads. The rosary, however, is no invention of the Papacy. It is of the highest antiquity, and almost universally found among

pagan nations. The rosary was used as a sacred instrument among the ancient Mexicans. It is commonly employed among the Brahmins of Hindustan; and in the Hindu sacred books reference is made to it again and again . . . In Tibet it has been used from time immemorial, and among all the

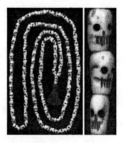

millions in the East that adhere to the Buddhist faith . . . In Asiatic Greece the rosary was commonly used, as may be seen from the image of the Ephesian Diana. In pagan Rome the same appears to have been the case."[121]

We could go on, but the purpose here is not to disparage the Catholic Church - only to demonstrate that there is an age old struggle to divert mankind from the truth, which continues to this day. The adversary has not just been sitting on the sidelines for the past two thousand years while the Christian church has been building in glory, strength, purity, and power. To the contrary, he has been busy, slowly and quietly deceiving, infiltrating, and undermining the Assembly - all the while building and establishing his kingdom and redirecting the worship of many toward himself rather than the Creator. Through the Christian religion he has continued to promote and perpetuate his Babylonian sun worship.

Of course this should not be a surprise because even in the First Century there were people who were preaching a false messiah as we read from Shaul: *"³ But I am afraid that just as Hawah was deceived by the serpent's cunning, your minds may somehow be led astray from your sincere and pure devotion to Messiah. ⁴ For if someone comes to you and preaches a Yahushua other than the Yahushua we preached, or if you receive a different spirit from the one you received, or a different gospel from the one you accepted, you put up with it easily enough."* 2 Corinthians 11:3-4. Shaul wrote these words before the Christian religion was established in Rome and through its formation many of his fears came to fruition.

The Christian religion has been propagating a false gospel and a false messiah for centuries. They have been

promoting a Hellenized Christ named Jesus when they should have been promoting a Torah observant Hebrew Messiah named Yahushua. Sun god worship has greatly influenced and permeated not only the Catholic Church but also most of the Christian religion through their various interpretations, doctrines and traditions. There were many different gods in the Roman culture

when the Christian religion was established - too many to deal with comprehensively in this text. We already visited the concept of Hellenism and determined that the Roman Empire was a polytheistic culture which worshipped many gods.

One of the pagan gods of particular importance to this discussion is that of Mithras, which was a Persian god said to have been created by Ahura-Mazda and incarnated into the human form. According to Persian legend, and in the typical pagan pattern, Mithras was incarnated into the human form and was born of Anahita, an immaculate virgin mother on December 25, 272 B.C.E.

Anahita was once worshipped as fertility goddess before her stature was reformed in the sixth and seventh centuries B.C.E. which was undertaken by Zarathustra (also known in Greek as Zoroaster), a prophet from the kingdom of Bactria. Anahita was said to have conceived Mithras, the savior, from the seed of Zarathustra preserved in the waters of Lake Hamun in the Persian province of Sistan. Mithras later ascended into heaven which was said to have occurred in 208 B.C.E.

The cult of Mithras was developed and expanded

by the Babylonians. Babylonian clergy assimilated Ahura-Mazda to the god Baal, Anahita to the goddess Ishtar (Easter), and Mithras to Shamash, their god of justice, victory, and protection and the sun god from whom King Hammurabi received his code of laws in the [16th]* century B.C.E. As a result of the solar and astronomical associations of the Babylonians, Mithras later was referred to by Roman worshippers as "Sol invictus," or the invincible sun. The sun itself was considered to be "the eye of Mithras." The Persian crown, from which all present day crowns derive, was designed to represent the golden sun disc sacred to Mithras.¹²²

These sun discs can be seen all throughout Christian art and are often called "halos." These halos are

placed above the heads of Christian characters considered to be divine or anointed in the same fashion that sun worshippers ascribe divinity to their gods. The word halo derives from the name of a sun god named "Helios" who was another prominent sun god that permeated Judaism as well as Christian theology as has already been mentioned throughout this text.

Helios, as we saw earlier in the synagogue at Tiberias and Bet Alpha, was a popular sun god and interestingly, the Greek New Testament actually replaces the name of Eliyahu (Elijah) with the name of the pagan sun god Helios. If you look at the Greek manuscripts you will see the Greek name Helios in place of the name Eliyahu. This certainly blows the argument out of the water concerning the inerrancy of the "original Greek" which so many Christians ascribe to. The reason why people did this was the same reason why people wanted to worship Shaul and Barnabas as pagan deities.

You see Helios was often represented as riding a chariot into the sun and since Eliyahu was taken up in a fiery chariot he resembled what they knew and were familiar with - paganism. Therefore, the people that copied and recopied the early manuscripts changed them to suit their beliefs. This was quite common - especially considering the fact that there were no professional copyists of the Messianic texts for hundreds of years. Therefore, there was no standard or uniformity.[123]

Now most modern translators recognize this error and have made the appropriate correction in their translations, regardless, one cannot help but wonder what other changes were made by the people who transmitted the earlier Greek texts. This is why I strongly encourage people to explore the underlying texts and translations of their Bibles in order to discern the original intent and meaning.

These clear errors should also make a person wonder about the various traditions which have been inherited from those Hellenized Christians. For instance, the fact that Mithras was born on December 25 should jump right off the page. Not surprisingly, every sun god throughout history was born on December 25 because they all derive from Babylon. As an example, in the Roman pagan system Attis was a son of the virgin Nana. His birth was celebrated on December 25. In the Greek pagan religion, Dionysus was a savior-god whose birth was observed on December 25. In the Egyptian pagan religion, Horus was a savior-god born of a virgin Isis on December 25.

The reason they were all born on December 25 was because in ancient times that was when the winter solstice occurred which was the shortest day of the year in the Northern Hemisphere. After that date, the days grew longer and it was a celebration of rebirth and it was the time that all sun gods were supposedly born. As a result of this traditional date to worship the birth of sun gods – Christians adopted the same date to worship their Christ. Therefore, we can see how pagan influences infiltrated into Christianity which now celebrates Christmas - the day that pagans celebrate the birth of their savior gods.

Etymologically speaking, a mass is traditionally a religious service involving a sacrifice. The Christ Mass was always a pagan celebration involving a ritual sacrifice. It has absolutely nothing to do with Yahushua the Messiah Who was most likely born during the Scriptural Feasts of YHWH.[124] At present, the winter solstice occurs on or around December 21, but the original date of December 25 has continued to control tradition.

The winter solstice was one of four major celebration times on the pagan calendar which divides the year into four seasons. The winter solstice, the summer solstice, the spring equinox and the autumnal equinox. This is where the pagan symbol of the sun wheel derives, which is the symbol of Baal. It is also the source of the swastika which is an ancient sun wheel.

It is a well known fact that Adolf Hitler was an avid pagan and his selection of the swastika was because of his involvement in sun worship. The swastika predates Nazi Germany by thousands of years.  Notice the Nazi symbol which depicts Mithra, represented by the bird, atop a wreath, which originates from the pagan fire wheel, which represents eternity. This was similar to various standards used by Roman soldiers and most will recognize this symbol on many flag poles in modern times. As we shall see in the next chapter, sun worship is all around us - we have just not been educated enough to recognize it for what it is - pagan.

The modern world is almost exclusively following the pagan solar system of reckoning time. The days of the week are named after pagan gods and goddesses. For instance: Sunday is the Day of the Sun, Monday is the Day of the Moon, Tuesday is Tyr's Day, Wednesday is Wooden's Day, Thursday is Thor's Day, Friday is Friga's Day and Saturday is Saturn's Day. The Scriptural calendar counts the days numerically one through six beginning on Sunday and the seventh day is the Sabbath.[125]

According to the Scriptural calendar, as with the days of the week, the months are numbered and not named. The first month begins at the sighting of the renewed moon when the barley is in the state of aviv.

 After that, the months continue to begin at the sighting of each renewed moon until the following barley harvest. The cycle revolves around the moon except for the daily cycle which revolves around the sun. A day begins in the evening at sundown, and ends the following evening.

This stands in stark contrast to the pagan system where a day begins and ends at midnight. Also under the pagan system the months are named, mostly after pagan

 gods. The first month, January, is named after Janus, the two headed Roman god. The second month, February, is named after the pagan goddess Februa. The third month, March, is named after the pagan god Mars. The fourth month, April, is named after the pagan goddess Aprilis. The fifth month, May, is named after the pagan goddess Maya. The

sixth month, June, is named after the pagan goddess Junio. The seventh month, July, is named after Julius Ceasar who was believed to have become a god and the same holds true for the eighth month, August, which was named after Augustus Ceasar.

The remaining months are very interesting because they reveal that originally the months went according to the Scriptural Calendar because the ninth month, September, derives from septu which means seven. The tenth month, October, derives from octo which means eight. The eleventh month, November, derives from novum which means nine and the twelfth month, December, derives from deca which means ten. Thus, the

names of the last four months actually reveal the general order which they should fall under the Scriptural calendar.

What does this all mean? Simply that most of the world is out of synch with the Creator's calendar and his clock - including the Christian religion. He has His own timetable within which He operates and within which those who love and serve Him are <u>supposed</u> to be operating, but they are not because they are completely engulfed in a pagan system. If you fail to understand the Creator's Calendar, you will never understand Bible prophecy because you will not be looking at the right time. For

instance, the world was holding its breath at Y2K believing that the year 2,000 was significant. The problem is that it had no significance on the Creator's Calendar. Sadly, most people do not even realize that there is another way of reckoning time nor do they know what time it is on the Creator's Calendar.[126]

Whether we choose to recognize it or not, the world is greatly influenced by ancient sun worship and the

world's largest religious system - the Roman Catholic Church - is no exception. The traditions and symbols of sun worship can be found throughout the Catholic Church - particularly at the Vatican in Rome

which is their world headquarters. The placement of this holy site of the Catholic church is quite disturbing for it is built on top of various pagan temples and tombs. It even contains an intact pagan cemetery. This is in direct

contravention to the notions of
set apartness and sanctification
as seen in the Scriptures and yet
this is fairly typical in the
Catholic religion. Later we will
see examples of how other
"alleged" holy sites are actually
revamped pagan worship sites.[127]

Besides the location, the architecture is littered
with pagan artifacts which are an abomination according
to the Scriptures. The large obelisk at the entrance of St.
Peter's Square is not a copy of an Egyptian obelisk, but
rather the very same obelisk that stood in Heliopolis in
Egypt which was the center of worship for none other than
Helios. Caligula had this obelisk brought from Heliopolis
to his circus on Vatican Hill between 37-41 C.E.

The obelisk is centered nicely in the middle of a
pagan sun wheel which fills the square.
Of course this is a fine compliment to
a statue of the sun god Tammuz which
is also located in the Vatican as well as
the statue of the sun god Jupiter, which
has been conveniently renamed Peter.
These sun god relics should feel right
at home in the "Holy City" called the
Vatican which sits in Rome on one of

the seven hills. (Revelation 17:9). Instead of destroying
these pagan sun god images, in accordance with Scriptural
directives, the Catholic Church collects them.

Similarly, most Christian Holy sites are actually
former pagan sites which have been adopted into
Christian lore and tradition. Sadly and shockingly, I

see Christians traversing around Yahrushalaim and the surrounding area visiting shrines which have been set up by Emperor Constantine's mother, Queen Helena, who  used sorcery and other questionable means to locate all of these alleged holy sites. For years, Christian Pilgrims have flocked to the Church of the Nativity in Bethlehem to see the supposed birth site of Yahushua.

The Church is located above a Mithra cave with a Mithra sun god symbol located on the supposed spot of the birth of the Messiah. While I was visiting this site  many years ago, I examined the cave and found it to be a dark, depressing, and oppressive Mithra cave located beneath a gloomy, sanctuary above which was divided into numerous sections by various Christian denominations. Notice the Mithra sunburst which is placed at the supposed site of the birth of Yahushua. This, of course, is not the site of His birth. He was not born in a cave - He was born in a manger.

This cave is just another example of how pagan sun god worship infiltrated Christianity in centuries past to the point where bewildered pilgrims herd to these sights like cattle, rarely questioning the authenticity or origins of these pagan shrines. They walk the Via Dolorosa and perform the "stations of the cross" through the streets of Yahrushalaim which did not exist at the time Yahushua was crucified - streets which are nearly 30 feet above the

streets where Yahushua would have walked, all the while believing that they are retracing his steps. A good example of this variance can be seen at the Damascus Gate which lies well above the original street level as excavations have exposed an ancient entrance to the city directly left and below the modern Gate.

As the pilgrims who traverse the Via Dolorosa draw to the completion of their fictitious journey they are led directly to the location where the former Temple of Aphrodite (Easter) was located. In fact, the pillars of the former temple are still visible to this day but instead of the temple of the fertility goddess you will now find the

Church of the Holy Sepulcher, where Yahushua was supposedly nailed to the cross, hung, laid out, and anointed and then placed into a tomb. How convenient that all of these events supposedly occurred on the site of a pagan temple. Now Christian Pilgrims come and kiss and rub personal effects on the stones hoping for some sort of anointing to rub off which they can then bring home to their friends and family.

As visitors proceed through that church, they will notice that it is divided into various sections as the different denominations have had their turf wars over the space. The infighting has gotten so bad that the keys to the

Church are held by a Muslim overseer so that one group of Christians cannot lock the others out. The entire building is filled with icons and idols and it has the look and stench of death. If this Church represents Christianity then Christianity is a pagan religion that is full of idolatry.

An idol is commonly defined as an image used as an object of worship, a false god, or a person or thing that is blindly or excessively adored. There are more idols today than ever existed in the entire history of mankind although nowadays it is not as easy to recognize an idol as it used to be because now idols are condoned and even encouraged by certain religious systems. The Catholic Church does not try to hide or excuse their involvement in idolatry and even flaunt it in the open for all to see.

While the adoration of idols, objects, and symbols is an obvious form of idolatry, there are other aspects of idolatry which are not so easy to recognize. Idols are not only small wooden or stone carvings that people used to set up in their homes. Now they are cars in their garages, money in their banks, clothes in their closets, jewelry in their safes, as well as their houses, their furniture, their High Definition TVs - you name it.

These are the objects and temptations which challenge us everyday as we try to live a life according to the instructions of our Creator. We expect these temptations and struggles when we are out in the world. On the contrary, we do not expect these things in our religious lives and activities. When we assemble together and worship with other servants of YHWH we do so with an expectation that we are no longer in the world, but have transcended into the spirit - a place where we can fellowship with a Holy (Set apart) Elohim.

It is typically shocking and even unthinkable to most people when you inform them that the Church they have been attending their entire life or the denomination that they belong to has been involved in harlotry and has perpetuated lies. While it is clearly evident in the Catholic Church, it is not so easy to detect in Protestant denominations, although it is still there. One of the first places you will find it is in the Holidays (Holy Days) that they celebrate.

Protestant Christians still observe the same pagan originated holidays established by the Catholic Church namely: Christmas and Easter. They still worship on Sunday and treat that day as their Sabbath as opposed to the Scriptural Seventh Day Sabbath.[128] They still fail to use the Name of YHWH or Yahushua. They still operate their organizations in the same Nicolaitan fashion as the Catholic Church and they still build their buildings reminiscent of the pagan temples of days gone by. So while their governmental structure may have changed, much of their doctrine remains the same. Therefore, on the exterior there are visible differences between Catholics and Protestants, although I believe they have more in common than most would either recognize or admit.

Now keep in mind that I grew up in and around these systems and I participated in them for most of my life. My observations are just as much a criticism of myself and my former beliefs and they are not meant to disparage or demean the individuals who are doing what they have been taught - people who are trying with all of

their hearts to worship the Almighty and do what is right. My criticism is toward the systems which have misled people, and as we shall see, these systems are not only religious in nature.

13

Paganism in Modern Society

I heard it proclaimed most of my life that America is a Christian nation and there is even an old court case wherein the Court allegedly affirms that fact.[129] With the continuous espousement of separation of church and state, a doctrine which has been read into the constitution, one would be hard pressed to prove that America is a nation which represents any particular religion.

While America was allegedly founded upon Scriptural principles we need to be honest - it is not a theocracy nor was it intended to be one. I know that most people believe that this is a Christian nation but that begs the question: What exactly is a Christian nation? Is it a nation that operates according to the Commandments of the Almighty? If that is true then America is disqualified by the fact that it permits the freedom of religion. YHWH does not want freedom of religion in His Kingdom nor will He tolerate His people worshipping other deities.

Regardless, America allows people to worship satan or any other god or goddess - it permits both paganism and atheism, Christianity, Judaism, Islam, or any one of countless religions -

not unlike the Hellenistic cultures of the Greco-Roman Era.

America tolerates things which the Scriptures consider abominable and condones things that the Scriptures prohibit. America does not even abide by the Ten Commandments. In fact, it continues to remove the Ten Commandments from all public buildings. Therefore, just applying the standard set by the Scriptures, America, as a nation, certainly does not serve YHWH.

On the other hand, if you knew nothing about this country and arrived as a traditional immigrant - simply based upon certain observations - you would be forced to

conclude that America is a pagan society. It even has a goddess to greet new immigrants into the "Promised Land." The Statue of Liberty represents the goddess of Liberty and is most likely the largest pagan statue ever erected in history. This giant goddess not only greets those who enter into the United States of America, but if they then proceed into New York State they are surrounded by her companions, the goddess of Freedom and the goddess of Justice as well as Mithra himself, all of whom adorn the New York State emblem.

The very fact that this country permits the use of these pagan statues and images disqualifies it from being a government based upon the Scriptures. If America were serving the Elohim of Yisrael

and obeying His Commandments, then paganism and idolatry would not be tolerated because that is what the Scriptures mandate. America would not condone the killing of unborn children, rampant adultery, rebellious children nor would it sanction same sex marriages because all of these actions constitute sin and require judgment.

America still claims to be one nation "under God," but that statement is meaningless because it does not specify *which* god it is under. If you had to make a judgment based upon outward appearances and the symbols used throughout the country, you would have to admit that it is

a pagan god. I say this because statues and idols of pagan gods and goddesses adorn our nation's federal and state capitals, America's courtrooms - even its currency. The nation's capital building is decked with a statue of the goddess of Freedom at its apex and it is also protected by the Roman god Mars. The U.S. Congress, which operates in this building, even offers the prayers of pagan clergy to open certain sessions.

What about the fact that our currency states: "In God We Trust." I am sorry to repeat that the phrase is quite meaningless because, once again, it fails to identify *the god* in which Americans supposedly trust. Many might respond: "we trust in

the god with the capital 'G' - you know - that God." No matter how you spell it, "god" is just a title and could mean anything or any god. The Creator of the Universe is

called Elohim in the Scriptures and we are told that His Name is YHWH.

It also may be useful to take a closer look at American currency, in particular the one dollar bill. The reverse side of every one dollar bill contains the Great Seal of the United States. Did they ever  teach you in school who designed the Great Seal or how this became the official seal of the country? You would think that something so common and so important would be taught to every child in every school in America, but it is not. In fact, it is a mystery to most Americans. Did anyone ever explain why there is a pyramid on this American seal? Any reasonable person should quickly ask: "What does a pyramid have to do with the United States of America?" After all, we do not have any pyramids in this country.

The Great Seal is actually a two sided seal with one side containing the pyramid and the other side containing the bird symbol, which has also been adopted  as the Presidential Seal. Both portions of the seal are littered with occult symbolism. It is alleged that the Great Seal was designed by Charles Thompson, William Barton and Pierre Eugene Du Simitiere in 1782 and it is reported by Freemason historian, Manly P. Hall that the original design included a Phoenix resting on a nest of flames. In older designs it is clear that the bird was, in fact, a phoenix which later morphed into a bird which now looks like an eagle.

This fact is important because the use of the

phoenix was supposed to symbolize a new nation being birthed, but the phoenix has much greater significance in mythology. The word "Phoenix" is a Greek name for a mythical bird which originated in Ancient Egypt known as  the Benu Bird. The Benu Bird, otherwise known as the Sacred Bird of Heliopolis was one of the primeval forms of the High God and, according to the Pyramid Texts and the Book of the Dead, represented in various forms, the manifestations of Atum, Ra, and Osiris. The Phoenix is directly associated with sun god worship. In the original seal, the stars above the head of the phoenix were all  hexagrams designed in a hexagram pattern, which still remains on the modern seal. The hexagram has a history of use in pagan cult practices and the fact that it is surrounded by a monstrance, a standard sun god symbol only adds to my suspicion of its usage.

The Benu Bird (Phoenix) was closely associated with a stone called the Benben Stone. The two names are derived from the same word, which means "to rise." The Benben stone was placed on the top of a tall column, an obelisk, to catch the first rays of the rising sun. The obelisk, with the Benben stone on its cap represents the perch rising from the Abyss, which the Benu Bird perched atop, about to call the world into existence. The capstones of pyramids have the same name, and may have had the same function. Obelisks were sometimes erected in pairs, one for the sun and one for the moon. When obelisks occur in pairs, they are called pylons.[130]

Notice that the pyramid on the Great Seal does not have a capstone. "[T]he pyramid with its missing capstone is profoundly significant because it alludes to Illuminati control of Freemasonry, but also to the mystery schools of ancient Egypt.

In occult terms, the elevated capstone is an allusion to the Great Pyramid with its missing capstone. In ancient Egypt, the pyramids were used as initiation chambers in the king-making rituals. Each pyramid had a capstone, made either of pure crystal or an alloy of some kind. This capstone was used to attract cosmic rays, which would induce spiritual illumination. The illuminated triangle with the all-seeing eye represents the missing capstone and its accompanying mysteries, both of which only survive now in symbolic form."[131]

The thirteen levels of the pyramid represent the thirteen levels of masonry. The all seeing eye is a Luciferian eye representing Osiris and Horus - Egyptian sun gods. The Roman numerals MDCCLXXVI translate into Arabic numerals as 1776, the year of the American Revolution, but also the year that the Illuminati was founded as well as the founding of the House of Rothschild. The Latin inscription surrounding the pyramid proclaims: "He has favored our undertaking - a new order for the ages." I doubt that many people ever took the time to translate the phrase. It is plain to anyone who looks close enough that there are things that have been set in motion long ago by powers that go beyond our elected officials.

There is another pagan symbol in this country which provides more insight into the god that America

serves. Everyone who visits the Nation's Capital has likely taken a photo of the giant obelisk, which represents the phallus of Baal. It is called the Washington Monument and it is located in the National Mall. I would hazard a

guess that it is the largest obelisk ever erected in the history of the world. Interestingly, on the aluminum cap of this immense phallic symbol one will find inscribed the words "Laus Deo" which means "Praise be to Deo." Some translate "Deo" to mean "God" but it was originally the name of a pagan

fertility goddess, Demeter, who was allegedly the mother of Dionysus, the pagan savior which we already discussed has striking similarities to Jesus.

Therefore, the god that America is "under" appears to be the sun god, Osiris. Knowing that all of these sun gods derive from Babylon, we realize that this is blatant Baal worship. In fact, most of the architecture of the capital city is patterned from the Greco-Roman style so it even looks like a pagan city filled with pagan temples and to top it all off - it

is designed in the shape of a pentagram - a symbol with profoundly pagan attachments.

The Supreme Court Building is adorned with sculptures of a variety of pagan gods. A review of the rest of the country reveals much of the same. The goddess of Justice is in most state and federal courts, overseeing how justice is meted out throughout the country. You will find her in most lawyer's offices and on many business cards and letterheads. Her name is Themis in the Greek culture

and Justicia in the Roman culture.

No matter how you say her name, she is a pagan goddess. True justice comes from Our Heavenly Father, not some pagan goddess. "*³ For I proclaim the Name of YHWH: Ascribe greatness to our Elohim. ⁴ He is the Rock, His work is perfect; for all His ways are justice, an Elohim of truth and without injustice; Righteous and upright is He.*" Devarim 32:3-4.

The symbol of Asclepius is seen throughout the medical profession. Known as Asklepios to the Greeks, he is considered a god of healing and was venerated in the ancient world as the patron deity of physicians. "His cult, established in the fourth century B.C.E., became common throughout the Greco-Roman world, and  even today his symbols - a staff and snake - are used universally as the symbols of medicine."¹³² The study and profession of psychiatry and psychology are named after Psyche who was a maiden loved by Eros, the god of love, and united with him after Aphrodite's jealousy was overcome and who subsequently became the personification of the soul.

Even the dollar sign ($) used to represent currency derives from the snake symbolism, which, in the case of money, most likely symbolizes the wand or caduceus carried by the god Mercury. Mercury is often pictured carrying a caduceus consisting of two snakes wrapped around each other, rather than a snake wrapped around a pole. The dollar sign was also used by medieval astrologers to denote the planet Mercury. In mythology, Mercury had rule over banking, commerce and financial transactions.

"It is traditional for banks to have sculpted models of either Mercury or the caduceus on their facades or doors. The Bank of England, in London, has a caduceus on either of its main doors. Above the main portal of the Federal Reserve Building, in Washington, D.C., is a sculpture of a female personification of America, holding a caduceus. This was sculpted in 1937, two years after the modern dollar bill was designed and printed."[133]

We already discussed the pagan elements of the solar calendar that we have inherited and we see from astronomy how all of the planets have been named after pagan gods and goddesses and the constellations have all been attributed to pagan characters and myths. In March 2004 NASA claimed to have discovered a tenth planet in our solar system which they promptly named Sedna after the Inuit goddess of the sea. I am not certain how the recent demotion of Pluto will affect Sedna but I find it intriguing that their natural

inclination was to attach a pagan label to the heavenly bodies which were specifically designed to be a witness to the Creator of the Universe.

The planets, stars, and the constellations were placed in the heavens for a reason. The Scriptures tell us that: *"Elohim said, Let there be lights in the firmament of the heavens to divide the day from the night; and **let them be for signs and seasons, and for days and years** . . ."* Beresheet 1:14. They are for signs and seasons, they tell the story of the Creator and His plan of restoration yet the pagans have taken hold of them and warped and twisted their true meaning through the occult. The Zodiac is a pagan adulteration of what is called mazeroth in Hebrew.[134]

The Scriptures are very clear that the people of Elohim are not even to utter the names of false gods, let alone have pictures and statutes of them strewn about their nation. What we see in the United States of America is similar to what happened to ancient Yisrael. Instead of tearing down the pagan symbols they ended up falling into idolatry.

Yisrael was commanded to rid the land of these symbols and practices. *"²You shall utterly destroy all the places where the nations which you shall dispossess served their gods, on the high mountains and on the hills and under every green tree. ³ And you shall destroy their altars, break their sacred pillars, and burn their wooden images with fire; you shall cut down the carved images of their gods and destroy their names from that place. ⁴ You shall not worship YHWH your Elohim with such things."* Devarim 12:2-4.

The reason for this commandment was to cleanse the land of these practices so that people would not be led astray and begin participating in the abominable acts. We can vividly see the need for this commandment in our present culture. People no longer obey these commands - even in the modern State of Israel. The landscape of modern Jerusalem is littered with minarets and steeples, domes and other pagan imagery.

The abominations which were prohibited by the Scriptures continue to be built and no one even appears to be concerned. In fact, they are even raising obelisks which were once fallen - in the name of archaeology.[135]

"[14] *Therefore, my beloved, flee from idolatry.* [15] *I speak as to wise men; judge for yourselves what I say.* [16] *The cup of blessing which we bless, is it not the communion of the blood of Messiah? The bread which we break, is it not the communion of the body of Messiah?* [17] *For we, though many, are one bread and one body; for we all partake of that one bread.* [18] *Observe Yisrael after the flesh: Are not those who eat of the sacrifices partakers of the altar?* [19] *What am I saying then? That an idol is anything, or what is offered to idols is anything?* [20] *Rather, that the things which the Gentiles sacrifice they sacrifice to demons and not to Elohim, and I do not want you to have fellowship with demons.* [21] *You cannot drink the cup of YHWH and the cup of demons; you cannot partake of YHWH's table and of the table of demons.* [22] *Or do we provoke the Master to jealousy? Are we stronger than He?*" 1 Corinthians 10:14-22.

Our senses are so dulled that most do not even recognize the pagan influences that surround us. We hear about mother nature and refer to her when we speak of the weather without even realizing that she is the same

Mother Earth that the pagans worship. We see the symbols for male and female which stem directly from ancient paganism. We tell our children that the Tooth Fairy is going to come into their room at night and take their teeth from under their pillow. We sing nice songs asking "Mr. Sandman" to bring us a dream.

We buy our children movies and take them to Disney World where magic and sorcery, fairies and witches are all glamorized and made into entertainment. I read a report once that indicated that the only time someone prayed in a Disney movie was when Gepetto prayed to the Blue Fairy. I haven't watched them all so I cannot say for sure if that is true, but the point is quite compelling.

The holidays that we celebrate generally all have pagan roots. Christmas, Easter, Halloween, and Valentine's Day are all pagan celebrations yet the majority of Christians are oblivious to the abomination that 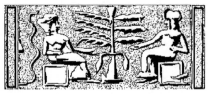 they are committing in the eyes of Elohim when they participate in these activities. As was already mentioned the December 25 celebration of Christmas is completely grounded in sun god worship. The tree which people cut down and then set up in their houses represents Nimrod and the traditional gold and silver balls which they would adorn the tree with represented his testicles - I am not making this stuff up! This type of conduct is clearly an abomination, yet most people do not even realize that they are repeating an ancient pagan rite.

This is the same thing that Yisrael was warned

about yet we have not learned from their example. "*2 Do not learn the way of the Gentiles; do not be dismayed at the signs of heaven, for the Gentiles are dismayed at them. 3 For the customs of the peoples are futile; for one cuts a tree from the forest, the work of the hands of the workman, with the axe. 4 They decorate it with silver and gold; they fasten it with nails and hammers so that it will not topple.*" Yirmeyahu 10:2-4 NKJV.[136]

The Christian religion, as a whole, has become so infiltrated with paganism that many Christians are stunned when their eyes are opened and they find out how many similarities that they share with sun worship. This really should not come as a surprise. After all, if people consider America to be the example of a Christian nation then all you need to do is look around, watch the news, or read a paper to deduce that something must be seriously wrong with Christianity.

America may be a Christian nation, whatever that means, but it surely is a pagan nation. With the history of legalizing and condoning the killing of unborn children and rampant sexual immorality, this nation is on the fast track to judgment. We need only to examine history to get a glimpse of what is in store for this nation and the world if they do not turn from their wicked ways.

Some believe that America is in store for judgment similar to that of Sodom. I believe that this is true but not specifically for the reasons one might think. The sin of Sodom was that she had: "*49 . . . pride, fullness of food, and abundance of idleness; neither did she strengthen the hand of the poor and needy. 50 And they were haughty and committed abomination before Me; therefore I took them away as I saw fit.*" Yehezqel 16:49-50 NKJV. This sounds like an accurate definition of the society that I live in as well as much of

the "modern" world.

The information provided in this chapter is simply a brief overview yet these facts alone should dispel any question of whether or not America is a pagan society. I would encourage readers throughout the world to take a fresh look at their own individual cultures to discern any imbedded pagan concepts or practices which may need to be exposed. This must be done through prayer so that the eyes of your understanding are opened, and it is a critical part of the process of Scriptural Restoration. Your prayer should mirror that of the Tehillim: "*²³ Search me, O Elohim, and know my heart; try me, and know my thoughts; ²⁴ and see if an idolatrous way is in me, and lead me in the way everlasting.*" Tehillim 139:23-24.

14

Scriptural Restoration

By now it should be clear to the reader that not only has society been compromised by pagan influences but so has the religion of Christianity. In the same fashion

that the Pantheon, a Greek Temple dedicated to the worship of all gods, was converted to a Christian Church in 607 C.E., so too we see that much church doctrine and tradition have been built upon a pagan foundation.

This is the same thing that happened to Yisrael and Yahudah and the Scriptures offer numerous examples of restoration that they experienced after falling away. These examples are helpful to those who currently desire restoration because they provide a blue print and a pattern. One example of restoration can be seen in King Hezekiah whose proper Hebrew name is Hizqiyahu. Hizqiyahu (חזקיהו) means "Yah has strengthened him." Yah is the poetic short form for the true Name of Elohim which is rarely used any longer. Hizqiyahu was the twelfth King of Yahudah and ascended the throne around 726 B.C.E. Let us read how he restored the kingdom during his reign.

"¹ Hizqiyahu became king when he was twenty-five years old, and he reigned twenty-nine years in Yahrushalaim. His mother's name was Abiyah the daughter of Zecharyah.² And **he did what was right in the sight of YHWH, according to all that his father David had done.** ³ In the first year of his reign, in the first month, **he opened the doors of the house of YHWH and repaired them.**⁴ Then he brought in the priests and the Levites, and gathered them in the East Square, ⁵ and said to them: Hear me, Levites! Now sanctify yourselves, sanctify the house of YHWH Elohim of your fathers, and carry out the rubbish from the holy place.⁶ For our fathers have trespassed and done evil in the eyes of YHWH our Elohim; they have forsaken Him, have turned their faces away from the dwelling place of YHWH, and turned their backs on Him.⁷ They have also shut up the doors of the vestibule, put out the lamps, and have not burned incense or offered burnt offerings in the holy place to the Elohim of Yisrael.⁸ Therefore the wrath of YHWH fell upon Yahudah and Yahrushalaim, and He has given them up to trouble, to desolation, and to jeering, as you see with your eyes.⁹ For indeed, because of this our fathers have fallen by the sword; and our sons, our daughters, and our wives are in captivity. ¹⁰ Now it is in my heart to make a covenant with YHWH Elohim of Yisrael, that His fierce wrath may turn away from us.¹¹ My sons, do not be negligent now, for YHWH has chosen

you to stand before Him, to serve Him, and that you should minister to Him and burn incense. ¹² Then these Levites arose: Mahath the son of Amasai and Yoel the son of Azariah, of the sons of the Kohathites; of the sons of Merari, Kish the son of Abdi and Azariah the son of Yahallelel; of the Gershonites, Yoah the son of Zimmah and Eden the son of Yoah;¹³ of the sons of Elizaphan, Shimri and Yeiel; of the sons of Asaph, Zecharyah and Mattaniah;¹⁴ of the sons of Heman, Yehiel and Shimei; and of the sons of Yaduthun, Shemaiah and Uzziel. ¹⁵ And they gathered their brethren, sanctified themselves, and went according to the commandment of the king, at the words of YHWH, to cleanse the house of YHWH.¹⁶ Then the priests went into the inner part of the house of YHWH to cleanse it, and brought out all the debris that they found in the temple of YHWH to the court of the house of YHWH. And the Levites took it out and carried it to the Brook Kidron. ¹⁷ Now they began to sanctify on the first day of the first month, and on the eighth day of the month they came to the vestibule of YHWH. So they sanctified the house of YHWH in eight days, and on the sixteenth day of the first month they finished. ¹⁸ Then they went in to King Hizqiyahu and said, We have cleansed all the house of YHWH, the altar of burnt offerings with all its articles, and the table of the showbread with all its articles.¹⁹ Moreover all the articles which King Ahaz in his reign had cast aside in his

transgression we have prepared and sanctified; and there they are, before the altar of YHWH. ²⁰ Then King Hizqiyahu rose early, gathered the rulers of the city, and went up to the house of YHWH. ²¹ And they brought seven bulls, seven rams, seven lambs, and seven male goats for a sin offering for the kingdom, for the sanctuary, and for Yahudah. Then he commanded the priests, the sons of Aaron, to offer them on the altar of YHWH. ²² So they killed the bulls, and the priests received the blood and sprinkled it on the altar. Likewise they killed the rams and sprinkled the blood on the altar. They also killed the lambs and sprinkled the blood on the altar. ²³ Then they brought out the male goats for the sin offering before the king and the assembly, and they laid their hands on them. ²⁴ And the priests killed them; and they presented their blood on the altar as a sin offering to make an atonement for all Yisrael, for the king commanded that the burnt offering and the sin offering be made for all Yisrael. ²⁵ And he stationed the Levites in the house of YHWH with cymbals, with stringed instruments, and with harps, according to the commandment of David, of Gad the king's seer, and of Nathan the prophet; for thus was the commandment of YHWH by His prophets. ²⁶ The Levites stood with the instruments of David, and the priests with the trumpets. ²⁷ Then Hizqiyahu commanded them to offer the burnt offering on the altar. And when the burnt offering began, the song

of YHWH also began, with the trumpets and with the instruments of David king of Yisrael.[28] So all the assembly worshiped, the singers sang, and the trumpeters sounded; all this continued until the burnt offering was finished.[29] And when they had finished offering, the king and all who were present with him bowed and worshiped.[30] Moreover King Hizqiyahu and the leaders commanded the Levites to sing praise to YHWH with the words of David and of Asaph the seer. So they sang praises with gladness, and they bowed their heads and worshiped. [31] Then Hizqiyahu answered and said, Now that you have consecrated yourselves to YHWH, come near, and bring sacrifices and thank offerings into the house of YHWH. So the assembly brought in sacrifices and thank offerings, and as many as were of a willing heart brought burnt offerings.[32] And the number of the burnt offerings which the assembly brought was seventy bulls, one hundred rams, and two hundred lambs; all these were for a burnt offering to YHWH.[33] The consecrated things were six hundred bulls and three thousand sheep.[34] But the priests were too few, so that they could not skin all the burnt offerings; therefore their brethren the Levites helped them until the work was ended and until the other priests had sanctified themselves, for the Levites were more diligent in sanctifying themselves than the priests.[35] Also the burnt offerings were in abundance, with the fat of the

peace offerings and with the drink offerings for every burnt offering. So the service of the house of YHWH was set in order.³⁶ Then Hizqiyahu and all the people rejoiced that Elohim had prepared the people, since the events took place so suddenly." 2 Chronicles 29:1-36.

The Scriptures record that King Hizqiyahu did what was right in the eyes of YHWH. He opened the doors of the House of YHWH and he repaired them. The Temple service had been shut down and he proceeded to cleanse the House and restore the priestly service, the Temple service, and Davidic worship. Next, King Hizqiyahu proceeded to keep the appointed times of YHWH which are prescribed in the Scriptures.

"¹ And Hizqiyahu sent to all Yisrael and Yahudah, and also wrote letters to Ephraim and Manasseh, that they should come to the house of YHWH at Yahrushalaim, to keep the Passover to YHWH Elohim of Yisrael.² For the king and his leaders and all the assembly in Yahrushalaim had agreed to keep the Passover in the second month.³ For they could not keep it at the regular time, because a sufficient number of priests had not consecrated themselves, nor had the people gathered together at Yahrushalaim. ⁴And the matter pleased the king and all the assembly. ⁵ So they resolved to make a proclamation throughout all Yisrael, from Beersheba to Dan, that they should come to keep the Passover to YHWH Elohim of Yisrael at Yahrushalaim, since they had not done it for a long time in the prescribed manner. ⁶ Then the runners went throughout

all Yisrael and Yahudah with the letters from
the king and his leaders, and spoke according to
the command of the king: **Children of Yisrael,
return to YHWH Elohim of Abraham,
Yitshaq, and Yisrael;** then He will return to
the remnant of you who have escaped from the
hand of the kings of Assyria.[7] And do not be like
your fathers and your brethren, who trespassed
against YHWH Elohim of their fathers, so that
He gave them up to desolation, as you see.[8] Now
do not be stiff-necked, as your fathers were,
but yield yourselves to YHWH; and enter His
sanctuary, which He has sanctified forever, and
serve YHWH your Elohim, that the fierceness
of His wrath may turn away from you.[9] For if
you return to YHWH, your brethren and your
children will be treated with compassion by those
who lead them captive, so that they may come
back to this land; for YHWH your Elohim is
gracious and merciful, and will not turn His face
from you if you return to Him. [10] So the runners
passed from city to city through the country
of Ephraim and Manasseh, as far as Zebulun;
but they laughed at them and mocked them.
[11]Nevertheless some from Asher, Manasseh,
and Zebulun humbled themselves and came to
Yahrushalaim. [12] Also the hand of Elohim was
on Yahudah to give them singleness of heart to
obey the command of the king and the leaders,
at the word of YHWH. [13] **Now many people, a
very great assembly, gathered at Yahrushalaim
to keep the Feast of Unleavened Bread in the**

second month. **¹⁴ They arose and took away the altars that were in Yahrushalaim, and they took away all the incense altars and cast them into the Brook Kidron.** ¹⁵ Then they slaughtered the Passover lambs on the fourteenth day of the second month. The priests and the Levites were ashamed, and sanctified themselves, and brought the burnt offerings to the house of YHWH. ¹⁶ They stood in their place according to their custom, according to the Torah of Mosheh the man of Elohim; the priests sprinkled the blood received from the hand of the Levites. ¹⁷ For there were many in the assembly who had not sanctified themselves; therefore the Levites had charge of the slaughter of the Passover lambs for everyone who was not clean, to sanctify them to YHWH. ¹⁸ For a multitude of the people, many from Ephraim, Manasseh, Issachar, and Zebulun, had not cleansed themselves, yet they ate the Passover contrary to what was written. But Hizqiyahu prayed for them, saying, May the good YHWH provide atonement for everyone ¹⁹ who prepares his heart to seek Elohim, YHWH Elohim of his fathers, though he is not cleansed according to the purification of the sanctuary. ²⁰ And YHWH listened to Hizqiyahu and healed the people. ²¹ So the children of Yisrael who were present at Yahrushalaim kept the Feast of Unleavened Bread seven days with great gladness; and the Levites and the priests praised YHWH day by day, singing to YHWH, accompanied by loud instruments. ²² And

Hizqiyahu gave encouragement to all the Levites who taught the good knowledge of YHWH; and they ate throughout the feast seven days, offering peace offerings and making confession to YHWH Elohim of their fathers. ²³ *Then the whole assembly agreed to keep the feast another seven days, and they kept it another seven days with gladness.* ²⁴ *For Hizqiyahu king of Yahudah gave to the assembly a thousand bulls and seven thousand sheep, and the leaders gave to the assembly a thousand bulls and ten thousand sheep; and a great number of priests sanctified themselves.* ²⁵ *The whole assembly of Yahudah rejoiced, also the priests and Levites, all the assembly that came from Yisrael, the sojourners who came from the land of Yisrael, and those who dwelt in Yahudah.* ²⁶ *So there was great joy in Yahrushalaim, for since the time of Solomon the son of David, king of Yisrael, there had been nothing like this in Yahrushalaim.* ²⁷ *Then the priests, the Levites, arose and blessed the people, and their voice was heard; and their prayer came up to His holy dwelling place, to heaven."* 2 Chronicles 30:1-27.

This is the mark of true restoration. The people had a powerful desire to obey the Word of Elohim. They did not just talk about being obedient, their words were supported by action. They rejoiced in doing what was right and their zeal was so great that they went above and beyond what was prescribed in the Word. When they were finished celebrating, they went and cleansed the land of all the worship of false gods.

"[1] Now when all this was finished, all Israel who were present went out to the cities of Yahudah and broke the sacred pillars in pieces, cut down the wooden images, and threw down the high places and the altars - from all Yahudah, Benyamin, Ephraim, and Manasseh - until they had utterly destroyed them all. Then all the children of Yisrael returned to their own cities, every man to his possession. [2] And Hizqiyahu appointed the divisions of the priests and the Levites according to their divisions, each man according to his service, the priests and Levites for burnt offerings and peace offerings, to serve, to give thanks, and to praise in the gates of the camp of YHWH. [3] **The king also appointed a portion of his possessions for the burnt offerings: for the morning and evening burnt offerings, the burnt offerings for the Sabbaths and the New Moons and the set feasts, as it is written in the Torah of YHWH.**" 2 Chronicles 31:1-3.

An interesting part of this passage is the fact that the King reached out to the Northern tribes, which were known as the House of Yisrael, who had drifted into pagan worship after the Kingdom of Yisrael had divided around 922 B.C.E. Hizqiyahu, the King of Yahudah, wanted to restore the divided kingdom, at least as far as worshipping their Elohim was concerned. The Scriptures make specific mention that Yisraelites from Ephraim, Manasseh, Issachar, and Zebulun came to Yahrushalaim. This must have been an amazing time. Some of the tribes from the divided kingdom of Yisrael and Yahudah were united in their desire to cleanse the land, and worship and obey their Elohim. Sadly, this restoration was not complete and it did not last - the tribes fell back into idolatry.

Another significant restoration can be seen during the reign of King Josiah. His proper Hebrew name is pronounced Yoshiyahu (יאשׁיהו) which means "healed

or supported by Yah." Young King Yoshiyahu was the sixteenth king of Yahudah and began his reign around 653 B.C.E. Let us read how he restored the Kingdom.

"*¹ Yoshiyahu was eight years old when he became king, and he reigned thirty-one years in Yahrushalaim. His mother's name was Yedidah the daughter of Adaiyah of Bozkath.² And **he did what was right in the sight of YHWH, and walked in all the ways of his father David; he did not turn aside to the right hand or to the left.**³ Now it came to pass, in the eighteenth year of King Yoshiyahu, that the king sent Shaphan the scribe, the son of Azaliyah, the son of Meshullam, to the house of YHWH, saying: ⁴ Go up to Hilkiyah the high priest, that he may count the money which has been brought into the house of YHWH, which the doorkeepers have gathered from the people.⁵ And let them deliver it into the hand of those doing the work, who are the overseers in the house of YHWH; let them give it to those who are in the house of YHWH doing the work, to repair the damages of the house - ⁶ to carpenters and builders and masons - and to buy timber and hewn stone to repair the house.⁷ However there need be no accounting made with them of the money delivered into their hand, because they deal faithfully. ⁸ Then Hilkiyah the high priest said to Shaphan the scribe, **I have found the Scroll of the Torah in the house of YHWH. And Hilkiyah gave the Scroll to Shaphan, and he read it.** ⁹ So Shaphan the scribe went to the king,*

bringing the king word, saying, Your servants have gathered the money that was found in the house, and have delivered it into the hand of those who do the work, who oversee the house of YHWH. ¹⁰ Then Shaphan the scribe showed the king, saying, Hilkiyah the priest has given me a scroll. **And Shaphan read it before the king.** ¹¹ **Now it happened, when the king heard the words of the Scroll of the Torah, that he tore his clothes.**¹² Then the king commanded Hilkiyah the priest, Ahikam the son of Shaphan, Achbor the son of Michaiyah, Shaphan the scribe, and Asaiyah a servant of the king, saying, ¹³ Go, inquire of YHWH for me, for the people and for all Yahudah, concerning the words of this Scroll that has been found; for great is the wrath of YHWH that is aroused against us, because our fathers have not obeyed the words of this Scroll, to do according to all that is written concerning us. ¹⁴ So Hilkiyah the priest, Ahikam, Achbor, Shaphan, and Asaiyah went to Huldah the prophetess, the wife of Shallum the son of Tikvah, the son of Harhas, keeper of the wardrobe. (She dwelt in Yahrushalaim in the Second Quarter.) And they spoke with her.¹⁵ Then she said to them, Thus says YHWH Elohim of Yisrael, Tell the man who sent you to Me, ¹⁶ Thus says YHWH: Behold, I will bring calamity on this place and on its inhabitants - all the words of the Scroll which the king of Yahudah has read - ¹⁷ because they have forsaken Me and burned incense to other gods, that they might provoke Me to anger with all the works of their hands. Therefore My wrath shall be aroused against this place and shall not be quenched.¹⁸ But as for the king of Yahudah, who sent you to inquire of YHWH, in this manner you shall speak to him, Thus says YHWH Elohim of Yisrael: Concerning the words which you have heard - ¹⁹ **because your heart was tender, and you humbled yourself before YHWH when you heard what I spoke against this place and against its inhabitants, that they would become a desolation and a curse, and you tore your clothes and wept before Me, I also have heard you, says YHWH. ²⁰ Surely, therefore, I will gather you to your fathers, and you shall be gathered to your grave in peace; and your eyes shall not see all the calamity which I will bring on this place.** So they brought back word to the king. ^{23:1} Now the king sent them to gather all the elders of Yahudah and Yahrushalaim to him.² The king went up to the house of YHWH with all the men of Yahudah, and with him all the inhabitants of Yahrushalaim - the priests and the prophets and all the people, both small and great. **And he read in their hearing all the words of the Scroll of the Covenant which had been found in the house of YHWH. ³ Then the king stood by a pillar and made a covenant before YHWH, to follow YHWH and to keep His commandments and His testimonies and His statutes, with all his heart and all his soul, to perform the words of this covenant that were** written in this Scroll. And all the people took a stand for the covenant. ⁴ And the king commanded Hilkiyah the high priest, the priests of the second order, and the doorkeepers, to bring out of the House of YHWH all the articles that were made for Baal, for Asherah, and for all the host of heaven; and he burned them outside Yahrushalaim in the fields of Kidron, and carried their ashes to Bethel. ⁵ Then he removed the idolatrous priests whom the kings of Yahudah had ordained to burn incense on the high places in the cities of Yahudah and in the places all around Yahrushalaim, and those who burned incense to Baal, to the sun, to the moon, to the constellations, and to all the host of heaven.⁶ And he brought out the wooden image from the House of YHWH, to the Brook Kidron outside Yahrushalaim, burned it at the Brook Kidron and ground it to ashes, and threw its ashes on the graves of the common people. ⁷ Then he tore down the Ritual booths of the perverted persons that were in the House of YHWH, where the women wove hangings for the wooden image.⁸ And he brought all the priests from the cities of Yahudah, and defiled the high places where the priests had burned incense, from Geba to Beersheba; also he broke down the high places at the gates which were at the entrance of the Gate of Yahshua the governor of the city, which were to the left of the city gate.⁹ Nevertheless the priests of the high places did not come up to the altar of YHWH in Yahrushalaim, but they ate

unleavened bread among their brethren. ¹⁰ And he defiled Topheth, which is in the Valley of the Son of Hinnom, that no man might make his son or his daughter pass through the fire to Molech.¹¹ Then he removed the horses that the kings of Yahudah had dedicated to the sun, at the entrance to the House of YHWH, by the chamber of Nathan-Melech, the officer who was in the court; and he burned the chariots of the sun with fire. ¹² The altars that were on the roof, the upper chamber of Ahaz, which the kings of Yahudah had made, and the altars which Manasseh had made in the two courts of the house of YHWH, the king broke down and pulverized there, and threw their dust into the Brook Kidron.¹³ Then the king defiled the high places that were east of Yahrushalaim, which were on the south of the Mount of Corruption, which Solomon king of Yisrael had built for Ashtoreth the abomination of the Sidonians, for Chemosh the abomination of the Moabites, and for Milcom the abomination of the people of Ammon.¹⁴ And he broke in pieces the sacred pillars and cut down the wooden images, and filled their places with the bones of men. ¹⁵ Moreover the altar that was at Bethel, and the high place which Yeroboam the son of Nebat, who made Yisrael sin, had made, both that altar and the high place he broke down; and he burned the high place and crushed it to powder, and burned the wooden image. ¹⁶ As Yoshiyahu turned, he saw the tombs that were there on the mountain. And he sent and took the bones out of the tombs and burned them on the altar, and defiled it according to the word of YHWH which the man of Elohim proclaimed, who proclaimed these words.¹⁷ Then he said, What gravestone is this that I see? So the men of the city told him, It is the tomb of the man of Elohim who came from Yahudah and proclaimed these things which you have done against the altar of Bethel. (See 1 Kings 13). ¹⁸ And he said, Let him alone; let no one move his bones. So they let his bones alone, with the bones of the prophet who came from Samaria. ¹⁹ Now Yoshiyahu also took away all the shrines of the high places that were in the cities of Samaria, which the kings of Yisrael had made to provoke YHWH to anger; and he did to them according to all the deeds he had done in Bethel.²⁰ **He executed all the priests of the high places who were there, on the altars, and burned men's bones on them; and he returned to Yahrushalaim. ²¹ Then the king commanded all the people, saying, Keep the Passover to YHWH your Elohim, as it is written in this Scroll of the Covenant.** ²² Such a Passover surely had never been held since the days of the judges who judged Yisrael, nor in all the days of the kings of Yisrael and the kings of Yahudah.²³ But in the eighteenth year of King Yoshiyahu this Passover was held before YHWH in Yahrushalaim. ²⁴ **Moreover Yoshiyahu put away those who consulted mediums and spiritists, the household gods and idols, all the abominations that were seen in the land of Yahudah and in**

Yahrushalaim, that he might perform the words of the Torah which were written in the Scroll that Hilkiyah the priest found in the House of YHWH.[25] *Now before him there was no king like him, who turned to YHWH with all his heart, with all his soul, and with all his might, **according to all the Torah of Mosheh**; nor after him did any arise like him."* 2 Kings 22:1-23:25.

The acts of King Yoshiyahu are also described in 2 Chronicles 34 through 35. From both of these accounts we see that when he was young, Yoshiyahu did what was right, he walked a straight path and *"did not turn aside, right or left."* Quite simply, he cleaned house. This account is not unlike what we observe today in the Land of Yisrael. Back then, the Temple was in ruins it was littered with idols and pagan worship.

Today, the Temple is completely destroyed and although Yahrushalaim was retaken in 1967 the Modern State of Israel has not rebuilt the House of YHWH nor have they cleansed the land. They have decided that world opinion and acceptance is more important than rebuilding and obeying YHWH. This is why they have not experienced true Scriptural restoration. These may sound like harsh words to a people and a country that have seen continuous conflict and great tragedy, but much of their problems are a direct result of their failure to obey the commandments. Now, I love the people and the land of Israel and it grieves me to see the continuous conflict and suffering that they are experiencing. I very much want to see peace in the land, but only the peace which YHWH has promised, not the contrived false promises of peace from men and their ill fated treaties and accords.

The Scriptures are resoundingly clear that Yisrael was given the land and would prosper so long as the Torah was obeyed. If they chose not to obey the Torah then they were not living according to the covenant and they would not live in the land - it is that simple. This is why we see them losing land little by little and this trend will continue until something changes. I doubt that King Yoshiyahu would have stood idle while paganism was rampant throughout the land, especially if he was in charge of the best trained, most sophisticated, and most powerful military force in the region.

The reason why he would not stand idle was because he found the Torah Scroll. He read the Words in the Torah and they struck him to his very core. The Words rang true and he realized that Yisrael had forgotten the covenant with Elohim. They had been disobedient. He read the Words and proclaimed them to the people. He confessed his sins and the sins of his fathers. He confirmed the covenant between himself and Elohim and set his heart to obey. This is called repentance although his restoration did not simply involve words. He took decisive action to obey. It was messy and it was bloody - it involved a lot of destruction, but oftentimes that is necessary for restoration because restoration involves tearing down and rebuilding.

The Modern State of Israel has been equipped with everything they need to obey the Torah. This would surely have worldwide repercussions, but they could withstand any wrath which may be brought on by their neighboring enemies - this has already been demonstrated in the past. Regardless, instead of doing things according to the Torah of YHWH, their leaders have chosen their own path

which is clearly not working.

Only when the Assembly of Yisrael unites under the banner of YHWH and truly repents will we see the type of restoration experienced by Yoshiyahu. Today we see the two religions that worship the Elohim of Yisrael, Christianity and Judaism, both having lost the Torah to a great extent. Christians do not even call it the Torah, they lump it in with other writings and refer to them all as the "Old Testament."

In Christianity, there is an overriding belief that those Scriptures are no longer directly applicable to "the Church." The Torah is treated more like a history book than it is Scriptures with power and relevance to modern day Believers. Christians feel that while there may be spiritual application to these writings, there is no real direct application to those Scriptures which were given to Yisrael. While it may contain some nice stories and lessons, selected passages are generally relegated to Sunday school. Therefore Christianity, which claims to serve the same Elohim as Yoshiyahu, has lost the Torah, just as it was lost prior to the days of Yoshiyahu, and Christianity now desperately needs restoration.

Judaism still reveres the Torah, but they do not necessarily obey the Torah. Adherents of Judaism have developed their Mishnah, which is a set of directives developed by the Rabbis, as well as the Talmud, which are voluminous teachings which have been compiled over the centuries. The weight which is placed upon the particular writings is determined by which sect or denomination that an individual Jewish person subscribes. Some zealously obey everything, while others pick and choose what to obey. Rabbinic authority has been created which provides the Rabbis with powers to interpret and reinterpret the Torah leading to inconsistencies and division.

A simple example of the inconsistency which exists in Judaism is the contradiction between the kippot and the tzitzit. The kippah, or yarmulke, is a trademark of Judaism and the Pope. Nowhere in the Torah will you find a commandment concerning the kippot, yet most of Judaism zealously adheres to this tradition.

To the contrary, tzitzit, which are tassels with a blue thread are commanded to be worn on two separate occasions in the Torah. (Bemidbar 15:38-39, Devarim 22:12). Now, as of the writing of this book, I think it is safe to say that most of Judaism does not obey the commandments

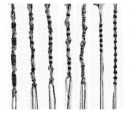

concerning the tzitzit and if they do, the majority do not place a blue thread in the tzitzit. There are technical and traditional reasons why they do not include the blue thread but the point is significant: most obey a tradition and not a commandment. Thus Judaism, as much as it would like to claim to be the gatekeeper to the Torah and the exclusive faith for all who desire to obey the Torah, has its own set of problems and is in serious need of restoration. We have not even broached the subjects of kabbalism and mysticism which have infiltrated Judaism along with other pagan rooted customs and traditions.

If both of these religions claim to be serving the Elohim of Yoshiyahu, and since his actions were pleasing to Elohim, then it seems logical that they both could look to him as an example for their restoration. The King first discovered the Torah, he read the Torah, and he responded to the Torah. He tore his clothing and wept as an act of remorse and humility. He realized that Yisrael had forgotten Elohim and they needed to be restored to the truth.

Prior to Yoshiyahu's repentance, the people in the Kingdom were obviously having "church" because the Temple was operating, it was just polluted with sun god, moon god, fertility goddess and other pagan devices and practices. This too is not unlike the religions of Christianity and Judaism. They are both functioning and probably few see any real problems, but both have inherited false customs and they too need to identify and get rid of the paganism and lies which have infiltrated their belief systems. They need to learn from Yoshiyahu - he identified the problems because he read the Truth in the Torah.

Only by the Torah can we measure what is acceptable worship and what is unacceptable. Only by the Torah can we measure what is acceptable conduct and what is unacceptable. By hearing the Truth Yoshiyahu's eyes were opened to the filth that surrounded him and he then began to obey. He repaired and cleansed the House of YHWH and restored Davidic worship. He began to keep the Appointed Times of YHWH and he cleansed the land of all false gods and pagan worship. He purified the Land by tearing down and destroying the statues and altars of false gods as well as the sun pillars (obelisks) which were spread throughout the land.

His actions are important because they provide some examples of how a person and a nation is to respond

when they discover that they have strayed from the ways of Elohim and need restoration. Sadly, the Modern State of Israel has not seen this type of restoration and is violating the commandments found in the covenant. They do not follow the Torah, except maybe observing the Sabbath - and even that observance is heavily influenced by Rabbinic ordinances.  Many outside the Orthodox community treat the Appointed Times as mere secular holidays and instead of going to Yahrushalaim in obedience to the Torah they leave Yahrushalaim and go on vacation elsewhere.

At the same time, the government allows paganism to thrive in the land. Minarets, which are phallic symbols attached to Mosques, litter <u>much of the land</u>. These are not unlike the Christian steeples which are generally only found within the vicinity of Yahrushalaim.

We can see a pattern for restoration from the examples of the two kings of Yahudah. They both discovered the Torah and realized that they were not obeying the Torah. Their response was to repent and covenant with YHWH to obey Him. They then proceeded to obey the Torah and restore true worship in the Land. They began to celebrate the Appointed Times of YHWH and they rid their lives and their land of idolatry and the worship of false gods. Now the average reader may think: That is all well and good for them, but what does this all have to do with me? The answer is: everything!

You see, most of us have this archaic notion that

idolatry is something that happened in the ancient world and no longer exists in our modern, educated, sophisticated Judeo-Christian society. A deeper look reveals that the modern world is in an even worse state than we read about in the examples found in the Scriptures. Those who desire to be part of the Congregation of Yisrael desperately need to participate in the restoration which is occurring right now.

Another wonderful blueprint for this restoration can be seen through the accounts of Nehemiah and Ezra. Nehemiah was a Hebrew official who was part of the Babylonian exile. His name is properly pronounced Nehemyah (נחמיה) and means "comforted by Yah." Ezra was a priest who was also exiled from the land. The name Ezra (עזרה) means "help" and may be a shortened form of Azariyah (עזריה) which means "Yah has helped." These two men were used by YHWH after both the House of Yisrael and the House of Yahudah had been exiled from the land. Both men heard the call to return and rebuild what had been destroyed by Nebuchadnezzar.

The walls of Yahrushalaim had been torn down and the gates were burned. The children of Yisrael had been scattered and the Temple service had ceased. When Nehemyah heard about the condition of Yahrushalaim and his people in about 447 B.C.E. he wept, fasted, and prayed. Nehemyah desired to help restore his people back to their land and to restore the worship of their Elohim.

The Scriptures record the following prayer uttered by him: "⁵ I pray, YHWH Elohim of heaven, O great and awesome Elohim, **You who keep Your covenant and mercy with those who love You and observe Your commandments,** ⁶ please let Your ear be attentive and Your eyes open, that You *may hear the prayer of Your servant which I pray before You now, day and night, for the children of Yisrael Your servants, and confess the sins of the children of Yisrael which we have sinned against You. Both my father's house and I have sinned.*[7] **We have acted very corruptly against You, and have not kept the commandments, the statutes, nor the ordinances which You commanded Your servant Mosheh.** [8] *Remember, I pray, the word that You commanded Your servant Mosheh, saying,* **If you are unfaithful, I will scatter you among the nations;** [9] **but if you return to Me, and keep My commandments and do them, though some of you were cast out to the farthest part of the heavens, yet I will gather them from there, and bring them to the place which I have chosen as a dwelling for My Name.** [10] *Now these are Your servants and Your people, whom You have redeemed by Your great power, and by Your strong hand.*[11] *O YHWH, I pray, please let Your ear be attentive to the prayer of Your servant, and to the prayer of Your servants who desire to fear Your Name; and let Your servant prosper this day, I pray, and grant him mercy in the sight of this man. For I was the king's cupbearer."* Nehemyah 1:5-11.

The prayer of Nehemyah is significant because it provides the outline of a prayer that gets heard by the Creator. First of all Nehemyah identifies by Name the One to Whom he is praying - YHWH. Next, he speaks of the covenant which was made between the Creator and Yisrael and he specifically addresses YHWH as: "*You Who keep Your covenant and mercy with* **those who love You and observe Your commandments.**" This sounds very inclusive and contrary to the predominate position in Judaism that the Torah is only for the Jews.

Nehemyah then confesses not only his sins, but the sins of his fathers. He acknowledges that those sins had consequences pursuant to the covenant, but he also remembered the promises that were contained within the covenant. The promises were contingent upon returning to the Creator by keeping and obeying His commands. Nehemyah asks that the prayer of **those who desire to fear the Name** of the Creator be heard. This prayer shows the heart of someone who confessed his sins, repented from his transgressions and desired to be restored to the Creator. This is a Hebrew praying, but it sounds an awful lot like a Christian prayer.

Repentance is heavily emphasized in Christianity for salvation, but it is not a Christian concept and to realize this we need only to look to the prophets. "*[19] Therefore this is what YHWH says: 'If you repent, I will restore you that you may serve me; if you utter worthy, not worthless, words, you will be my spokesman. Let this people turn to you, but you must not turn to them. [20] I will make you a wall to this people, a fortified wall of bronze; they will fight against you but will not overcome you, for I am with you to rescue and save you,' declares YHWH. [21] 'I will save you from the hands of the wicked and redeem you from the grasp of the cruel.'*" Yirmeyahu 15:19-21.

Yehezqel also speaks of repentance: "*[6] Therefore say to the House of Yisrael, Thus says YHWH Elohim: **Repent, turn away from your idols, and turn your faces away from all your abominations.** [7] For anyone of the House of Yisrael, or of the strangers** who dwell in Yisrael, who separates himself from Me and sets up his idols in his heart and puts before him what causes him to stumble into iniquity, then comes to a prophet to inquire of him concerning Me, I YHWH will answer him by Myself. [8] I will set My face against that man and make him a sign and a proverb, and I will cut him off from the midst of My people. Then you shall know that I am YHWH.'*" Yehezqel 14:6-8.

Notice that He is speaking to the House of Yisrael and the strangers who dwell with them. If you haven't already figured it out, you will begin to see that Elohim's promises are available to anyone who wants to dwell with Him. In this case, He is speaking to the House of Yisrael and those who dwell with them because these are the ones who were subject to the covenant. Obviously, Elohim does not prophesy punishment to someone for breaking His covenant when they are not a part of the covenant - like the Christian religion which did not even exist at that time.

Many Christians get confused when they read the prophets because they are not sure how they apply to them - if at all. The answer is simple: if you are born into the covenant or take hold of a covenant, it applies to you. Yehezqel goes on to give some advise regarding repentance to the House of Yisrael by stating: "*30 Therefore I will judge you, O House of Yisrael, every one according to his ways, says YHWH Elohim. Repent, and turn from all your transgressions, so that iniquity will not be your ruin.*31 *Cast away from you all the transgressions which you have committed, and get yourselves a new heart and a new spirit. For why should you die, O House of Yisrael?* 32 *For I have no pleasure in the death of one who dies, says YHWH Elohim. Therefore turn and live!*" Yehezqel 18:30-32.

Restoration is always preceded by repentance and as we already discovered, they mean the same thing in Hebrew. This message of repentance was repeated by Kepha on the Day of Pentecost, which is an Appointed Time of YHWH better known as the Feast of Shavuot: "*19 Repent therefore and be converted, that your sins may be blotted out, so that times of refreshing may come from the presence of*

YHWH, [20] and that He may send Messiah Yahushua, who was preached to you before, [21] whom heaven must receive **until the times of restoration of all things**, which Elohim has spoken by the mouth of all His holy prophets since the world began." Acts 3:19-21.

Most Christians have been taught that the "Church" began on Pentecost (Shavuot). What they fail to realize is that this was an Appointed Time established by YHWH and it is the same Appointed Time hundreds of years earlier when YHWH gave the Torah to Yisrael at Mt. Sinai. I hope that the pattern is abundantly clear. The Torah was written on tablets of stone on Shavuot at Sinai and the Torah was written on the hearts and minds of those obedient Yisraelites who were in Yahrushalaim celebrating the Feast of Shavuot after the death and resurrection of Messiah.[137]

Now getting back to Nehemyah we will see the significance of another Appointed Time - Sukkot. Nehemyah recognized the need for change, he confessed his transgression and resolved himself to turn back to Elohim, to guard His commandments and to do them. Nehemyah's prayer was heard and he received favor from his sovereign and was permitted to return to Yahrushalaim to rebuild. This restoration started with the House of Yahudah and consisted of a physical restoration of Yahrushalaim. Nehemyah and the remnant rebuilt the walls of the city. They then set up the doors and Nehemyah appointed gatekeepers. The walls and gates are for a defense - the remnant needed to defend themselves. Things were then set in order, singers and priests were appointed and proper worship was restored.

Things were not easy, the remnant was surrounded

by enemies. While they worked they were threatened, but they called upon their Elohim. They worked together and they worked hard. Some built while others defended. Even the builders were involved in the defense, they bore a load with one hand and a weapon in the other. False prophets were sent and gave false prophecies intended to spread fear because they were hirelings sent by the enemy. (Nehemyah 6:12-13). Regardless, the people stayed focused on their goal and true to their task. They did not listen to the lies of the enemy nor did they get discouraged. They carried on and completed the work.

This sounds a lot like the Modern State of Israel which currently consists of a remnant of those who were scattered abroad. They have worked hard for decades to rebuild their cities and their newly formed nation. Just as Nehemyah and Ezra received permission from Babylonian authorities to return and rebuild, so too, the Modern State of Israel received permission from the United Nations to return and rebuild. The big difference between the restoration under Nehemyah and Ezra was that their primary goal was to rebuild "The House of YHWH" and rebuild Yahrushalaim so that they could worship.

The Modern State of Israel is largely a secular state - polls have shown that the vast majority of the population is not "religious." The motivation of most of their founders was not so much to rebuild so that they could worship. If that were the case they would have rebuilt the Temple decades ago. To the contrary, the driving force was Zionism, a secular movement designed to establish a land that Jews could call their own, free from the persecution and slaughter that they had experienced for centuries. That is not to say that none of the nation's

founders were motivated by their religious convictions. I am simply stating that the Torah was not necessarily at the foundation of Zionism

In some instances, Zionism has become a religion of sorts. According to Yisrael Harel, the most respected of the settler movement's political commentators: "Zionism, including the religious brand, never relied on miracles. It created them . . . That is how we produced the solutions to our greatest difficulties. But that was when we still had faith in our capabilities and the justice of our cause."[138]

I am not saying that settling the land is a bad motivation, in fact, I agree that the Promised Land should be settled - but it should be settled only by those who follow and obey the instructions of YHWH. Every example of true Scriptural restoration has been motivated by a desire to return to Elohim and obey His commands. This was not the sole motivation for the Modern State of Israel so currently, while their return was miraculous and no doubt aided or permitted by YHWH, it is not a complete restoration. The Modern State of Israel is not obeying the Torah and until the nation turns to Elohim wholeheartedly, they will not see restoration and the peace promised within the Scriptures. Their continuing suffering will not bring about the blessings of Elohim, only their obedience will.

One of the most significant portions of the Book of Nehemyah which relates with this generation is found in Chapter 8. "*And when the seventh month came, the children of Yisrael were in their cities. And **all the people gathered together as one man** in the open square that was in front of the Water Gate; and they told Ezra the scribe to bring the Scroll of the Torah, which YHWH had commanded Yisrael.² So Ezra the*

priest brought the Torah before the assembly of men and women and all who could hear with understanding on the first day of the seventh month.[3] **Then he read from it in the open square that was in front of the Water Gate from morning until midday, before the men and women and those who could understand; and the ears of all the people were attentive to the Torah Scroll.** [4] *So Ezra the scribe stood on a platform of wood which they had made for the purpose; and beside him, at his right hand, stood Mattithiah, Shema, Anaiah, Uriyah, Hilkiyah, and Maaseiyah; and at his left hand Pedaiyah, Mishael, Malchiyah, Hashum, Hashbadana, Zecharyah, and Meshullam.*[5] *And Ezra opened the book in the sight of all the people, for he was standing above all the people;* **and when he opened it, all the people stood up.**[6] *And Ezra blessed YHWH, the great Elohim. Then all the people answered, Amen, Amen! while lifting up their hands. And they bowed their heads and worshiped YHWH with their faces to the ground.* [7] *Also Yahshua, Bani, Sherebiyah, Yamin, Akkub, Shabbethai, Hodiyah, Maaseiyah, Kelita, Azariyah, Yozabad, Hanan, Pelaiyah, and the Levites, helped the people to understand the Torah; and the people stood in their place.*[8] *So they read distinctly from the scroll, in the Torah of Elohim; and they gave the sense, and helped them to understand the reading."*
Nehemyah 8:1-9.

There is much that we can glean from this passage. To begin with, the passage mentions the day that the people assembled, the first day of the seventh month. This was an Appointed Time of YHWH known as The Day of Trumpets or Teruah (תרועה) in Hebrew. (Vayiqra 23:24). This was a High Sabbath, a set apart gathering. The priests not only read the Word, but they taught the people and helped them to understand the Word. The Word would have been read in Hebrew and many people did not

understand the language.

The Hebrew word meturgam (מתרגם) means translator and there were those who would translate the Torah as it was read. This was common after the exile when people spoke different languages from the countries to which they had been dispersed. I believe that this is a critical point for Believers in this generation. Many people read the Word, but they do not necessarily understand what the Word is saying because of the language barrier as well as inherited customs, traditions, and doctrines which conflict with the Torah and cloud their understanding. They need a correct translation and instruction to properly understand the Word.

Now let us continue with this important lesson from Nehemyah: "⁹ And Nehemyah, who was the governor, Ezra the priest and scribe, and the Levites who taught the people said to all the people, This day is set apart to YHWH your Elohim; do not mourn nor weep. For **all the people wept, when they heard the words of the Torah.** ¹⁰ Then he said to them, Go your way, eat the fat, drink the sweet, and send portions to those for whom nothing is prepared; for this day is set apart to our Master. Do not sorrow, for the joy of YHWH is your strength. ¹¹ So the Levites quieted all the people, saying, Be still, for the day is set apart; do not be grieved. ¹² And all the people went their way to eat and drink, to send portions and rejoice greatly, because they understood the words that were declared to them." Nehemyah 8:9-12.

Ask yourself: When is the last time that you wept when you heard the Word read aloud? That should give us all food for thought and prayer. The fact that the people wept means that it had significance to them. It impacted their lives. The Levites gave instruction on how to respond

to the Word. They taught them about the Appointed Time and they instructed the people to celebrate the set apart day.[139]

I am sure that everybody was in awe at what just happened so the next day all the elders, priests, and Levites gathered to Ezra to study the Torah. *"14 And they found written in the Torah, which YHWH had commanded by Mosheh, that the children of Yisrael should dwell in booths during the feast of the seventh month, 15 and that they should announce and proclaim in all their cities and in Yahrushalaim, saying, Go out to the mountain, and bring olive branches, branches of oil trees, myrtle branches, palm branches, and branches of leafy trees, to make booths, as it is written. 16 Then the people went out and brought them and made themselves booths, each one on the roof of his house, or in their courtyards or the courts of the house of Elohim, and in the open square of the Water Gate and in the open square of the Gate of Ephraim. 17 So the whole assembly of those who had returned from the captivity made booths and sat under the booths; for since the days of Yahshua the son of Nun until that day the children of Yisrael had not done so. And there was very great gladness.18 **Also day by day, from the first day until the last day, he read from the Scroll of the Torah of Elohim.** And they kept the feast seven days; and on the eighth day there was a sacred assembly, according to the prescribed manner."* Nehemyah 8:14-18.

This was a powerful thing that happened. All of the people learned about another Appointed Time known as the Feast of Sukkot (סכות) or the Feast of Booths. This is a very special time when people are instructed to go up to Yahrushalaim and dwell in succas also known as booths or mangers. These temporary structures were meant to remind the children of Yisrael of when they sojourned in

the wilderness. (Vayiqra 23:33).[140]

How interesting it is to read that this Feast had not been observed since the days of Yahshua. It is generally understood that Yahshua died at the age of 110 around 1380 B.C.E. Therefore, over 1,000 years had elapsed since the children of Yisrael had kept the Feast. Also, there is no mention that they observed the Day of Atonement better known as Yom Kippur (יום כפר) which falls on the tenth day of the seventh month. (Vayiqra 23:27).

The Feasts which occur in the seventh month are extremely significant, especially in the days to come. Sukkot, which is also called "The Feast of Tabernacles," has prophetic significance for the end times and just as those of the remnant started celebrating this Feast once they read about it, so too is the remnant today. Many are beginning to learn about the Appointed Times and they are celebrating them, sometimes without knowing anything about them - they are simply acting out of obedience. These special times do not belong to any particular religion or ethnic group, they are YHWH's (Vayiqra 23:2) and they are for all those who worship and desire to obey the Elohim of Yisrael.[141]

What we read about in this passage involving Nehemyah and Ezra was likely at the end of a Sabbath Year in year 1 because it appears that the entire Torah was read to the Assembly during the Feast. This was commanded to be done every seven years. "[10] *At the end of every seven years, at the appointed time in the year of release, at the Feast of Tabernacles,* [11] *when all Yisrael comes to appear before YHWH your Elohim in the place which He chooses, you shall read this Torah before all Yisrael in their hearing.* [12] **Gather the people together, men and women and little ones, and** *the stranger who is within your gates, that they may hear and that they may learn to fear YHWH your Elohim and carefully observe all the words of this Torah,*[13] *and that their children, who have not known it, may hear and learn to fear YHWH your Elohim as long as you live in the land which you cross the Yarden to possess.*" Devarim 31:10-13.

Notice that it was not just the descendants of Yisrael that were to hear, learn, fear, and obey, but also the stranger who is within their gates, which means a person not of natural descent that chooses to dwell with Yisrael. We will see this time and time again that YHWH intended all people to know Him and obey His Torah, not just native Yisraelites.

The pattern that we see with Nehemyah and Ezra is critical. They studied and read the Torah and they wept because they understood that they had lost something. Through reading the Scriptures they saw that they had forgotten the Appointed Times and commandments of their Elohim. Their immediate response was to obey. They didn't necessarily realize how or why they were doing certain things, they simply obeyed.

According to the Book of Ezra, when they fell into transgression by taking foreign wives their response was to acknowledge their trespass. They prayed, confessed, and again, they wept. They then made a covenant with Elohim to put away their foreign wives - which they did. (Ezra 10:1-4). They were not joking around. These words resonate from that passage: "*Let it be done according to the Torah. Arise, for the matter is upon you . . . Be strong and act.*" Ezra 10:3-4.

Be strong and act! This is the message to the remnant during this present age. Just as Nehemyah and

Ezra heard the call to return, restore, and rebuild, so too are many throughout the world hearing a call to return, restore, and rebuild. Ask yourself: When is the last time that you stood in an assembly and heard the Torah read aloud for hours with all the people attentive to the Word? This would be a very good start for someone who wants to be restored. If you do not understand, then you need to be taught how it applies to your life. This is one of the purposes of this book, but it is no substitute for the actual Word.

Therefore, I would suggest that you get a hold of the Torah, open to the first page in Beresheet, and start reading through to the end of Devarim. Read it with the understanding that it is your heritage and it applies to you. Through this process you will begin to lay the foundation for restoration in your life. This is the same Word that Ezra, Hizqiyahu, and Yoshiyahu read, it is the same Word that the Messiah and His disciples read. The "Old Testament" it turns out is not so "old" after all. It contains knowledge and power necessary for the people of Elohim to be restored. Just as the remnant of Yisrael had so many times forgotten the Torah and then rediscovered the Torah, so it is with the remnant of this present day.

15

Truth versus Tradition

It is stated in the prophecies that knowledge will increase in the latter days. *"But thou, O Daniel, shut up the words, and seal the book, even to the time of the end: many shall run to and fro, and knowledge shall be increased."* Daniel 12:4 KJV.

We are currently experiencing a time when knowledge is increasing at a breathtaking pace. We are also witnessing a restoration of things that have been lost for centuries. According to the prophecies, the altar and sacrifices will someday be restored. The Temple Mount Institute in Yahrushalaim has prepared all of the clothing, implements, and instruments to conduct the sacrificial service. The Ark of the Covenant has allegedly been found along with the Tabernacle and there are now unblemished red heifers in existence. All of the pieces of the puzzle seem to be falling into place as all eyes focus on Al-Haram al-Qudsi al-Sharif, the alleged location of the Temple Mount in Yahrushalaim.[142]

Despite the fact that the stage is being set for the culmination of many prophetic events, some do not recognize their significance because the Christian religion has propagated an anti-Semitic Replacement Theology for centuries. The doctrine comes in many shapes and sizes and under different names, but generally it teaches that Yisrael had their chance and blew it - as a result, now the "Church" has taken her place. This teaching is not supported by any Scriptures and regardless of what any man teaches, the Christian "Church" has not replaced Yisrael.

The Creator of the Universe is still in control and His plan has remained unchanged from the beginning of time. The Messiah will be returning for a Bride without spot or wrinkle and if the Christian "Church" were that Bride, then the Messiah would not be returning for an awfully long time due to her current condition which, quite frankly, is a mess.

What many fail to realize is that the Creator has always had a remnant of those who believed and obeyed Him. This remnant does not necessarily belong to the same denomination, sect, or religion. Most of the remnant probably do not even know each other and at any given time an individual may only see part of the grand plan.

It is this remnant which is being prepared for the coming Messiah, not a particular religious group. It does not matter what congregation you belong to. What matters is the condition of your heart. Today, we see people who think that if they belong to a certain assembly or speak, act, and dress a certain way then they will somehow get their ticket to paradise. They might be in for a big surprise.

In fact, most of humanity is living in a dream world which is not based upon the truth and reality contained within the Scriptures. This is why the voice is crying from heaven: *"Come out of her, my people, lest you*

share in her transgressions, and lest you receive of her plagues." (Revelation 18:4). The remnant needs to wake up from this dream state, separate from Babylon and enter into the reality which Elohim has prepared for them.

I like to use the movie called "The Matrix" as an example of what is happening in the world today. If you can get past the violence it really has quite a fascinating plot. The story basically involves a young man who is living a fairly ordinary life until he is contacted by someone who offers to show him the truth. The man is given the option of remaining ignorant and going back to his regular existence or taking the plunge and learning the truth of his existence.

He decides that he wants to find out the truth and ends up discovering that he has been living his life inside The Matrix which is basically an enormous computer program. His body has been living in a comatose state along with millions of other human beings who are all plugged into The Matrix, living their lives in an alternate, imaginary reality. You see the machines had taken over the world and were breeding human beings for energy. The best way to control them was to keep them preoccupied through the alternate, imaginary reality until it was time to process them.

In many ways this is exactly what is happening today to most of the population of the world. There are systems in place which are not real, they are made up simply to distract people from the truth. Political, religious, scientific, educational, and entertainment systems have been developed which have clouded and distorted reality in such a way that most people believe that it is normal to

go to work Monday through Friday, take Saturday off and clean, go shopping or have a barbeque, go to Church on Sunday morning, watch sports in the afternoon, and start the process all over again on Monday.

The American dream consists of obtaining an education, finding a job, getting married, buying a house, having children, raising a family, going on vacations, and saving for retirement so hopefully you can enjoy a few "golden years" before you get some disease and die. I am obviously being facetious and simplistic, but essentially this is the line that many of us have been fed all of our lives and this is what we come to accept as normal.

Many westerners now live in a very materialistic culture which has become a powerful distraction to most people - including myself. There are so many neat products and gadgets to buy, use, and wear that you could spend your entire life on a spending spree and never get it all. Some people strive their entire lives trying to obtain things that they thought would make them happy, only to find out that they were wrong.

Others never obtain the things they strive for and think that they are a failure. We all fall prey to some extent or another - after all we are human and subject to the temptations that surround us. The key is to remember that there will come a day when this world will be judged - not by water but by fire. (Malachi 4:1-6). On that day, everything will burn like wood, hay, and stubble, except for those eternal riches which we have laid up. (1 Corinthians 3:12-15).

The problem is that the lifestyle which we have come to accept as normal is not what our Creator considers

normal and the American dream is not necessarily pleasing to Him. We do not always feel the need to check in with Him on these issues because it is so deeply ingrained within us that we would never question whether these desires are acceptable. Instead of selling all to follow Him we are often absorbed in building our nestegg for retirement.

For those of us who were raised in the "Church," we were taught a certain way of doing things and a certain way of speaking which oftentimes has no basis in Scripture. I like to call it the cattle mentality. Most of us are being herded through life like cattle in a slaughterhouse although if you are holding this book in your hand and reading these pages you have a choice.

You can either stick with the herd and continue on the way that you have lived until it is your time to "retire," or you can jump the fence and find out what is really going on. We have all heard the saying that the grass always looks greener on the other side of the fence; in this case it is true. You may like your life just the way it is, but if you believe that you have an eternal soul, then you owe it to your future to find out the truth of your existence.

Let's start with a simple reality check. One of the first things that we learn as children is how to tell time and the days of the week. It would surprise many people to know that according to Elohim's reckoning of time, the day starts after sunset, not at twelve o'clock midnight. The first day of the week is Sunday, not Monday and we already discussed the fact that the names for the days of the weeks and months are all named after pagan gods or have pagan influences. Our entire calendar system is based upon a solar system which was influenced by sun god worship.

In sharp contrast, the Creator has His own calendar which is set forth in the Scriptures and is based upon the lunar cycle. So at any given time you may think that you know what day, week, month, or year it is, but you will be wrong if you are operating under the World's calendar. You also will not know when to celebrate the Appointed Times which, as we have seen, are an integral part of the restoration process. Ask yourself if you know what time it is on the Creator's calendar. If you do not - this would be a great place to start in your own personal restoration.[143]

Of course, this is just the tip of the iceberg and ultimately you begin to see a pattern develop. It appears that the adversary, also known as hashatan,[144] has actually been very busy throughout the millennia trying to take as many of Elohim's Creation down with him as possible. He has not just been attending black sabbath services in remote areas, conducted by dark robed worshippers.

Rather, he has been plotting and influencing some of the most powerful people and nations throughout human history to accomplish his objective. He wants to be worshipped like Elohim by the entire world, not just some deranged fringe group. As a result of this desire, he has been fashioning a kingdom on this earth which will culminate with him being seated in the Holy of Holies (Daniel 11:31), a place set apart for Elohim alone. At the same time, the Creator of the Universe has allowed him to continue because He is also building His Kingdom, "on earth as it is in Heaven."

There is a cosmic battle going on as these two kingdoms are warring in both the physical and the spiritual realms. We are dealing in multiple dimensions, but sadly, most of the world is not aware of this struggle because they are drifting through their lives in The Matrix. Reality is passing them by while they spend their time at work, surfing the net, or watching television. Instead of living in reality, they are watching "reality" television.

In fact, most people do not realize that the plan of Elohim is actually depicted right above our heads in the stars for all to see. The battle of the universe is written in the sky. Most people have heard of the zodiac and astrology, which is the pagan study of the stars, but you might be surprised to know that the planets and the stars were originally placed there by the Creator of the Universe for a specific purpose.

They not only help us to keep time, but they also tell the story of His creation and salvation that He has offered to the world. This is what King David meant when he said: "*¹ The heavens declare the glory of Elohim; the skies proclaim the work of his hands. ² Day after day they pour forth speech;* **night after night they display knowledge.** *³ There is no speech or language where their voice is not heard. ⁴* **Their voice goes out into all the earth, their words to the ends of the world.**" Tehillim 19:1-4. Every star and planet has a name. "*He counts the number of the stars;* **He calls them all by name.**" Tehillim 147:4 NKJV.

The names are not the pagan names attributed to them by the occult, rather they were named by YHWH. These names were known to mankind before they were scattered across the earth and the languages were confused at Babel (Beresheet 11:9). To this day, most cultures continue to understand that there are meanings and stories represented by the constellations and the movement of the planets. Sadly, as with the calendar, hashatan distorted the things of Elohim to draw people into his kingdom.

Once you get the names and meanings straight, it is amazing what truths the Creator has placed in the sky for all to see. This should not come as any wonder to those who at least read the first page of Beresheet because the Creator said that they would be *"for signs and appointed times, and for days and years."* Beresheet 1:14.

What signs and what Appointed Times, you might ask. Well for one - how about the birth of the Messiah.[145] As was mentioned previously, Yahushua was NOT born of December 25, the ancient date of the winter solstice, which was the date established for the birth of numerous sun gods. It is likely that the "Wise men" were aware of the signs in the heavens and this was what prompted their journey to find the Messiah.

With the advent of computers we are now able to follow the courses of celestial bodies and literally travel back in time. We can look at the sky from any vantage point on Earth at any moment in history on a laptop computer. We now believe that they saw a great sign in the Heavens which occurred on the first day of the seventh month at the end of the fourth millennium, which just so happened to be the Day of Trumpets, Yom Teruah, when shofars are blown, as a rehearsal. On that year, they announced the birth of the Messiah.

The sign in the sky which announced the birth of the Messiah likely consisted of the following: The Star named Tsemach (צמח) which means "The Branch" a title given to the Messiah, aligned in the left hand of the Hebrew constellation named Bethula, which means "The Virgin" (commonly referred to as Virgo). Above her head was the constellation Ariel (commonly called Leo) which represents the Lion of the Tribe of Yahudah. Between His

front paws was the star HaMelech (המלך), which means "The King", which came into conjunction with the planet Jupiter, which in Hebrew is HaTzedek (הצדיק), which means "The Righteous One." (Beresheet 49:10).[145]

Some believe that Yahushua was born on that day while others believe that He was born two weeks later during Succot, also known as the Feast of Mangers, the Feast of Booths or the Feast of Tabernacles when all those who follow YHWH are directed to go to Yahrushalayim and build mangers (succas) and dwell in them for seven days. Since Yahushua was born in Bethlehem and not Jerusalem it does not seem possible for Him to be born during Succot.

Beyond the incorrect date of His birth, most manger scenes are inaccurate when they show the baby Jesus in a manger with the "Three Wise Men" looking over Him. To begin, the  Scriptures do not mention three wise men, but rather three gifts of gold, frankincense, and myrrh. There were probably many more than three, and they most likely would have had a large entourage to carry and protect the gifts and supplies necessary for such a long journey which would have taken time to assemble. The only witnesses to the birth and the infant according to the Scriptures were the shepherds, who would not have been living outside in the middle of winter (Luke 2) which supports the fact that this event occurred during the fall.

There is ample evidence to prove that the "wise men" found Yahushua in the Galilee - not in Bethlehem.

One significant reason is because after Yahushua was circumcised on the eighth day in accordance with the Torah and after the days of purification were completed according to the Torah, Yoseph and Miryam took Him to Yahrushalaim to present Him before YHWH and "to offer a sacrifice according to what is said in the Torah of YHWH, a pair of turtledoves or two young pigeons." Luke 2:34.

What this passage of Scripture is telling us is that they presented a sacrifice which a *poor person* would bring to the Temple. According to the Torah: "*⁶ When the days of her purification are fulfilled, whether for a son or a daughter, she shall bring to the priest a lamb of the first year as a burnt offering, and a young pigeon or a turtledove as a sin offering, to the door of the tabernacle of meeting.⁷ Then he shall offer it before YHWH, and make atonement for her. And she shall be clean from the flow of her blood. This is the Torah for her who has borne a male or a female. ⁸ **And if she is not able to bring a lamb, then she may bring two turtledoves or two young pigeons** - one as a burnt offering and the other as a sin offering. So the priest shall make atonement for her, and she will be clean.*" Vayiqra 12:6-8.

Since they did not bring a lamb, then they must have been poor. This is inconsistent with the myth that the Messiah and His family were loaded up with gold and other gifts on the night He was born. The wise men clearly did not appear the night of the birth, only the shepherds were witnesses to the baby. (Luke 2:12). The wise men were nowhere near the manger (succca) in Bethlehem because the Scriptures say: "**And coming into the house**, they saw the Child with Miryam His mother, and fell down and did reverence Him . . ." Mattityahu 2:11.

The wise men appeared at the "house" - not at the manger when Yahushua was a "child" - not a baby. They actually found Yahushua almost two years after His birth and it was only then that they worshipped Him and gave Him gifts. It was after that point that they were warned in a dream not to return to Herod. (Mattityahu 2:12). Herod had already learned from the wise men exactly what time the star appeared. That is why, when he learned that he had been duped by them he ordered all children two years old and younger to be killed. Yoseph was also warned in a dream to flee to Mitsrayim and he now could afford the trip because he had just been given the resources necessary for the journey. (Mattityahu 2:13).

Just who were these "wise men" seems to be the mystery of the ages although it is possible to piece together their identity through a historical analysis. We know that at the time of the Birth of Yahushua the Roman Empire and the Parthian Empire were experiencing somewhat of a détente. The wise men described in the Scriptures were likely from Persia, members of the Megistanes, very high officials from the Parthian Empire.[146] The historian Josephus strongly implies that the Parthians were Yisraelites formerly deported by the Assyrian Empire.[147]

We know from history that the Prophet Daniel was a gifted and brilliant Yisraelite who was brought captive to Babylon by Nebuchadnezzar. He belonged to the Tribe of Yahudah and was from nobility in the Kingdom of Yahudah. He experienced great favor, esteem and power in the Babylonian Empire and was given the governorship of the province of Babylon, and the headinspectorship of the sacerdotal caste, which consisted of the scholars, educators and scientists, including the astrologers, astronomers, magicians, sorcerers, priests and the like, also known as Magi or wise men.

Later, when the Persians conquered the Babylonians, Daniel continued his administratorship in that Empire as well. He was given the unique responsibility of being the principal administrator of two world empires - not something many people can put on their resume. One of the titles given to Daniel was Rab HarTumaya (חרטמיא רב) - the Chief of the Magicians. When he continued in this role - a Yisraelite, functioning in a traditional hereditary Median priesthood, it resulted in the plot which got him thrown in the lion's den from which he was miraculously delivered.

As a result of his prominence in both the Babylonian and Persian empires, Daniel likely had great riches, but he was a eunuch with no descendants. This was a barbarous custom for those who served in the oriental courts but it begs the question: What happened to the wealth of this man who had no progeny? Being a prophet of the Most High he was given wisdom, knowledge and revelation beyond any man of his time and he was told to "*close up and seal the words of the scroll until the time of the end.*" (Daniel 12:4). Daniel likely knew when the Messiah would come, or at least the signs to look for, since he was a prophet who was given very specific time frames for future events.

As such, it is believed by some that he passed on his riches through the Parthian Magi with instructions to bring his wealth to the Messiah when the sign of His birth was seen in the Heavens. When the Magi saw this sign, they knew that it signaled the birth of the Hebrew Messiah. Since the prophecies indicated where the Messiah would be born (Michayahu 5:2-5) and where He would dwell (Yeshayahu 9:1), they knew where to look for Him.[148]

Their entourage would have been enormous, likely in the thousands. They would have brought a small army with them since they were Parthian dignitaries traveling within the Roman Empire carrying great riches. This is why Herod and all of the inhabitants of Yahrushalaim were "disturbed" and "troubled" by their arrival. (Mattityahu 2:3). This is a scene which most people will not be presented with in Sunday School but it is supported by history and the Scriptures. The information is all readily available but we have not necessarily been looking in the right places for the answers to our questions. Sometimes we do not even know what questions to ask.

Another fable that was passed on to me through Church School was the fact that David was a little boy when he killed Goliath in the Valley of Elah. We read about this incident in I Shemuel 17 and are told that David was the youngest of the eight sons of Yishai. It never says his age but he was obviously older than a little boy. He was charged with the responsibily of tending his father's sheep which was not an easy task. He traveled back and forth from Bethlehem to his brothers with supplies which is not likely something a young child would be doing by himself.

One time when he journeyed to meet his brothers while they were engaging the Philistines, David spoke to King Shaul regarding fighting Goliath. We read in a modern translation that the King's response was as follows: "*You are not able to go out against this Philistine and*

fight him; you are only a boy, and he has been a fighting man from his youth." 1 Shemuel 17:33 NIV. This is where the tradition has developed that David was a little boy, but the tradition does not correspond with the facts which are presented in the Scriptures.

Part of the problem stems from the translation of the Hebrew word for boy - na'ar (נער) which can mean: "youth," but also means: "babe, child, young one or young man." The context in which King Shaul described David was a comparison between David and Goliath and their requisite military training and skills. No doubt, Goliath was a professionally trained soldier while David was a shepherd. In terms of military training - David was a boy compared to Goliath.

David was obviously smaller than Goliath, who was a giant, but from the text we can clearly see that he must have been a very large young man. He had already killed a lion and a bear, with his bare hands and a club - not a slingshot. (1 Shemuel 17:36). Also, he wore King Shaul's armor, mail, helmet, and sword and was about to wear them into battle when he changed his mind, not because they did not fit him, but **because he had not tested them.** (1 Shemuel 17:39). Now King Shaul was described as a large man, taller than any of his people (1 Shemuel 9:2) and his armor would have no doubt been heavy. He would not have recommended that David wear his armor if it did not come close to fitting him. You would not put heavy armor on a little boy, who would not be able to bear its weight, rather they would have found some that fit him.

Since King Shaul's armor obviously fit David, then David must have been a large young man. Further, after David struck Goliath with the stone he proceeded to unsheathe the very heavy sword of the Philistine giant and lop off his head. Again, not something a little boy could do. David later used that sword as his own. (1 Shemuel 21:9).  Therefore, the story of David, the small shepherd boy, defeating Goliath, the Philistine Giant, is a myth perpetuated over time. It is a distortion of reality which most people now accept as truth.

How about the fact that the Scriptures never tell us  that Adam and Hawah ate an apple from the tree of knowledge of good and evil - yet chances are good that most people believe that to be undisputed truth. The apple was likely derived from the fact that Sophia, the goddess of wisdom, was often depicted with an apple. Again, we have a tradition which is not found in the Scriptures but is often portrayed as truth.

These are just a few simple examples of inherited traditions which do not stand the test of truth - yet many of us grew up believing these stories as if they are truth. They affect the way that we read and understand the Scriptures and they often give us a warped understanding of the truth.

These examples, along with the others provided throughout this book, should offer the reader a glimpse of the problem which runs deep through the Christian religion

- a religion that has developed doctrines and traditions which directly oppose or are simply not supported by the Scriptures. The religion of Judaism is guilty as well. The Talmud and their oral traditions are filled with stories and interpretations which are often fabrications that alter the truth contained within the Torah.

The Messiah is not pleased with any religious system which usurps the Torah with the traditions, customs and commandments of men. This is why He quoted Yeshayahu when He confronted the Pharisees by proclaiming: "*6 Well did Yeshayahu prophesy of you hypocrites, as it is written: This people honors Me with their lips, but their heart is far from Me. 7 And in vain they worship Me, teaching as doctrines the commandments of men.*" Mark 7:6-7.

As we yearn for restoration, it is critical that we examine our doctrines and beliefs to insure that they are consistent with the Torah - otherwise we will be grouped in with those Pharisees. We will be hypocrites saying that we follow YHWH but doing so only with our lips and not through our walk - believing and practicing lies instead of the Truth.

16

In the End

The lack of study and understanding of the Hebrew language and culture as they relate to the Torah of YHWH is the source of many of the problems in Christianity. The Torah "is the foundation for" the entire plan of Elohim, and is essential to anyone who desires to live a life of obedience which is pleasing to YHWH. You cannot have His Spirit within you and disagree with that statement because it is His Spirit that writes the Torah on our hearts and minds.

From beginning to end, the Torah instructs us in the Righteous path. In fact, the first word in the Scriptures, Beresheet (בראשית), actually tells the entire plan of creation - but you will only see it in Hebrew.[149] There is incredible information found within the books, paragraphs, sentences, words and individual letters and marks of the Hebrew Scriptures.

As I continue my study of the Hebrew Scriptures, I appreciate the passage which proclaims: "*Oh, the depth of the riches both of the wisdom and knowledge of Elohim!*" Romans 11:33. I also understand what is meant by the following: "*For the Word of Elohim is living and active. Sharper than any double-edged sword, it penetrates even to dividing soul and spirit, joints and marrow; it judges the thoughts and attitudes of*

the heart." Hebrews (Ibrim) 4:12.

It is believed these letters contained in the Messianic Scriptures were written between 50 and 95 C.E. which, along with the other Epistles of Shaul, are some of the earliest "New Testament" manuscripts known to exist. They are referring to the Tanak, in particular, the Torah. None of the Messianic writings were considered to be "the Word of Elohim" save for the Prophecy of Yahushua, not Yahanan, called The Revelation. (see Revelation 1:1).

In fact, when the Epistles were written, many of the Gospels had not even been written. The Torah, The Prophets, and the Writings were the only documents considered to be Scriptures for hundreds of years.[150] The Torah is unique from all of the other Scriptures. It was the Torah that was described as *"living and active."* Regrettably, many modern day Believers do not view the Torah with the same enthusiasm as did early disciples.

In fact, it appears that most of Christianity has forgotten the Torah and failed to see its relevance. Instead of seeing the Torah as The Way, The Truth, The Life and The Light, they may never experience true repentance and restoration. Just as a person must recognize that they have transgressed the Torah in order to repent, they must recognize that Torah observance is an integral part of restoration.

The Great Commission to go out into the world and make disciples of all nations (i.e. Gentiles) has somehow been twisted to "go out into all of the world and get as many people as you can to say a simple prayer and make a profession of faith." Then get them "plugged into a local church" so they attend regularly and start paying their tithes.

Regrettably, this is not what it means to make disciples. The term disciple generally always refers to a pupil or a taught one. This term is rendered in the Tanak as the Hebrew word Talmid (תלמיד) which means one "instructed," as in Yeshayahu 8:16; 50:4, or "taught" in 54:13.

In the Messianic writings, the word disciples is rendered in the Greek as mathetes (ματηετεσ), "learner," and occurs frequently. The meaning applies to one who professes to have learned certain principles from another and maintains them on that other's authority. It is applied principally to the followers of Yahushua (Mattityahu 5:1; 8:21; etc.); sometimes to those of [Yahanan the Immerser] (9:14) and of the Pharisees (22:16). It is used in a special manner to indicate the twelve (10:1; 11:1; 20:17).[151]

Therefore, a disciple is one who studies and learns and it also implies a lifestyle, not just a simple prayer. It involves following in the footsteps of your Rabbi – living just as He lived. Sadly, the modern Christian religion is not so concerned with the "quality" of the convert, but rather the "quantity" of the converts. It has become a numbers game to many and the pastor with the biggest congregation and the largest building is the most successful of the bunch. We have seen from the headlines how destructive and misleading this form of religion has become as scandal upon scandal rocks this religion of prosperity.[152]

The religion is more aptly described as "Churchianity" because rather than focusing on going out and making disciples of all the nations, it often revolves around going to, and staying in, "Church" buildings. This religion finds it important to build buildings, fix buildings, clean buildings, have services, meetings, meals

and activities in these buildings and hopefully fill them with people so that they can start a building project and either expand the present building or build a new one.[153]

These buildings are typically designed in the same fashion as a Greek pagan temple, with rows of pews facing an "altar." (Yirmeyahu 4:7). The attendees file into the rows and look at the backs of the heads of other attendees, sing some songs, listen to a sermon, and leave the "House of the Lord" after shaking some hands and feeling good that they just had some "fellowship."

Rarely does any intimate fellowship occur at these gatherings and this is not the Assembling of the Believers which the Scriptures refer to in Hebrews (Ibrim) 10:25. The Scriptural assembling referred to in this text primarily occurs at the Appointed Times found in Vayiqra 23. These assemblies would take place in Yahrushalaim at the one and only House of YHWH.

Other than those Appointed Times, when we assemble in our local communities on Shabbat or at other times we should all be prepared to participate and minister to one another as priests rather than laity. As we read in Ephesians 5:19 and Colossians 3:16, we are encouraged to teach and admonish one another - not file into a building and listen to one person who is paid to do a job.

This religion is so messed up that you might find three or four different "temples" all within a one block radius. They talk about saving the world but they cannot even get along with their own members who live in the same community - church splits and divisions are rampant. The Believers in any particular town, village, or city are not even united enough to meet in the same building, they have to build different buildings and call their sub-sect

something different than the others in order to properly identify what they believe as opposed to the people who meet in other buildings.

I am obviously being a bit sarcastic and I am generalizing, but I trust that my point is clear. If you want to get offended because I ruffled your feathers or criticized your traditional way of living, you can go ahead and do so. I grew up in this system and spent most of my life immersed in this culture so I have every right to criticize it although it is not my purpose to offend - only to reveal how ludicrous this is and how displeased the Messiah is with those who claim to follow Him.

Instead of uniting under His banner, Christians have all made up their own banners and then scattered into their separate buildings which they treat like clubhouses. Rabbinic Judaism is equally guilty of this type of conduct and they have acted similarly with their synagogues and their various denominations.

The Scriptures have been massaged and manipulated by both of these religions in order to support and perpetuate their systems. Neither religion represents the way things are meant to be and they will not continue in this fashion much longer. There will soon be a shaking which will force these people out of their buildings which will fall on them if they do not get out into the world where the Good News is supposed to be spoken, taught, and lived.

There is only one building which is called the Temple, more accurately called The House of YHWH, and there is only one place where He has chosen to place His Name.[154] The Prophet Yehezqel provides a description of a restored Land, a restored Yahrushalaim, and a restored

Temple. He describes a vivid picture of the healing that will take place when the promised restoration occurs. (see Yehezqel 47-48).

The Prophet Yeshayahu describes a renewed heaven and a renewed earth. Most English translations use the word "new" but when we look to the Hebrew we see that it is the same root as with the renewed moon and the renewed Covenant - hadash (חדש). *"17 For behold, I create renewed heavens and a renewed earth; and the former shall not be remembered or come to mind. 18 But be glad and rejoice forever in what I create; for behold, I create Yahrushalaim as a rejoicing, and her people a joy. 19 I will rejoice in Yahrushalaim, and joy in My people; the voice of weeping shall no longer be heard in her, nor the voice of crying."* Yeshayahu 65:17-19

This prophecy speaks of the restoration of all creation and we are provided with a vivid description of the Renewed Yahrushalaim in the prophecy of Yahushua as described by Yahanan in The Revelation. The city is adorned like a bride - beautiful. As in Yehezqel, there were 12 gates, each having the name of one of the tribes of Yisrael. In other words, you must be part of the Assembly of Yisrael to enter through the gates.

This city represents the restored Eden. It is a set apart place which is guarded and protected. *"1 And he showed me a pure river of water of life, clear as crystal, proceeding from the throne of Elohim and of the Lamb. 2 In the middle of its street, and on either side of the river, was the tree of life, which bore twelve fruits, each tree yielding its fruit every month. The leaves of the tree were for the healing of the nations. 3 And there shall be no more curse, but the throne of Elohim and of the Lamb shall be in it, and His servants shall serve Him. 4 They shall see His face, and His Name shall be on their foreheads. 5 There shall*

be no night there: They need no lamp nor light of the sun, for YHWH Elohim gives them light. And they shall reign forever and ever." Revelation 22:1-5.

Within its gates YHWH dwells with those who obey His Torah. "*14 Blessed are those who do His commandments, that they may have the right to the tree of life, and may enter through the gates into the city. *15 But outside are dogs and sorcerers and sexually immoral and murderers and idolaters, and whoever loves and practices a lie.*" Revelation 22:14-15. You cannot enter if you are lawless - if you do not obey the Torah, but those who obey can enter and partake of the Tree of Life - just as Adam and Hawah in the beginning.

This is the restoration of all things. When YHWH created Adam and Hawah they originally had no choice where they would live - they were placed in the garden. They were given the ability to choose, but only after the fact. They later chose to disobey which meant that they would no longer dwell in the presence of YHWH. The plan of restoration implemented by YHWH allowed Him to find a people who would willingly choose to obey Him - a people whose only desire is to dwell with Him. It also allowed for atonement for our transgressions.

If you are one of His set apart people, then it is time to recognize the pagan influences and the traditions of men that you may have inheritied, participated in and practiced - beliefs and practices which may place you outside of the garden, outside of the gates, outside of the Kingdom. It is time to repent of our transgressions and return to YHWH. It is time to start living in a manner worthy of your calling - according to the purity and truth as taught by the Messiah - the Living Torah. It is time

for the Bride to get ready for her Bridegroom so that she is found to be without spot or blemish when He comes to fulfill His promise of betrothal.

It is time for Restoration!

Endnotes

[1] Elohim (אלהים) is technically plural but that does not mean more than one Creator. The singular form is El (אל) and could refer to any "mighty one", but because the plural is used to describe the Creator, it means that He is qualitatively stronger or more powerful than any singular El (אל). In Hebrew, the plural form can mean that something or someone is qualitatively greater, not just quantitatively greater. We see in the first sentence of the Scriptures that "In the Beginning Elohim created" the Hebrew for "created" is bara (ברא) which literally is "He created." It is masculine singular showing that while Elohim is plural He is masculine singular. For an excellent discussion of the Hebrew Etymology of the Name of Elohim, I recommend *His Name is One* written by Jeff A. Benner, Virtualbookworm.com Published 2002.

[2] Understanding the significance of names is an important part of understanding the Scriptures. Our Creator places great importance on names, particularly His own. The Sefer Hoshea gives an excellent example of how names are used by Elohim to demonstrate His purpose and plan. Hoshea was commanded to marry Gomer, a harlot. They had three children together named Jezreel, Lo-Ruhamah and Lo-Ammi. Jezreel is Yisre'el (יזרעאל) in Hebrew and means "El scatters" or "El sows." Lo-Ruhamah (לארחמה) means "no mercy" and Lo-Ammi (לעאמי) means "not my people." Therefore, the Creator was teaching that He would scatter the House of Yisrael, that He would not have mercy upon them, that they would then not be considered His people any longer and He would not be considered their Elohim. The prophecy does not stop there because He states that their numbers would be as the sand of the sea, a promise given to Abraham and Ya'akov. He then states that they would be gathered together with the House of Yahudah (Hoshea 1:11). This regathering is a prophesied event which has yet to occur. The marriage and subsequent redemption of Gomer is critical to understanding this prophecy. Hoshea, which

means "salvation" is a clear reference to the Messiah and was the original name of Yahshua (Joshua). He married a prostitute, which represents the House of Yisrael. Instead of remaining true to her Husband she continues to prostitute herself. Hoshea later redeems (purchases) her for a price (15 shekels of silver and one and one half omer of barley). This is symbolic of the redemption that the Messiah has paid for His Bride. This subject is discussed in greater detail in the Walk in the Light series book entitled "Names."

3   Yirmeyahu (ירמיהו) is the proper transliteration for the Hebrew name of the prophet commonly called Jeremiah.

4   Judaism originally developed a tradition NOT to speak the Name of YHWH because they claimed that it was ineffable - unspeakable. This is a false and baseless tradition since the Name of YHWH was clearly spoken throughout all of the Tanak and at no time were we ever commanded NOT to speak the Name. The tradition was initiated in an effort to protect the Name from being blasphemed, but it ended up suppressing and hiding the Name from the world. Scribes later altered vowel points in the Hebrew texts so as to hide the actual pronunciation of the Name from people. As a result, many people ended up pronouncing the Name of the vowel pointing instead of the consonants. Thus, the title Adonai was spoken wherever the Name was supposed to be spoken. When it came time to translate the Hebrew Texts into the English language, we find that most translators adopted the tradition that the Name was ineffable and therefore replaced the Name of YHWH with the title "The Lord" and replaced the word Elohim with the title "God."

5   The Torah (תורה) is generally found within and consists of the first five books of the Hebrew and Christian Scriptures. Traditionally, it is contained in a Scroll and the first scroll was written by Moses (Mosheh) and placed within the Ark of the Covenant. The Torah is often referred to as "The Law" in many modern English Bibles. Law is not a very accurate word to describe the Torah which often results in the Torah being confused with the laws, customs, and traditions of the religious leaders as well as the laws of particular countries.

The Torah is more accurately defined as the "instruction" of YHWH for His set apart people. The Torah contains instruction for those who desire to live righteous, set apart lives in accordance with the will of YHWH. Contrary to popular belief, people can obey the Torah. (Devarim 30:11-14). It is the myriads of regulations, customs and traditions which men attach to the Torah that make it impossible and burdensome for people to obey. The names of the five different "books" are transliterated from their proper Hebrew names as follows: Genesis - Beresheet, Exodus - Shemot, Leviticus - Vayiqra, Numbers - Bemidbar, Deuteronomy - Devarim.

[6] Mosheh (משה) is the proper transliteration for the name of the Patriarch commonly called Moses.

[7] Ancient Hebrew is a visual language wherein every letter has a visual meaning and tells a story. When those letters are put together, their meanings combine to form concepts. I have made it a part of my studies to look beyond the Modern Hebrew to the Ancient Hebrew pictographs to find out the original concepts behind various words. This adds a whole new dimension to the study of the Scriptures which is both exciting and authentic. I highly recommend that you visit www.ancient-hebrew.org which has a considerable amount of information.

[8] Tetragrammaton is the word used to describe the four letter Name of the Creator (יהוה) often written as YHWH in English. A detailed discussion of the Name is found in the Walk in the Light Series book entitled "Names."

[9] There are at least 47 other instances in the Tanak where Yah (יה) is located in the Hebrew text but all of the modern English versions reflect the title "The LORD" instead of the Name. When people say Hallelu<u>Yah</u> (הללויה) they are saying a Hebrew word which means "praise be to Yah." Yah is the short form of the full Name of YHWH. While some pronounce it as Yeh, the real debate revolves around how the end of the Name is pronounced. The third Hebrew letter in the Name is vav (ו). While the vav (ו) now has a "v" sound in Modern Hebrew, it is believed that it had a "w" sound in ancient Hebrew. Many of our ancestors in the

faith contained the Name of YHWH within their names. For instance, the correct Hebrew name of the Prophet called Isaiah is Yeshayahu. It is spelled יְשַׁעְיָהוּ in Hebrew, and it ends with the first three letters of the Name of YHWH. This is not the only name where this occurs and those three letters are usually always pronounced: "yahu" or "yahuw." The final Hebrew letter hay (ה) has an "h" sound. Therefore, many pronounce the Name as Ya-hu-wah. I believe that a key to the correct pronunciation is found in the name commonly called "Judah." The first time that we see the name Judah in the Scriptures is when Leah conceives her fourth son: "*And she conceived again and bore a son, and said, 'Now I will praise YHWH.' Therefore she called his name Judah.*" Beresheet 29:35. The name Judah, properly pronounced Yahudah, stems directly from her statement "*Now I will praise YHWH.*" Many people interpret Yahudah to simply mean "praise," but as we can see, this is not correct. The name which is commonly spelled and pronounced Judah in English is spelled 𐤄𐤃𐤅𐤄𐤉 in ancient Hebrew or יהודה in Modern Hebrew. Notice the similarity between יהודה (YHWDH) and יהוה (YHWH). The only difference is the dalet (ד) which has a "D" sound. If we take the dalet (ד) out of Yahudah we are left with YHWH, the Name of the Creator. Therefore, if you believe that the Name of YHWH consists of all consonants then it would likely be pronounced Yahuwah rather than Yahweh. It also seems consistent with the name of the first woman whose name meant "life giver." The name Hawah (חוה) actually ends with the same two letters as YHWH (יהוה) so Yahuwah would be a consistent pronunciation. There are many different people who believe in many different pronunciations. "John H. Skilton, *The Law and the Prophets*, pp. 223, 224, prefers 'Yahoweh'. The Assyrians transcribed the Name as 'Ya-u-a', so Mowinckle and other scholars prefer 'Yahowah'. Some scholars prefer 'Yehowah', because that is the way the Massoretes vowel-pointed it.(Whether this vowel pointing of the Name was done in truth, or whether it was done to 'disguise' the Name, in accordance with the instruction given in the Mishnaic text of *Tamid* vii.2 (= *Sota* vii.6), we do not know for certain. There is also the Rabbinical interpretation of the Massoretic text saying that the vowels e, o and a were added to the Name as a *Qere perpetuum* which means that the reading of Adonai or Elohim is to be used instead. However, there is no definite proof that the Massoretes originally did it for this reason)." (*The Scriptures*, Institute for Scripture Research, 1998, p. xii.) In this period of restoration which the Assembly is currently experiencing, it is important to remain teachable. I have very good friends who have different opinions and I certainly do not consider the pronunciation to be a point of contention since it is still the subject of debate and speculation. Some pronounce it Yahweh while others pronounce it Yahuwah - still others pronounce it Yahovah and Yahavah. The point is that we are all trying to get it right.

[10] This definition of restoration is gleaned from a variety of sources.

[11] Beresheet is the transliteration of the Hebrew word בראשית which is often translated as Genesis. It means "in the beginning" and it is the name of the first book found in the Scriptures as well as the first word in that book. Keep in mind that I use the word "book" very loosely because in this modern day we use books in codex form which are bound by a spine and generally have writing on both pages. By using the word "book" we create a mental image regarding manuscripts which may not be accurate. Manuscripts such as the Torah and other writings in the Tanak were written on scrolls, so instead of the word book, it is more accurate to refer to the scroll or the sefer (ספר) when referring to these ancient manuscripts. Therefore, the "book" of Beresheet would be more accurately described as Sefer Beresheet ספר בראשית since it originally came as a scroll.

[12] Biblesoft's New Exhaustive Strong's Numbers and Concordance with Expanded Greek-Hebrew Dictionary. Copyright © 1994, 2003 Biblesoft, Inc. and International Bible Translators, Inc.

[13] *Panorama of Creation*, Dr. Carl E. Baugh, Creation Evidences Museum, 1989.

14 Hawah (חוה) means "giver of life" or "mother of all living." It is interesting to note that Adam did not name his wife until after their transgression.

15 It is important to point out that Elohim told The Man: "*¹⁶ Of every tree of the garden you may freely eat; ¹⁷ but of the tree of the knowledge of good and evil you shall not eat, for in the day that you eat of it you shall surely die.*" Beresheet 2:16-17. Now Adam was responsible for teaching the woman the commandments which were given to him. Sadly, we see that he either did not teach them properly or the woman misinterpreted them because we read that during her encounter with the serpent she added to the commandment by stating: "*We may eat the fruit of the trees of the garden; but of the fruit of the tree which is in the midst of the garden, Elohim has said, 'You shall not eat it, nor shall you touch it, lest you die.'*" Beresheet 3:2-3. Elohim never said that they could not touch the tree, the commandment only concerned eating from the tree. The Scriptures repeatedly command not to add to or take away from the commandments and we can see what happens when we disobey – we fall into temptation and we sin.

16 It is interesting to note that the first commandment which was broken referred to food. The Scriptures provide specific commandments concerning what is food to be eaten and what is not food. For some reason, there are many people who believe that Jesus changed or nullified those instructions which is absolutely false. No one has the authority to add to or to take away from the commandments and it is absurd to think that the Creator instructed us what to put into our bodies so that we could remain healthy and blessed then changed His mind and now allows us to eat things which He calls abominable. This subject is treated at length in the Walk in the Light series book entitled "Kosher."

17 The probability against the evolution from a common ancestor with chimps to modern man, using these figures, is 153 quadrillion (153 followed by 15 zeros) to one. www.thetrumpet.com. This calculation is on the conservative side. In reality, the theory of evolution is impossible.

18 Tehillim (תהלים) is a proper transliteration for the word

Psalms. The Book of Psalms would thus be rendered Sefer Tehillim.

[19] Charles Darwin himself described evolution as absurd. "To suppose that the eye with all its inimitable contrivances for adjusting the focus to different distances, for admitting different amounts of light, and for the correction of spherical and chromatic aberration, could have been formed by natural selection, seems, I confess, absurd in the highest degree." —Charles Darwin. There are numerous resources which provide a solid refutation of evolution as well as support for creation science. Here is a link with some interesting sites: http://emporium.turnpike.net/C/cs/links.htm.

[20] Throughout history we can observe the tendency of technologically advanced cultures to see themselves as superior to less advanced cultures. This can lead to an array of prejudices and beliefs which can prove catastrophic. A famous line from the Declaration of Independence proclaims "We hold this truth to be self evident that all men are created equal . . ." Thomas Jefferson wrote those words over two centuries ago and yet we continually see that much of the world either does not believe this message or does not understand it. It simply means that a wealthy American or European westerner is not one bit better than the poorest African tribesman or Middle Eastern Bedouin. It means that the most righteous Christian or Jew is not better than the most debased pagan. It means that there is no Master Race as the Nazis tried to ascribe to the Aryans nor was Yisrael better than any of the Nations because they were chosen for a particular purpose by YHWH. There is nothing which makes a person from the Tutzi tribe inherently better or worse than a person of the Hutu tribe - neither philosophies, tribal identities, nor scientific advancement make a person better or worse than another in terms of evolutionary development. I have been to many third world countries and it is easy to look at them as primitive because they lack the modern conveniences such as plumbing and electricity which many of us are used to. This is dangerous because the people are not less human, they simply lack technology and

that is not always a bad thing. We need to be very careful not to cloud the issues and make these inappropriate distinctions. Evolution has opened the door to justify some people's deep seeded hatred and prejudices by supporting the notion that one group of people is better than another. Those who follow YHWH should never adopt such an attitude toward others knowing that we all come from Adam who was made in the Image of YHWH.

21 *The Gay Science*, Friedrich Nietzsche (1882, 1887) para. 125; Walter Kaufmann ed. (New York: Vintage, 1974), pp.181-82.]

22 Lyell originally started his career as a lawyer, but later turned to geology. His zoological skills aided in his extensive studies and observations throughout the world. He became an author of The Geological Evidence of the Antiquity of Man in 1863 and Principles of Geology (12 editions). Lyell argued in this book that, at the time, presently observable geological processes were adequate to explain geological history. He thought the action of the rain, sea, volcanoes, and earthquakes explained the geological history of more ancient times. Lyell rebelled against the prevailing theories of geology of the time. He thought the theories were biased, based on the interpretation of Genesis. He thought it would be more practical to exclude sudden geological catastrophes to vouch for fossil remains of extinct species and believed it was necessary to create a vast time scale for Earth's history. This concept was called Uniformitarianism. The second edition of Principles of Geology introduced new ideas regarding metamorphic rocks. It described rock changes due to high temperature in sedimentary rocks adjacent to igneous rocks. His third volume dealt with paleontology and stratigraphy. Lyell stressed that the antiquity of human species was far beyond the accepted theories of that time. www.mnsu.edu/emuseum/information/biography/klmno/lyell_charles.html. See also www.victorianweb.org/science/lyell.html.

23 For interesting articles on the various methods of dating see www.cs,unc.edu/~plaisted/ce/dating.html.

24 For a detailed discussion on the Torah, see the Walk in the

Light series book entitled "The Law and Grace."

[25] *The Nephilim and the Pyramid of the Apocalypse*, Patrick Heron, Xulon Press 2005.

[26] There are numerous legends concerning who killed Nimrod and the sources are often obscure. There are some who suggest that it was Esau who actually killed Nimrod. See *Targum Jonathan* on Beresheet 25:27.

[27] Pirke R. El. xxiv.; "Sefer ha-Yashar" l.c.; comp. Gen. R. lxv. 12. http://www.jewishencyclopedia.com/view.jsp?artid=295 &letter=N&search=nimrod.)

[28] *Nimrod and Babylon: The Birth of Idolatry*, Steve and Terri White http://koinonia-all.org/bible/nimrod.htm. The Name of YHWH and the title Elohim replaced by author for consistency.

[29] *The Pagan Origin of Easter*, David J. Meyer, Last Trumpet Ministries International, PO Box 806, Beaver Dam, WI 53916, www.lasttrumpetministries.org/tracts/tract1.html.

[30] *ibid, The Nephilim and the Pyramid of the Apocalypse.*

[31] *ibid, The Nephilim and the Pyramid of the Apocalypse* see also http://tourpagan.itgo.com/archi/page2.html.

[32] www.pantheon.org/articles/z/zeus.html "Jupiter" created on 03 March 1997; last modified on 26 May 1999 (Revision 2). 228 words. by Micha F. Lindemans.

[33] See *Fossilized Customs* by Lew White ISBN 0-9583453-6-7 (www.fossilizedcustoms.com) *Too Long in the Sun* by Richard M. Rives, Partakers Publications (www.toolong.com) and *The Two Babylons* by Alexander Hislop, Book Jungle, ISBN 1-5946248-4-4

[34] Abram (אברם) was the original name of our Patriarch who is often called Abram. His name was later changed to Abraham (אברהם).

[35] Yitshaq (יצחק) is the correct transliteration for the Hebrew name commonly called Isaac.

[36] Ya'akov is a proper transliteration for the name which is often called Jacob in English, the same name as the patriarch whose name was changed to Yisrael and who fathered the Tribes of Yisrael. It is also the correct Hebrew name for the disciple traditionally called James.

37   Shlomo (שלמה) is the proper English transliteration for the Hebrew name which is traditionally pronounced as Solomon.

38   The Northern Tribes known as the House of Yisrael, repeated the same sin the Children of Yisrael had originally committed at Sinai. They worshipped a calf, which was an Egyptian god - this was idolatry. Not only did they worship the same god, they made two of them and they worshipped at two locations which were not ordained by YHWH. They also established appointed times which were in contravention with the Torah. They broke the covenant and were judged - they committed adultery and received a certificate of divorce from YHWH. (Yirmeyahu 3:8).

39   Yahudah (יהודה) is the proper English transliteration for the Hebrew name often pronounced as Judah.

40   Benyamin is the proper transliteration for the name which is often pronounced as Benjamin because there is no "J" in Hebrew.

41   Yaroboam (ירבעם) is the proper English transliteration for the Hebrew name which is typically spelled Jeroboam in English Bibles.

42   Yehezqel (יהזקאל) is the proper Hebrew transliteration for the Prophet commonly called Ezekiel.

43   The American Heritage Dictionary.

44   Shaul (sha ool) is the proper transliteration for the name of the apostle commonly called Paul.

45   The proper transliteration for the name of the person often called Cain in the Scriptures is Qayin (קין) and the proper transliteration for the name of the person often called Abel in the Scriptures is Hebel (הבל). It is very interesting to view the sacrifices which were rendered by these two because it reveals a pattern which is repeated in Scriptures and shows us behavior which is pleasing and that which is displeasing to YHWH. We read in Beresheet that "in the process of time" they both provided an offering to YHWH. In the Hebrew we read miqetz yamiym (מקץ ימים) which literally means "in the end of days." It seems clear that this was an Appointed Time when both knew that an offering was expected of them.

The Scriptures reveal that Qayin brought an offering of the fruit of the ground to YHWH and Hebel ALSO brought the firstborn of his flock and their fat. In other words, Hebel brought an offering of the fruit of the ground to YHWH but he also brought the firstborn of his flock. The Hebrew word used for flock is tsone (צֹאן) which implies a goat or a lamb. I believe that this was likely the time of the Passover when all are required to offer a goat or a lamb. (Shemot 12:5). Passover is one of three times in the Torah when males are to appear before YHWH at an appointed time and place, to present an offering. The two other major feasts are Sukkot and Shavuot - during both of these feasts they would have been required to present the firstfruits of their labors which they had sown in the field. (Shemot 23:14). During the Passover and the Feast of Unleavened Bread, we bring a lamb or a goat offered with its' fat and in the midst of Unleavened Bread we also present the Firstfruits (resheet - beginning) of our crops. Now many believe that the Appointed Times were created at Sinai but this is not supported by the Scriptures. I believe that the Torah and the patterns found within the Feasts go back to the beginning. YHWH repeatedly tells us that He has declared the end from the beginning. (Yeshayahu 41:26, 46:10, 48). His patterns and His ways go all the way back to the beginning and are demonstrated through cycles - one of those cycles being harvests. Throughout the Scriptures we see the terms "in the beginning" (beresheet) referring to the beginning of a harvest or the firstfruits of a harvest and the term "in the end of days" (miqetz yamiym) referring to the end of that harvest. Many interpret this passage with Qayin and Hebel as if to show that raising animals was better than tilling the ground, but that has nothing to do with it. We see that Hebel offered his firstfruits while there was no mention of this for Qayin. Also note that the offering of Hebel involved blood while the offering of Qayin did not. Thus the offering of Qayin was not acceptable - it did not include blood and he did not receive atonement. As a result, he was overtaken by sin and he ultimately did shed blood - the blood of his brother. This provides us with the patterns of Messiah's fulfillment

of the Passover.

The Torah provides instructions regarding what is considered to be food. Not all animals were meant to be consumed. The Creator made certain animals that can be eaten and others which are not meant to be eaten because their particular function would make them inappropriate to be eaten. These instructions are meant for our good to keep us healthy, they are not meant to deprive us of any delicacies. Christians have missed considerable health blessings because of their treatment of this subject. They believe that since they are not "under the law" they can now eat anything. Sadly, nothing could be further from the truth. The Messianic Scriptures actually state that "Jesus declared all foods clean" but this particular passage does not provide for the abolition of the dietary instructions as so many believe. Let us take a closer look at the passage in the Good News according to Mark from the NIV Translation. ""¹⁴ *Again Jesus called the crowd to Him and said, 'Listen to Me, everyone, and understand this. ¹⁵ Nothing outside a man can make him unclean by going into him. Rather, it is what comes out of a man that makes him unclean.' ¹⁷ After he had left the crowd and entered the house, his disciples asked him about this parable. ¹⁸ 'Are you so dull?' he asked. 'Don't you see that nothing that enters a man from the outside can make him unclean? ¹⁹ For it doesn't go into his heart but into his stomach, and then out of his body. (In saying this, Jesus declared all foods "clean.")*" Mark 7:14-19 NIV. Notice the information in parenthesis at the end of this passage of Scripture. The parenthesis means that this statement is not in the original manuscript but rather it was a translator's notation, a very ignorant one at that! Yahushua was not declaring all foods clean in this Scripture and He never made that statement. It is simply astounding that a translator would put such an erroneous notation at the end of a passage where the Messiah specifically asks "Are you so dull?" It is as if the Messiah is asking that question of the translator. The point of His teaching was that it is the heart that gets defiled, not the body. Eating something unclean does not turn someone into an unclean being. Eating pig does not turn a person into pig, they are still human. They do not turn into the unclean animal – instead their body eventually eliminates the unclean thing. Regardless, eating a pig is still considered an abominable act because swine is not defined as "food" in the Torah. There are various other quotes from Shaul which people use to justify violating the dietary instructions. None of them accomplish that goal when they are translated correctly and read within their proper context. The subject of the Scriptural dietary instructions is discussed in detail in the Walk in the Light series book entitled "Kosher."

47 The exact boundaries of the Promised Land are hotly disputed because the specific location of the reference points are not known. What is clear is that the Land covenant has never been completely fulfilled and we look forward to the future fulfillment of this covenant.

48 Yisrael (ישראל) is the English transliteration for the Hebrew word often spelled Israel.

49 Egypt is the modern word used to describe the land inhabited by the descendents of Mitsrayim, who was the son of Ham (Beresheet 10:6). Thus, throughout this text the word Mitsrayim will be used in place of the English word Egypt since that is how it is rendered in the Torah.

50 www.answers.com/topic/midian.

51 Shemot (שמות) is the transliteration for the Hebrew word which is often written Exodus in English Bibles. Shemot actually means: "names."

52 Vayiqra (ויקרא) is the transliteration for the Hebrew word which is often written Leviticus in English Bibles. Vayiqra means: "called."

53 *Ancient Egypt*, Lorna Oakes and Lucia Gahlin, Barnes & Nobles Books, 2003, Page 283.

54 The word "Bible" has traditionally been the word used to describe the collection of documents considered by Christianity to be inspired by Elohim - I prefer the use of the word Scriptures. The word Bible derives from Byblos which has more pagan connotations than I prefer, especially when referring to the written Word of Elohim. This subject is discussed in greater detail in the Walk in the Light Series book entitled "Scriptures."

55   Pictures from www.biblelarkeologi.no/exodusklippenhoreb. htm. It is my understanding that Jim and Penny Caldwell as well as the late Ron Wyatt located and photographed this site. I would encourage the reader to visit their websites and read about their exciting adventures. You can visit these sites at www.wyattmuseum.com and www.jimandpenny.com.

56   *The Exodus Case*, Dr. Lennart Möller, Scandinavia Publishing House 2002.

57   The maps that you have in the back of your Bible are wrong because tradition has taken precedence over the truth. The process by which Queen Helena discerned the supposed locations of Scriptural cites was conducted using divination and sorcery. She was, after all, a pagan sun worshipper as was her son/lover - Emperor Constantine.

58   Yahushua is the correct Hebrew Transliteration of the patriarch we often call Joshua. The Name means "Yah saves" or "Yah is salvation" and it is the same name as the Messiah as defined in Matthew (Mattityahu) 1:21. Some also spell and pronounce it as Yahshua which is the short form. In this text I will use the shortened form when referring to the patriarch known as Joshua so as to avoid confusion with Messiah.

59   The story of Ruth is a story for our day - you should stop and read it now. It is not a difficult story to read and understand so I will simply point out some things to think about when you read it. Notice that the family of Naomi were from Bethlehem in the Land of Yahudah. They were from the Tribe of Yahudah although they were in the land of Moab because Yisrael was under a famine. Yisrael had no king – they were in the period of the judges yet the name of Naomi's husband Elimelech means: "my Elohim is King" which gives us a hint that this story is about YHWH as King. The only reason Yisrael would be in famine is if they were being cursed which means that they were not obeying the terms of the covenant made at Sinai and renewed at Moab. So where does Naomi and her family go - back to the Torah - they went to Moab. There Naomis' two sons marry Moabite women - who would then become part of their family. We read that not only did Naomis' husband die while they were in Moab

but so did her sons. Typically when one son would die he would take on the responsibilities of his brother's family but in this case all of the men had died and the women and their hope of producing seed had effectively been "cut off." The women were free to leave their connection with Yisrael and remain in Moab but Ruth "clung" to Naomi and took Naomis' Elohim as her own. They then return to Yisrael together and the story of Ruth coming to the Land of Yisrael starts "in the beginning" (beresheet) of the barley harvest. This is highly significant because we know that it is around the beginning of the first month because the month begins when the renewed moon is sighted and the barley is in the state of Aviv. The barley is then harvested in the first month as the people prepare, among other things, for the feast of Passover which is all about redemption. In Vayiqra 23, we are provided a detailed account of what are traditionally known as the feasts of YHWH which are divided into two groups; the early harvest and the latter harvest. The latter harvest feasts all occur in the seventh month and immediately preceding their description, the Torah provides something specific concerning these times. *"When you reap the harvest of your land, you shall not wholly reap the corners of your field when you reap, nor shall you gather any gleaning from your harvest. You shall leave them for the poor and for the stranger: I am YHWH your Elohim."* Vayiqra 23:22. YHWH is specifically showing that He will make provision for the Gentiles through His Appointed Times and this sets the stage for the process of being redeemed and grafted in by Ruth who was previously joined to Yisrael and cut off.

The mikvah is where the Christian doctrine of baptism derives although it did not begin with Christianity and was commanded by YHWH long before Messiah came. It was a natural thing for Yisraelites to do. In fact, there were hundreds of mikvahs at the Temple and it was required that a person be immersed in a mikvah prior to presenting their sacrifice. The Hebrew word for baptize is tevila (טביל) which is a full body immersion that takes place in a mikvah (מקוה) which comes from the passage in Beresheet 1:10 when

YHWH "gathered together" the waters. The mikvah is the gathering together of flowing waters. The "tevila" immersion is symbolic for a person going from a state of uncleanliness to cleanliness. The priests in the Temple needed to tevila regularly to insure that they were in a state of cleanliness when they served in the Temple. Anyone going to the Temple to worship or offer sacrifices would tevila at the numerous pools outside the Temple. There are a variety of instances found in the Torah when a person was required to tevila. It is very important because it reminds us of the filth of sin and the need to be washed clean from our sin in order to stand in the presence of a holy, set apart Elohim. Therefore, it makes perfect sense that we be immersed in a mikvah prior to presenting the sacrifice of the perfect lamb as atonement for our sins. It also cleanses our temple which the Spirit of Elohim will enter in to tabernacle with us. The tevila is symbolic of becoming born again and is an act of going from one life to another. Being born again is not something that became popular in the seventies within the Christian religion. It is a remarkably Yisraelite concept that was understood to occur when one arose from the mikvah. In fact, people witnessing an immersion would often cry out "Born Again!" when a person came up from an immersion. It was also an integral part of the Rabbinic conversion process, which, in many ways is not Scriptural, but in this sense is correct. For a Gentile to complete their conversion, they were required to be immersed, or baptized, which meant that they were born again: born into a new life. Many people fail to realize that this concept is not a Christian concept because of the exchange between Messiah and Nicodemus. Let us take a look at that conversation in the Good News according to Yahanan: "¹ *Now there was a man of the Pharisees named Nicodemus, a ruler of the Yahudim.* ² *He came to Yahushua at night and said, 'Rabbi, we know you are a teacher who has come from Elohim. For no one could perform the miraculous signs you are doing if Elohim were not with him.'* ³ *In reply Yahushua declared, 'I tell you the truth, no one can see the kingdom of Elohim unless he is born again.'* ⁴ *'How can a man be born when he is old?' Nicodemus*

asked. 'Surely he cannot enter a second time into his mc
womb to be born!' ⁵ Yahushua answered, 'I tell you the truth, no
one can enter the kingdom of Elohim unless he is born of water and
the Spirit. ⁶ Flesh gives birth to flesh, but the Spirit gives birth to
spirit. ⁷ You should not be surprised at my saying, You must be born
again. ⁸ The wind blows wherever it pleases. You hear its sound,
but you cannot tell where it comes from or where it is going. So it is
with everyone born of the Spirit.' ⁹ 'How can this be?' Nicodemus
asked. ¹⁰ 'You are Yisrael's teacher,' said Yahushua, 'and do you
not understand these things? ¹¹ I tell you the truth, we speak of
what we know, and we testify to what we have seen, but still you
people do not accept our testimony. ¹² I have spoken to you of earthly
things and you do not believe; how then will you believe if I speak of
heavenly things? ¹³ No one has ever gone into heaven except the one
who came from heaven-the Son of Man. ¹⁴ Just as Mosheh lifted up
the snake in the desert, so the Son of Man must be lifted up, ¹⁵ that
everyone who believes in him may have eternal life.'" Yahanan
3:1-15. Nicodemus was not surprised by the fact that a person
needed to be "born again." His first question: "How can a
man be born when he is old?" demonstrated he did not see how
it applied to him, because he was already a Yahudim. His
second question "How can this be," only affirmed that fact.
And this is why Yahushua said: "You are Yisrael's teacher
and do you not understand these things." In other words, "you're
supposed to be the one teaching Yisrael about these spiritual
matters and you're not. You think only the Gentiles need
to be immersed and born again, but you all need it because
you are all sinners and this needs to be taught to everyone,
not just the Gentiles." So you see, being born again through
immersion was not new to Yisrael. This is why many readily
were immersed by Yahanan the Immerser - they understood
their need. It was often the leaders who failed to see their
need for cleansing because they were blinded by the notion
that their Torah observance justified them. It is important to
note that the tevila must occur in "living waters" - in other
words, water which is moving and ideally which contains
life. These living waters refer to the Messiah. In a Scriptural
marriage, a bride would enter the waters of purification prior

to her wedding. These are the same waters that we are to enter when we make a confession of faith and become part of the Body of Messiah - His Bride. A bride also enters the waters of separation when her niddah period has ended so that she can be reunited with her husband.

61 King David repeatedly extolled the Torah throughout the Psalms (Tehillim). In fact, the entire Tehillim 119, the longest of the Tehillim, is about the Torah. I would encourage every reader to read this portion of Scripture, recognizing that the entire text is about the Torah.

62 Replacement Theology basically teaches that the church replaced Yisrael. The Yisrael that we read about in the "Old" Testament was "physical" Israel while the "church" is "spiritual" Yisrael. The word "church" is a man-made word generally associated with the Catholic and Christian religions. In that context, it is typically meant to describe the corporate body of faith. It is used in most modern English Bibles as a translation for the Greek word ekklesia (εκκλεσια) which generally refers to the "called out assembly of YHWH." The word "church" derives from pagan origins and its misuse is part of the problem associated with Replacement Theology which teaches that the "Church" has replaced Yisrael, which in Hebrew is called the qahal (קהל): "the called out assembly of YHWH." The Hebrew "qahal" and Greek "ekklesia" are the same thing: The Commonwealth of Yisrael. Therefore, the continued use of the word "church" is divisive and confusing. It gives the appearance that "the church" is something new or different from Yisrael. This subject is described in greater detail in the Walk in the Light Series book entitled "The Redeemed."

63 Dispensationalism in its most recent popular form derived primarily from the Bible School movement in the United States and the Scofield Bible. Dispensationalism promotes the replacement of the "old" with the "new". It teaches that the "church" has replaced Yisrael and that grace has replaced the "law" among other things. This doctrine has no support in the Scriptures and is merely a way for men to explain the changes which have occurred within Christianity over the

past two thousand years. It is a very dangerous doctrine which has pervaded most of modern Christianity. I call it dangerous because it completely distorts the plan of the Creator of the Universe as described in the Scriptures and actually alters the way that people read the Scriptures. It justifies lawlessness by advocating the abolishment of the commandments. It teaches that the commandments were only for the "Jews" leaving Christianity in a quandary because the Messiah, Who is the "Word That Became Flesh," obeyed the commandments and instructed those who loved Him to obey His commandments which are not just to love one another as is commonly taught. (John 14). In fact, He specifically stated that He did not come to abolish the "Law". (Matthew 5:17). Dispensationalism is discussed in greater detail in the Walk in the Light series book entitled "The Law and Grace."

[64] The name of the Disciple commonly known as John in the English was a Hebrew and therefore had a Hebrew name. In Hebrew his name means "YHWH has given." Many pronounce his Hebrew name as Yochanan (יוחנן) but that pronunciation loses the Name of YHWH. According to McClintock and Strong it is "a contracted form of the name Jehohanan." Therefore, in an effort to keep the original flavor of the name I use the Yahonatan, Yahuhanan or Yahanan when referring to the Hebrew Disciple traditionally called John.

[65] Kepha is the proper transliteration for the Hebrew name of the disciple commonly called Peter.

[66] *Backgrounds of Early Christianity*, Everett Ferguson, Second Edition, William B. Eerdmans Publishing Company, 1993, p.11.

[67] *The Origins of Christianity and the Bible* - The cultural background of early Christianity, www.religious-studies.info.

[68] ibid, *The Origins of Christianity and the Bible*.

[69] ibid, *The Origins of Christianity and the Bible*. (Items in brackets added by this author for clarity and consistency of the text).

[70] In this context, I am using the word to refer to an adherent to the religion of Judaism. At other times, I may use it in the traditional sense for the sake of continuity or consistency.

[71]   *The Scriptures*, Institute for Scripture Research, (1998) p. 1216.

[72]   http://jacksonsnyder.com.

[73]   Yeshayahu (ישעיהו) is the proper transliteration for the Prophet commonly called Isaiah. His name in Hebrew means "YHWH saves."

[74]   For the sake of clarity, I use Yahushua when referring to The Messiah, Son of YHWH and I use the short form Yahshua when referring to the son of Nun.

[75]   In this sense, I am using the word in its common usage which could mean an ethnic descendent of one of the twelve tribes or someone who subscribes to the religion of Judaism. I am clarifying because I believe that words are powerful tools for learning or for disinformation depending on whether or not they are used wisely and correctly.

[76]   The name of the Prophet commonly called Micah (מיכה) is the contracted form of Michayahu (מיכיהו) and means: "who is like Yah."

[77]   Mattityahu (מתתיהו) is the proper transliteration of the Hebrew name which is often spelled Matthew in English. The name contains the Name of YHWH and means "gift of Yah."

[78]   Eliyahu is the correct transliteration of the Hebrew name for the prophet of Yisrael commonly called Elijah. The name means: "YHWH is Elohim."

[79]   I grew up thinking that John the Baptist was the first Baptist. As we already saw in Endnote 64 the proper Hebrew name would have been Yahanan. He was the son of a priest which meant that he was also a priest although he was not serving in the Temple. He was in the wilderness immersing people which was a common practice for those who desired to repent and prepare themselves to worship YHWH. Many in those days rejected the Temple in Yahrushalaim as corrupted so some who were looking for True Spiritual cleansing went to Yahanan the Immerser – not John the Baptist.

[80]   The existence of the Hebrew version of Mattityahu has caused quite a stir in the scholarly community as well as those who believe in the "original Greek." Many people

treat Greek as if it were a holy language in the same sense that Hebrew is the holy tongue. Not so - the Greek language was a pagan language and was generally considered to be an "unclean" language among Yisraelites. Therefore, we should not be surprised to find Messianic texts written in Hebrew since the early Assembly likely consisted of mostly all native Yisraelites. That is not to say that these Yisraelites did not speak Greek because some of them probably did, but I would expect that there were many texts written in Hebrew that have since been lost or destroyed. Strangely, it was with the great influx of Greek speaking Gentile converts that likely caused the high volume of Greek copies which resulted in our ability to preserve so many of these writings and determine the original meaning – even though we do not have the original documents. The Good News according to Mattityahu is special because we have numerous witnesses to the fact that it was originally written in Hebrew. "Papias (ca. 60-130 CE), bishop of Hierapolis wrote that 'Matthew collected the oracles in the Hebrew language, and each interpreted them as best he could.' Irenaeus wrote in Adv. Haer. 3.1.1: 'Matthew also issued a written Gospel among the Hebrews in their dialect while [Kepha] and [Shaul] were preaching at Rome and laying the foundations of the [Assembly]' Origen quoted by Eusebius, H.E. 6.25.4 wrote: 'As having learnt by tradition concerning the four gospels, which alone are unquestionable in the [Assembly of Elohim] under heaven, that first was written that according to [Mattityahu], who was once a tax collector but afterwards an apostle of [Yahushua Mashiach], who published it for those who from Judaism came to believe, composed as it was in the Hebrew language.' Eusebius, H.E. 3.24.6 wrote: '[Mattityahu] had first preached to Hebrews, and when he was on the point of going to others he transmitted in writing in his native language the [Good News] according to himself, and thus supplied by writing the lack of his own presence to those from whom he was sent.'" Quoting from *Hebrew Gospel of Matthew* by George Howard, Mercer University Press 1995 pp. 157-158. The source text for The Hebrew Gospel of Matthew translated by George Howard derives from a treatise entitled Evan Bohan (אבן בוחן) which means: "The Touchstone." It was written by Shem-Tob ben-Isaac ben-Shaprut in the 14th Century. It was not intended to be favorable toward Christianity, in fact, it was meant to assist Jews to argue the Scriptures with Christians. This is why some people have a problem with the text because it uses the slur (יש"ו) Yesu whenever referring to Yahushua. Regardless of that fact, Shem-Tob probably would have desired to have an accurate translation on doctrinal matters so that his readers could properly present their arguments against the Christians. If they had a flawed text they would, in turn, present flawed arguments. Therefore, I find the text to be incredibly helpful in my studies. Passages such as Mattityahu 2:23 which have confounded Christians for centuries suddenly are seen in a different light.

[81] The Septuagint is the common name for the Greek translation of the Hebrew Scriptures - The Tanak. Septuagint often rendered as LXX means "70" because tradition has it that 72 scholars translated the text. The Septuagint can be extremely useful when we study the "New Testament" because it acts as a bridge between the New Testament Greek and the Hebrew in the Tanak.

[82] See *Trench Word Studies and Fausset's Bible Dictionary*, Electronic Database 1998 by Biblesoft.

[83] Maimonides is probably best known for his teaching that there are 613 Mitzvot in the Torah. The quote is provided in what he details as Mitzvot 309. I do not condone the concept of listing and numbering the Mitzvot because, in my opinion, it oversimplifies and minimizes the Torah which is not a two dimensional list of do's and don'ts, but rather a spiritual instruction which is "living and powerful." The other commentary referenced in this end note comes from *The Aryeh Kaplan Anthology I.* by Aryeh Kaplan Mesorah Publications 1991 ISBN 0899068669.

[84] According to George Howard's analysis of the Shem-Tob Hebrew Matthew (Mattityahu) there were various comments made by Shem-Tob within the manuscript which pointed out the similarities between Yahushua and the Gemara. One

in particular was concerning the statement by Yahushua in Mattityahu 5:17 that He did not come to destroy the Torah but to fulfill. The comments provide that Yahushua's intention was "not to add a word to the words of the Torah nor to subtract any." This of course was a foundational commandment in the Torah and appears to be an accurate interpretation of the text which not only provides clarity to the statement made by Yahushua but also shows the perfect consistency between the Torah of Mosheh and the Ministry of Yahushua.

[85] *The Hebrew Yeshua vs. the Greek Jesus*, Nehemia Gordon, Hilkiah Press (2005).

[86] For a good treatment of the rise of Rabbinic Judaism I recommend the book *Rabbi Akiba's Messiah: The Origins of Rabbinic Authority* by Daniel Grubner, Elijah Publishing (1999).

[87] The Seventh month contains the Appointed Times commonly referred to as "the Fall Feasts." These Appointed Times include the Day of Trumpets, The Day of Atonement and Sukkot (The Feast of Tabernacles). These are shadow pictures or rehearsals of things to come and they will include the return of the Messiah, Judgment, and Him dwelling (tabernacling) with His people. The prophet Zecharyah states that Sukkot will be observed from year to year throughout the millennial reign. (Zecharyah 14:16). During Sukkot we are commanded to go to Yahrushalaim and build sukkas – which are temporary dwellings – also called a booth or a manger. This was the structure that Messiah was born in when "*the Word became flesh and tabernacled among us.*" Yahanan 1:14. These Appointed Times are discussed in more detail in the Walk in the Light Series book entitled "Appointed Times."

[88] The religious leaders had developed 39 primary categories of work which was prohibited on the Sabbath along with numerous subcategories. They most likely defined the actions of the disciples as falling in the category of reaping.

[89] The Pharisees, through their traditions and man-made rules had made the Sabbath a burden for people and had placed their yoke around the necks of men. A good example of the

difference between the "yoke" of the Torah and the "yoke" of the Pharisees can be seen concerning the Sabbath. While the Torah only has a few specific commands concerning the Sabbath, the Takanot of the Pharisees and the Rabbis consists of hundreds, if not thousands of rules and regulations. The yoke of the Torah is light and is meant to guide us in the paths of righteousness while the yoke of men becomes a burden that few, if any, can bear.

To fully understand the plan of the Creator we must know His Appointed Times which are clearly described in the Torah. When we keep these appointments, He meets with us and we are blessed. Just as Yahushua fulfilled the Torah by bringing fullness and meaning to the Feast of Pesach (Passover) Unleavened Bread, Firstfruits and the Feast of Shavuot (Pentecost) – we await His fulfillment of the remaining Feasts. A more detailed discussion of the feasts may be found in the Walk in the Light series book entitled "Appointed Times."

As mentioned previously, Rabbinic Judaism is not the same religion as that of the Yisrael that we read in the Scriptures. Rabbinic Judaism is a religion which was developed largely because of the Great Revolt. After the siege on Yahrushalaim and the destruction of the Temple by Titus in 70 A.D., the Pharisees and possibly only surviving Sanhedrin member Yochanan ben Zakkai founded an Academy at Yavneh which became the center of Rabbinic Authority. His predecessor Gamaliel II continued to solidify the power base of the Pharisaic Sect of the Hebrews who, through their cooperation with the Roman Empire, were able to survive the near annihilation which was suffered by the other Yisraelite sects such as the Sadducees, the Essenes, the Zealots, the Sicarii and the Nazoreans. There were still other sects of Yisraelites which history provides scant detail such as the Therapeutae and those who composed the "Odes of Solomon." In any event, the Pharisees, through the enhancement of Rabbinic authority and the leadership of Rabbi Akiba developed into the leading Yisraelite sect which is now known as Rabbinic Judaism. While Rabbinic Judaism claims to stem directly from Yisrael it is not much different from the Roman Catholic church claiming a direct line of "Popes" to Shimon Kepha. These claims of authority are quite meaningless as neither religious system represents the pure faith found in the Scriptures. Rabbinic Judaism, while it may consist of mostly genetic descendents of Abraham, Yitshaq and Ya'akov, is not Yisrael. In other words, you do not have to convert to Judaism to become part of the Commonwealth of Yisrael (i.e. the Kingdom of Elohim) nor do you have to accept Talmudic teaching to follow Elohim. Rabbinic Judaism does not have a Temple nor a priesthood and their Rabbinic power structure is not supported or condoned by the Scriptures. This is why the Talmud, which is not Scripture, is so important in Rabbinic Judaism, because it lends credence to their newly devised system. When the Messiah returns He will set things straight. He will find and lead His sheep and He will not need any Catholic Priests, Christian Pastors, or Jewish Rabbis to help Him.

[92] Erubin 21b. Whosoever disobeys the rabbis deserves death and will be punished by being boiled in hot excrement in hell. Hagigah 27a. States that no rabbi can ever go to hell. Baba Mezia 59b. A rabbi debates God and defeats Him. God admits the rabbi won the debate. All quotes and sources taken from *Quotes 'With Attitude' from the Jewish Talmud Commentary* By Don Talbot. See Endnote 101.

[93] Read what the 12th Century Babylonian Sage Maimonides, also known as Rambam, wrote concerning this issue: "If there are 1000 prophets, all of them of the stature of Elijah and Elisha, giving a certain interpretation, and 1001 rabbis giving the opposite interpretation, you shall 'incline after the majority' (Shemot 23:2) and the law is according to the 1001 rabbis, not according to the 1000 venerable prophets. And thus our Sages said, 'By God, if we heard the matter directly from the mouth of Joshua the son of Nun, we would not obey him nor would we listen to him!' . . . And so if a prophet testifies that the Holy-One, Blessed be He, told him that the law of a certain commandment is such and such, or [even] that the reasoning of a certain sage is correct, that prophet

must be executed . . . as it is written, 'it is not in heaven' (Devarim 30:12). <u>Thus God did not permit us to learn from the prophets, only from the Rabbis who are men of logic and reason.</u>" Ibid Gordon, Nehemia, Appendix 3, Page 83.

In my opinion, Rambam "destroyed the Torah" through this interpretation. In Torah study, it was common to refer to a bad interpretation as "destroying the Torah" while a good interpretation would "fulfill the Torah." Rambam misquoted Scripture in an effort to derive from it what he wanted – an excuse to solidify the power of the Rabbis. Rambam used this reasoning to justify the execution of any prophet who prophesied that the Rabbis are wrong on any point of interpretation.

[94] *Our Father Abraham, Jewish Roots of the Christian Faith*, Marvin R. Wilson William B. Eerdmans Publishing Company, Grand Rapids Michigan 1989 p. 65.

[95] en.wikipedia.org/wiki/Bar_Kokhba's_revolt. There are many problems with both Bar Kokhba and Rabbi Akiba and to properly understand the development of Judaism and Christianity it is critical to understand the essence of the Revolt. Rabbi Akiba, the father of Rabbinic Judaism supported a man who was clearly a false Messiah. He even manipulated facts to support the Messiahship of Bar Kokhba whose real name, ironically, was Bar Kosiba which can mean: "son of a liar." For a very good discussion on this subject see *Rabbi Akiba's Messiah: The Origins of Rabbinic Authority* by Daniel Gruber, Elijah Publishing (1999) ISBN: 0-9669253-1-9.

[96] *Come Out of Her My People*, C.J. Koster, Institute for Scripture Research (1998) p. 65.

[97] http://www.mechon-mamre.org/jewfaq/gentiles.htm.

[98] In Israel if you visit the remains of Korazim in the Galilee region you will find the head of Medusa engraved in the wall of the synagogue. You can also find pentagrams and hexagrams engraved on synagogues in the region – both of these symbols have long been associated with the occult. For further discussion on hexagram read: *Six-Pointed Star: Its Origin and Usage* by O. J. Graham, The Free Press 777, 2001.

[99] *Our Hands Are Stained With Blood*, Michael L. Brown, Destiny

Image, 1992, pp. 89-90.

[100] *Our Hands Are Stained With Blood* ibid pp. 90-91.

[101] Menahoth 43b-44a. A Jewish man is obligated to say the following prayer every day: "Thank you God for not making me a gentile, a woman or a slave." Rabbi Meir Kahane, told CBS News that his teaching that Arabs are "dogs" is derived "from the Talmud." (CBS 60 Minutes, "Kahane").Rabbi Yitzhak Ginsburg declared, "We have to recognize that Jewish blood and the blood of a goy are not the same thing." (NY Times, June 6, 1989, p.5). Rabbi Ya'akov Perrin said, "One million Arabs are not worth a Jewish fingernail." (NY Daily News, Feb. 28, 1994, p.6). According to Yebamoth 98a. All gentile children are animals. According to Abodah Zarah 36b. Gentile girls are in a state of niddah (filth) from birth. According to Abodah Zarah 22a-22b. Gentiles prefer sex with cows. Sanhedrin 58b. If a heathen (gentile) hits a Jew, the gentile must be killed. Sanhedrin 57a. A Jew need not pay a gentile the wages owed him for work. Baba Kamma 37b. If an ox of an Israelite gores an ox of a Canaanite there is no liability; but if an ox of a Canaanite gores an ox of an Israelite...the payment is to be in full. Baba Mezia 24a . If a Jew finds an object lost by a gentile ("heathen") it does not have to be returned. Sanhedrin 57a. When a Jew murders a gentile, there will be no death penalty. What a Jew steals from a gentile he may keep. Baba Kamma 37b. The gentiles are outside the protection of the law and God has "exposed their money to Israel." Baba Kamma 113a. Jews may use lies ("subterfuges") to circumvent a Gentile. All quotes, sources and interpretations taken from *Quotes 'With Attitude' from the Jewish Talmud Commentary* By Don Talbot www.rense.com/general21/tal.htm.

[102] The word Gentile is thrown around a lot as if a person in that group is the member of another species - when in fact a Gentile was simply someone who was not part of the Commonwealth of Yisrael. Some other words used to describe this category of people were: Heathens, Goyim or Nations. They were those who did not worship the Holy One of Yisrael and instead, worshipped false gods. The word

Gentile refers to one who is NOT a Yisraelite - one who does NOT follow YHWH - one who is NOT in the Kingdom. When someone, by faith, enters the set apart Assembly, you cannot continue to call them a Gentile, which means heathen or pagan because the label no longer applies. If you followed YHWH it meant that you joined with Yisrael and you were a Yisraelite - you did not convert to Judaism. While Judaism is an offshoot of Yisrael, it is very different from the Yisrael described in the Tanak. Shaul was ministering to the Gentiles in order to draw them into the Kingdom of Yisrael - not any particular religion or denomination. Therefore, a Gentile convert is one who <u>used</u> to be a Gentile but repented and was joined to the set apart Assembly. That is why I do not like the use of labels such as "Jewish Believers" and "Gentile Believers." These distinctions do not apply once you have joined the Assembly.

103 The reader should look at the entire text of Acts 15 and read it in context. The issue being addressed by the council was whether circumcision was a prerequisite to salvation - Not whether the Gentile converts needed to obey the Torah - that was a foregone conclusion. This matter is discussed in greater detail in the Walk in the Light series book entitled "The Law and Grace."

104 *The End of History the Messiah Conspiracy*, Dr. Philip Moore, Ramshead Press International, 1996.

105 Justin Martyr was a second century Christian apologist referred to as one of the Ante-Nicene fathers which simply means that he lived before the Roman Catholic Church was founded in Rome. It is important to remember that the Roman Church has controlled and influenced Church History. Justin was born a pagan around 100 C.E. and died in Rome around 165 C.E. He likely converted in Ephesus around 132 C.E. It is important to recognize that we can only know this man through his writings which clearly show that he had some problems with his doctrine very early on and this is one of the people who supposedly laid the foundation for the Roman Church. No doubt his writings are very important in a historical sense, but as with any man we must "test the

spirit" when examining his writings. Just because he lived a long time ago does not mean that he had more truth. This is the same with many of the early "Church Fathers."

[106] Origen of Alexandria, English Translation (185-254 A.D.)

[107] John Chrysostom (344-407 A.D.).

[108] *The Changing Face of Antisemitism: From Ancient Times To The Present Day*, Walter Laqueur (Oxford University Press: 2006), p.48. ISBN 0-19-530429-2. 48 Yohanan [Hans] Lewy, "John Chrysostom" in Encyclopedia Judaica (CD-ROM Edition Version 1.0), Ed. Cecil Roth (Keter Publishing House: 1997). ISBN 965-07-0665-8.

[109] St. Augustine (c. 354-430 A.D.) *Confessions*, 12.14 www.yashanet.com/library/fathers.htm.

[110] Peter the Venerable from *"The Roots of Christian Anti-Semitism"* by Malcolm Hay.

[111] Martin Luther - *"The Jews and Their Lies"* Part One.

[112] Martin Luther - 1543, Translated by Martin H. Bertram, *"On The Jews and Their Lies, Luther's Works, Volume 47"*; Philadelphia: Fortress Press, 1971.

[113] Martin Luther - 1543 *Of The Unknowable Name and The Generations of Christ.*

[114] Excerpt from *"Ad Quaelstiones et Objecta Juaei Cuiusdam Responsio,"* by John Calvin; The Jew in Christian Theology, Gerhard Falk, McFarland and Company, Inc., Jefferson, NC and London, 1931.

[115] The Wycliffe Biographical Dictionary of the Church, p. 366.

[116] *The Heretics*, p. 327

[117] *Hunted Heretic* by Roland H. Bainton (Beacon Press, 1953), p. 207.

[118] *The Popes Against the Jews*, David I.Kertzer, Vintage Books, 2001, pp. 27-28.

[119] It seems that almost every religious system has its own hierarchy and power structure which places the masses, also known as the laity, at the bottom of the power pyramid. This is where we get the term Nicolaitan. Two Greek root words "nico" and "laos" are brought together to form "nicolaitan." Nico means "to conquer or bind" while Laos means "the

common people." This notion of conquering or ruling over the common people is what Yahushua called the doctrine of the Nicolaitans and it was the only thing that I am aware of that He said He hated. (Revelation 2:15). There are clearly those servants who speak and teach the truth who do so with legitimate authority. The Temple service also had very explicit regulations and there were certain functions that only the Levites, Cohens, or High Priest could perform. Ultimately, when we are talking about assembling together and worship there is a need for order and it is perfectly fine that individuals are given the authority to coordinate and serve the assembly. The important distinction is that those servants do not have the authority to "rule over" the individuals that they are serving. Each and every Believer has the opportunity to commune with the Creator and receive instruction directly from Him. That is what He wants and He does not like men, particularly religious "leaders," sticking their noses where they do not belong. It always bothered me to observe people running to the Pastor, Priest, or Rabbi whenever they had a problem instead of running to their High Priest - Yahushua. While fellowship is important and we have much to learn from our brethren, it is a bad habit to get into.

[120] Ya'akov is a proper transliteration for the Hebrew Patriarch commonly called Jacob.

[121] *The Two Babylons*, Alexander Hislop, Chick Publications, pp. 187-188.

[122] Mithraism: an essay by David Fingerhut, www.ukans.edu.

[123] Textual criticism is a necessary aspect of restoration when the motivation of the "critic" is to discern the original meaning of a document. This is particularly important concerning the "New Testament" manuscripts because there are no original "autographs" of any "New Testament" manuscripts. Today, there are somewhere around 25,000 to 30,000 texts, some of which are merely fragments, all of them being copies of copies of copies. There are numerous variations in these texts which require diligent efforts to discern which variation best represents the original text. Most of the time these variations are inconsequential syntax matters but there are some very

important variations that can effect doctrinal issues. Now some textual critics endeavor upon their quest with the exclusive purpose of disproving the validity of the Scriptures. I understand the realities of the fact that we are dealing with writings almost 2,000 years old. It is incredible that we have so many texts of documents that involve our faith. I find it to be an exciting endeavor and it in no way diminishes my faith to admit that the New Testament copies are not perfect.

124 The Messiah was likely born in the seventh month in the year 3998 according to the Hebrew Lunar calendar or in the month of September in the year 3 B.C.E. according to the Roman Solar calendar.

125 For a more detailed discussion on the Sabbath I would recommend the Walk in the Light Series book entitled "The Sabbath."

126 The Creator's reckoning of time is discussed at length in the Walk in the Light series book entitled "Appointed Times." It is critical that anyone who claims to follow the Almighty understand His times and seasons in order to synchronize their lives with His plan.

127 *The Vatican's Pagan Cemetery* By Barbie Nadeau Oct. 13, 2006 - Just inside the Vatican's fortified walls, directly below the street connecting its private pharmacy and its members-only supermarket, lies a 2,000-year-old graveyard littered with bizarre, often disturbing displays of pagan worship. Under one metallic walkway, the headless skeleton of a young boy rests in an open grave. At his side, a marble replica of a hen's egg, which to pagans represented the rebirth of the body through reincarnation. Nearby, countless skeletons lie scattered among the remnants of terra cotta vases used in pagan ceremonies. The underground air is damp with the smell of wet dirt, and the clay tubes used by the pagans to feed their dead with honey and syrup still protrude, fingerlike, from the ground. Walking among the exposed bones of any ancient graveyard would be chilling enough. But when it's a pagan necropolis directly beneath Vatican City, arguably Christianity's holiest shrine, then the situation redlines right into completely unnerving. Or it would be if

it weren't so enthralling, especially for anyone who has ever pondered Roman Catholicism's pagan roots. The Necropoli dell'Autoparco (literally Necropolis of the Parking Garage), a 2,000-year-old burial ground, which opens to the public Oct. 20, offers a rarely seen glimpse of the close ties between pagans and Christians during the Augustan era (23 B.C.-14 A.D.). "You see a mix of social class and even religious beliefs here," says Francesco Buranelli, director of the Vatican Museums, who believes that including the pagan graveyard as part of the Vatican's museums will foster awareness of the roots of Catholicism and the importance of its Roman history. www.informationliberation.com/?id=16977.

[128] The Catholic Church has made no bones about the fact that they "changed" their Sabbath from the seventh day to the first day – Sun Day. They consider this to be their "mark" of authority and they do not try to find reasons in the Scriptures for such a change – because you will not find it in the Scriptures. The seventh day is still the Sabbath day. For more information concerning this important subject see the Walk in the Light series book entitled "The Sabbath."

[129] *Church of the Holy Trinity v. United States*, 143 U.S. 226 (1892). While the subject of this case was not to decide whether or not America is a Christian Nation – Justice Brewer in his decision writes: "beyond all these matters no purpose of action against religion can be imputed to any legislation, state or national, because this is a religious people." He then proceeds to present a dissertation on American religious history and several pages later makes the following comment: "These, and many other matters which might be noticed, add a volume of unofficial declarations to the mass of organic utterances that this is a Christian nation." I will let you be the judge as to what this actually means – if anything at all.

[130] www.phoenixfestivals.com

[131] *The Occult Conspiracy* by Michael Howard (Rochester, Vermont: Destiny Books 1989), pp. 84-86.

[132] *Healing waters*, Estee Dvorjetski, Biblical Archaeology Review, July/August 2004, Vol. 30, No. 4, Page 21.

[133] *The Secret Symbols of the Dollar Bill*, David Ovason, Harper

Collins Publishers 2003 p. 10.

134 Some interesting information concerning the Mazzaroth can be found in the following books: *Mazzaroth* by Frances Rolleston Weiser Books 2001; *The Witness of the Stars* by E.W. Bullinger Kregel Publications; *The Gospel in the Stars*, Joseph A. Seiss, Kregel Publications 1972.

135 There is an incredible archaeological site in Israel between Haifa and Tel Aviv known as Caesarea which was the place where the Apostle Shaul was imprisoned on his way to Rome. At this location there are ancient ruins of a circus where they would conduct chariot races – among other things. Traditionally, the Romans who were sun worshippers would place obelisks at the center of the arena. At this particular site the archaeologists discovered a fallen obelisk which they raised in direct contravention to the Torah. This reflects the attitude that modern day Israel has concerning the application of the Torah.

136 Christianity and Judaism are loaded with pagan influences. Christianity has rejected the Scriptural Appointed Times and has adopted pagan holidays such as Christmas and Easter. Christianity has rejected the seventh day Sabbath and replaced it with SunDay worship – the traditional day for sun worship. These issues and many others are discussed throughout the Walk in the Light series including "The Sabbath," "Appointed Times" and "Pagan Holidays."

137 The Appointed Times described in Vayiqra 23, as well as other portions of the Torah, are often erroneously referred to as the Jewish Holidays. This is a grave mistake because YHWH specifically says that these are "My appointed times." They belong to no ethnic or religious group. This topic is discussed in greater detail in the Walk in the Light series book entitled "Appointed Times." For the purposes of this discussion, it is important to point out that the Feast of Pentecost takes place 50 days after the Feast of Firstfruits which occurs during the Feast of Unleavened Bread. Pentecost, also known as Shavuot (weeks), is one of three feasts when all males are commanded to go up to Yahrushalaim. While at the Feast, you would go to the Temple, or rather House of YHWH, for prayer

and offerings, particularly during the morning (9:00 am) and evening (3:00 pm also known as the 9th hour). Contrary to popular belief, on the day of Pentecost, the Disciples were not huddled in the upper room, which was no doubt quite small. Rather they were in the House of YHWH at 9:00 am for the Feast. This is how such a crowd from around the world could gather to witness the outpouring and the speaking in many languages. These were all of the Torah observant Yisraelites who were present for the Feast. The Scriptures record that 3,000 were added to the faith and baptized, or rather immersed. There were hundreds of mikvahs at the Temple where people would cleanse themselves before entering the House of YHWH, this is how they were able to immerse so many people. "Shavuot was a shadow of things to come for the body of Mashiach. Consider the "Appointed Times" we should be observing, as we have been enjoined to YHWH as Yisrael through His Covenant (Eph. 2:8-13). These are listed as the Sabbath (weekly), Passover, Unleavened bread, Shabuoth (called "Pentecost"), and the appointments of the seventh moon, Yom Teruah, Yom Kaphar (Kippur), and Sukkoth (Tabernacles), and are carefully explained so all Israel will observe them and see YHWH's redemption plan for them. YHWH uses agricultural metaphors to represent His "redemption plan" for Yisrael, and Yahushua's work is accomplishing that redemption through all of these "<u>shadows</u>." They are literally shadows (metaphoric teachings) for Yisrael. Now, consider the following correction of the translation we are all familiar with: "Let no man therefore judge you in meat, or in drink, or in respect of a festival, or of the new moon, or of the Sabbath days which are a shadow of things to come for the body of Messiah." Colossians 2:16-17. Normally we see the word <u>but</u> in the last phrase. However, these "shadows" are intended to be <u>for</u> the body of Mashiach, not ignored as Christianity has done. The word commonly translated as <u>but</u> instead of <u>for</u> is the Greek word "de", and can mean a variety of things in English. It is a primary particle that can mean: but, and, or, also, yet, however, then, so, or <u>FOR</u>. In the last phrase, the word <u>is</u> does not exist in any of the received Greek texts; it is in italics in the KJV because <u>is</u> was added, and not in the Greek Received Text). These festivals are shadows of things to come, and certainly are for the body of Messiah. The body of Mashiach is Yisrael. Shavuot is an "annual" Sabbath day, a shadow of our Redemption. Through the Covenant we are wedded to Yahushua, our Redeemer, the Husband of all Yisrael." - Contributed by Lew White.

[138] *The Settlers' Crisis, and Israel's,* Hillel Halkin, Commentary Volume 119, Number 3, March 2005, Page 41.

[139] Yom Teruah means: "the day of trumpets or blasting." It is the Appointed Time which occurs on the first day of the seventh month. It is the only feast which coincides with the renewed moon - rosh hodesh - and therefore occurs at a day and an hour that no man knows. It begins the sequence of the fall feasts which contain incredible end time prophetic significance.

[140] Succot, also known as the Feast of Booths or the Feast of Tabernacles is specifically mentioned as a celebration which will occur every year when the Messiah reigns from Zion. All the Nations, not just Jews, will be required to celebrate or they will be punished. This is perfectly consistent with the notion that the Appointed Times belong to YHWH and that it is the time when His Creation will meet with Him. (see Zecharyah 14).

[141] This subject is discussed in greater detail in the Walk in the Light series book entitled "The Appointed Times."

[142] The location of the former House of YHWH is unanimously believed to be on the site known as Al-Haram al-Qudsi al-Sharif, or the Noble Sanctuary, to Arabs and Muslims where the Dome of the Rock and the Al Aqsa Mosque currently stand. The site is also known as the Har HaBayit or the Temple Mount to Jews and Christians. Interestingly, this location does not readily concur with many historical accounts which describe the size and location of the Temple as well as the fact that it was completely destroyed by the Romans which was consistent with the Prophecy given by Yahushua that *"not one stone will be left on another; every one of*

them will be thrown down." Luke 21:6 NIV. There are clearly thousands of original stones surrounding the Al-Haram al-Qudsi al-Sharif. Many argue that this was simply a retaining wall so it doesn't count but the fact remains that this structure was not completely destroyed in 70 C.E. - yet historical accounts describe that Yahrushalaim and the Temple were completely razed by the Romans under Titus. One structure which was not destroyed was the Praetorium also known as Antonia Fortress - which was Roman property and was not considered to be part of Yahrushalaim. This structure was enormous - described as a self contained city immediately north of the Temple which housed the entire Xth Roman Legion consisting of approximately 5,000 soldiers along with additional support personnel. In typical Roman fashion it would have contained streets, markets, a hospital, religious temples, parade grounds, store houses, cooking, eating, bathing, and recreational facilities and the like. There is no way that the traditional site of Antonia Fortress could have contained all of this and it seems much more consistent that the Fortress was actually located on the Al-Haram al-Qudsi al-Sharif which would have placed the actual Temple site to the South in the City of David at the Gihon Spring. Interestingly, modern Archaeology seems to confirm the fact that the Xth Legion "camped" at the Al-Haram al-Qudsi al-Sharif. In an article entitled *Hadrian's Legion Encamped on the Temple Mount* found in Biblical Archaeology Review November/December 2006, Eilat Mazar details significant artifacts which reveal the presence of the Xth Legion on the Al-Haram al-Qudsi al-Sharif. The author theorizes that the Romans "camped" on the site without considering the fact that it was actually the site of the Fortress. Very recently an enclosed road has been discovered underground which connected Roman baths to the site which was used before and after the destruction of the Temple. This makes perfect sense if the Al-Haram was a Roman Fortress, but it makes no sense if it was the site of the Temple. Regardless, people rarely consider that the Temple Mount was not the site of the Temple. This may very well be the result of the fact that tradition has overwhelmed the actual evidence so people now have to find explanations when the two do not coincide. This is an important part of the restoration process, setting aside our traditions and examining the evidence from a new and fresh perspective. I am not stating that I know where the site of the former Temple was located, only that we need to be willing to change our tradition and inherited understanding of matters when necessary. For a more detailed discussion on this alternate theory regarding the site of the Temple see *the Temples that Jerusalem forgot*, Ernest L. Martin, ASK Publications 2000 ISBN 0-945657-95-1.

[143] The issue of the Creator's Calendar is discussed more thoroughly in the Walk in the Light series book entitled "Appointed Times."

[144] HaShatan in Hebrew means "The Adversary." Many believe that a name of Shatan is "Lucifer" but this is merely a fabrication. It is only found one place in the Scriptures, namely Yeshayahu 14:12 which in the New King James Version proclaims: *"How you are fallen from heaven, O Lucifer, son of the morning."* The only problem is that this is not an accurate translation from the Hebrew text which should read: *"How you have fallen from heaven heylel ben shachar."* "Heylel ben shachar" can be literally translated as: "shining one, son of dawn." The Hebrew text makes no mention of the name Lucifer and it was Jerome who apparently first made the translation when he translated the Scriptures into the Latin language. Lucifer is actually a Latin word used to describe the morning star or rather Venus. It is a word written in a language that did not exist at the time that the Hebrew Scriptures were written and it does not necessarily have any direct connection with Shatan.

[145] It is believed by many that this was the great sign in the sky as described in Revelation 12:1-2: *"Now a great sign appeared in heaven: a woman clothed with the sun, with the moon under her feet, and on her head a garland of twelve stars."* NKJV. Modern calculations using computer generated models have determined that this sign likely occurred in September in the year 3 B.C. on the Gregorian Calendar. For more information

on the birth of Yahushua see the Walk in the Light Series book entitled "Appointed Times."

[146] *The "Lost" Ten Tribes of Israel . . . Found!* Steven M. Collins, CPA Book Publisher 1995 4th Printing p.268.

[147] *Antiquities of the Jews*, 11.5.2, from The Works of Josephus, translated by Whiston, W., Hendrickson Publishers 1987 13th Printing. p 294.

[148] I believe that function of the Parthian Magi was actually an anointing ceremony wherein they anointed Yahushua as the King of Yahudah.

[149] As explained above in footnote 7, the ancient Hebrew language consisted of pictographs. The word Beresheet is the first word in the Scriptures and actually summarizes the Scriptures. The word Beresheet spelled in ancient Hebrew looks like this: ☩⊐ᐧᐤ⅄ᐤᘉ. I would encourage the reader to begin their study of the Ancient Hebrew language at "the beginning" and see that power of the Scriptures and the truth of YHWH: *"Declaring the end from the beginning, and from ancient times things that are not yet done."* Yeshayahu 46:10. The study of the ancient language will truly strengthen your faith and provide deeper insights into the Word which is *"living and powerful and sharper than a two edged sword."* (Hebrews 4:12, Revelation 2:12-16).

[150] For hundreds of years after the death and resurrection, there was no such thing as the New Testament. The Scriptures were the Tanak - The Torah, The Prophets and The Writings. While there were many writings circulated throughout the Assembly, none were considered to be Scriptures until they were "canonized." Canonization is a man-made concept which determines whether certain writings are accepted as Scripture and therefore included in the Bible. The canonization of the modern day Bible took place at the Council of Laodicea in Phrygia Pacatiana somewhere between 343 A.D and 381 A.D. A commonly accepted date is 364 A.D. although no one can say for certain when the Synod took place. This subject is addressed in detail in the Walk in the Light Series book entitled "Scriptures."

[151] The New Unger's Bible Dictionary. Originally published by

Moody Press of Chicago, Illinois, 1988.

¹⁵² It appears that Modern Christianity is obsessed with buildings. While "Mega-Churches" are on the rise all throughout the world, most mainline denominations that have perfectly suitable buildings for assembling, are dwindling in numbers. I have always had a tendency to avoid the obsession with buildings. Many times people flock to these "Mega-Churches" because they market themselves well - they have "exciting" worship or "dynamic" teaching, but at the end of the day what might be drawing these large crowds is the fact that they are being entertained. Often the people flock into these "coliseums" to see and hear a particular individual which can become nothing more than a cult of personality. I understand that the Assembly needs to meet, but it should never be at the expense of all or most of the financial resources of the congregation. It always disappoints me when I see people going into debt over building funds or the entire budget of an assembly going toward salaries, heating, and air conditioning bills along with other maintenance costs associated with their buildings. I have seen assemblies become so obsessed with their buildings that their entire lives and all of their social activities revolve around the structure and they forget the really important things - the world around them. Their obsession with buildings and individuals can become a form of idolatry. When this occurs, things can often end with tragic results. No man can live up to the expectations of people when he becomes an idol and no faith can survive within the four corners of a building. Our example, Yahushua HaMashiach walked and His disciples followed. We must be careful not to become so comfortable in our pews that we cannot leave them when Messiah calls us to follow Him. If we look to men, we are always going to be disappointed. That is why our head is The Messiah - not our Pastor, Priest, Mula, Imam, Cleric, Lama, Guru, or Rabbi. (Ephesians 5:23 - Messiah is the head of the Assembly).

¹⁵³ A provocative discussion regarding assembling in Church buildings versus homes can be found in the book *Houses That Changed the World* by Wolfgang Simson, Authentic Lifestyle

2003 ISBN 1-85078-356-X.

Of course we now are living Temples if we have the Spirit (Ruach) dwelling within us but there is still great significance in the actual location of the former Temples in Yahrushalaim.

Appendix A

Tanak Hebrew Names

Torah - Teaching

English Name	Hebrew	English Transliteration
Genesis	בראשית	Beresheet
Exodus	שמות	Shemot
Leviticus	ויקרא	Vayiqra
Numbers	במדבר	Bemidbar
Deuteronomy	דברים	Devarim

Nebi'im - Prophets

Joshua	יהושע	Yahushua
Judges	שופטים	Shoftim
Samuel	שמואל	Shemu'el
Kings	מלכים	Melakhim
Isaiah	ישעיהו	Yeshayahu
Jeremiah	ירמיהו	Yirmeyahu
Ezekiel	יחזקאל	Yehezqel
Daniel	דניאל	Daniel
Hosea	הושע	Hoshea

Joel	יואל	Yoel
Amos	עמוס	Amos
Obadiah	עבדיה	Ovadyah
Jonah	יונה	Yonah
Micah	מיכה	Mikhah
Nahum	נחום	Nachum
Habakkuk	חבקוק	Habaquq
Zephaniah	צפניה	Zepheniyah
Haggai	חגי	Chaggai
Zechariah	זכריה	Zekaryah
Malachi	מלאכי	Malachi

Kethubim – Writings

Psalms	תהלים	Tehillim
Proverbs	משלי	Mishle
Job	איוב	Iyov
Song of Songs	שיר השירים	Shir ha-Shirim
Ruth	רות	Ruth
Lamentations	איכה	Eikhah
Ecclesiastes	קהלת	Qohelet
Esther	אסתר	Ester
Ezra	עזרא	Ezra
Nehemiah	נחמיה	Nehemyah
Chronicles	דברי הימים	Divri ha-Yamim

Appendix B

The Walk in the Light Series

Book 1   Restoration – A discussion of the pagan influences that have mixed with the true faith through the ages which has resulted in the need for restoration. This book also examines true Scriptural restoration.

Book 2   Names – Discusses the True Name of the Creator and the Messiah as well as the significance of names in the Scriptures.

Book 3   Scriptures – Discusses the origin of the written Scriptures as well as many translation errors which have led to false doctrines in some mainline religions.

Book 4   Covenants – Discusses the progressive covenants between the Creator and His Creation as described in the Scriptures which reveals His plan for mankind.

Book 5   The Messiah – Discusses the prophetic promises and fulfillments of the Messiah and the True identity of the Redeemer of Yisra'el.

Book 6   The Redeemed – Discusses the relationship between Christianity and Judaism and details how the Scriptures identify True Believers. It reveals how the Christian doctrine of Replacement Theology has caused confusion as to how the Creator views the Children of Yisra'el.

Book 7   Law and Grace – Discusses in depth the false doctrine that Grace has done away with the Law and demonstrates the vital importance of obeying the commandments.

Book 8   The Sabbath – Discusses the importance of the Seventh Day Sabbath as well as the origins of the tradition concerning Sunday worship.

Book 9   Kosher – Discusses the importance of eating food prescribed by the Scriptures as an aspect of righteous living.

Book 10   Appointed Times – Discusses the appointed times established by the Creator, often erroneously considered to be "Jewish" holidays, and critical to the understanding of prophetic fulfillment of the Scriptural promises.

Book 11   Pagan Holidays – Discusses the pagan origins of some popular Christian holidays which have replaced the Appointed Times.

Book 12   The Final Shofar – Discusses the walk required by the Scriptures and prepares the Believer for the deceptions coming in the End of Days.

The series began as a simple Powerpoint presentation which was intended to develop into a book with twelve different chapters but ended up being twelve different books. Each book is intended to stand alone although the series was originally intended to build from one section to another. Due to the urgency of certain topics, the books have not been published in sequential order.

For anticipated release dates, announcements and additional teachings go to:
www.shemayisrael.net

Appendix C

The Shema

Deuteronomy (Devarim) 6:4-5

Hear, O Israel: The LORD our God, the LORD is one!
You shall love the LORD your God with all your heart,
with all your soul, and with all your strength.

Traditional English Translation

שמע ישראל יהוה אלהינו יהוה אחד
ואהב את יהוה אלהיך בכל⁻ לבבך ובכל⁻ נפשך ובכל⁻ מאדך

Hebrew Text

Shema, Yisra'el: YHWH Elohenu, YHWH echad!
V-ahavta et YHWH Elohecha b-chol l'vavcha u-v-chol
naf'sh'cha u-v-chol m'odecha.

Hebrew Text Transliterated

Appendix D

Shema Yisrael

Shema Yisrael was originally established with two primary goals: 1) The production and distribution of sound, Scripturally based educational materials which would aid individuals to find and Walk in the Light of Truth. This first objective was, and is, accomplished through Shema Yisrael Publications; and 2) The free distribution of those materials to the spiritually hungry throughout the world along with Scriptures, food and clothing for the poor, the needy, the widow, the orphan, the sick, the dying and those in prison. This second objective was accomplished through the Shema Yisrael Foundation and through the Foundation people were able to receive a tax deduction for their contributions.

Sadly, through the Pension Reform Act of 2006 Congress severely restricted the operation of donor advised funds which, in essence, crippled the Shema Yisrael Foundation by requiring that funds either be channeled through another Foundation or to a 501 (c)(3) organization approved by the IRS. Since we operated very "hands on" by putting cash and materials directly into the hands of the needy in Third World Countries, we were unable to effectively continue operating the Foundation with the tax advantages associated therewith.

Therefore, Shema Yisrael Publications has effectively functioned in a dual capacity to insure that both objectives continue to be promoted, although contributions are no longer tax deductible. To review some of the work being accomplished you can visit www.shemayisrael.net and go to the "Missions" section.

To donate, make checks payable to: Shema Yisrael Publications and mail to:

Shema Yisrael
123 Court Street •Herkimer, New York 13350

You may also call 1-866-866-2211 to make a donation
or receive more information.